Seeing Color

Indigenous Peoples and Racialized Ethnic Minorities in Oregon

Edited by
Jun Xing
Erlinda Gonzales-Berry
Patti Sakurai
Robert D. Thompson, Jr.
Kurt Peters

UNIVERSITY PRESS OF AMERICA,® INC.
Lanham • Boulder • New York • Toronto • Plymouth, UK

Copyright © 2007 by
University Press of America,® Inc.
4501 Forbes Boulevard
Suite 200
Lanham, Maryland 20706
UPA Acquisitions Department (301) 459-3366

Estover Road
Plymouth PL6 7PY
United Kingdom

Library of Congress Control Number: 2007924985
ISBN-13: 978-0-7618-3726-8 (paperback : alk. paper)
ISBN-10: 0-7618-3726-4 (paperback : alk. paper)

Contents

Foreword

THE BROWNING OF OREGON

Seeing Color is an important new departure for the history of people of color. First the anthology concentrates on a single state which throughout much of its history was overwhelmingly white, Protestant and native-born. Indeed the image of the early settlers marching relentlessly across the Great Plains and Rocky Mountains destined for the verdant Willamette Valley is deeply ingrained in the state's history, heritage and political culture. Most Oregonians took as a matter of fact, and a substantial minority as a matter of pride, the designation of the state as one of the "whitest" in the nation.

Oregon, as this volume establishes, has a far richer, more racially and ethnically complex history which includes a vast array of people normally not associated with the rugged pioneer women and men who established the first settlements and farms in what was in the antebellum period a remote land. Moreover, even the legacy of racism that an earlier generation of scholars discovered in the territorial period debates over slavery and the migration of African Americans into the state is now found to be an incomplete, though not incorrect rendering of Oregon's past. To be sure, Oregon's legacy of racism continues to stand out in sharp relief but that racism was manifested in various and sundry ways against different people at different times and on occasion against the same group in differing ways over time.

However painful the reminder of the legacy of racism in the state, this anthology also shows the persistent efforts by various groups of color to establish or maintain their presence in the face of staunch opposition. Witness the efforts of the first Oregonians, the Native Americans in the 20th centuries, to retain their lands, language and cultural heritage even as they responded to new challenges and in the late 20th Century to new opportunities as reflected in the rise of gaming. Note the 19th Century groups often overlooked in the state's history, the Chinese and the Kanakas (Hawaiians) in the 19th Century who are included in this panorama of peoples in the history of the state. The volume also incorporates 20th Century groups such as the indigenous Mixtec people from Mexico who are often rendered invisible in the much larger discourse on Mexicano or Latino migration. We are also reminded of the small and long unnoticed Arab American populace in the state from whose ranks emerged Vic Atiyeh, who in 1979 became the first governor of Arab descent in the United States. Yet the remarkably quiet and successful assimilation of this population was challenged for the first time by the response to the events of September 11, 2001.

Seeing Color reminds us of the irony of Oregon's racialist history, of laws which generate unintended consequences. Peggy Pascoe's contribution for example studies the convoluted and tortured history of Oregon's law of miscegenation which provided a model for other states precisely because it expanded beyond the two groups normally involved, blacks and whites, to include various other groups of color. Her article also shows how that expansion proved the law's undoing in the 1950s as a broad based coalition came together to remove the odious statute.

Note also the rise of Oregon's prison industrial complex as profiled by David J. Leonard and Jessica Hulst. They analyze the phenomenon by following the curious growth of a successful clothing line, *Prison Blues,* on the rising levels of incarceration of African Americans, Native Americans and Latinos as a consequence of the 1990s anti-crime initiatives such as Measures 11 and 49.

Finally, *Seeing Color's* thorough and informative historical, sociological and political studies of the major 19th and 20th Century groups—African Americans, Asian Americans, Latinos and Native Americans—are interspersed with poignant personal accounts such as those by scholars Ed Edmo and Lani Roberts, whose descriptions of their respective childhood histories in the Dalles were separated by race and yet united by the common aspiration to dare to image a world where color did not categorize or confine.

Seeing Color is a powerful reminder of the ability of race to unnecessarily limit and often painfully divide people but it is simultaneously a testament to the common humanity that unites all of the people of Oregon, the nation and the world.

Quintard Taylor
Scott and Dorothy Bullitt Professor of History
University of Washington

Introduction: From the Legacy of Ing "Doc" Hay to Reading Ethnicity in Oregon History

Jun Xing

The idea of this project was conceived in 2002. After teaching in Colorado for almost ten years, I was very excited about my pending move to Oregon. One day, I came across a black and white 1887 print photo of a Chinese doctor by the name of Ing Hay. He was from John Day, a small town in northeastern Oregon. Intrigued, I immediately went to find the internet source of the photo, part of a CNN.com article, and learned the fascinating story of Doctor Hay and the Kam Wah Chung Museum (meaning "Golden Flower of Prosperity") which is dedicated to his memory (and the memory of other Chinese mining pioneers in the frontier West).[1]

The Kam Wah Chung Museum, on the National Register of Historic Places, is a unique state heritage site. The building, constructed as a trading post on The Dalles Military Road in 1867, was once the social and commercial center of a small but booming Chinese community in northeastern Oregon.[2] In 1887, two Chinese immigrants, Ing "Doc" Hay and his life-long friend and business partner Lung On, bought the Kam Wah Chung & Co. building and made it their home until 1948. Unlike other parts of the country where Chinese immigrants were being harassed, lynched and even massacred, these two men were welcomed by the local community and became two of its most prominent citizens. Lung On opened a general store for Chinese miners and white settlers, sold "bootleg" whiskey during Prohibition and opened the first automobile dealership in Eastern Oregon in 1909. Ing "Doc" Hay, a master herbalist, operated a successful clinic and became a local legend.[3] Doc Hay died in 1952 at the age of 89. His nephew, Bob Wah, donated the Kam Wah Chung building to the City of John Day in 1955. After being locked for twenty years, it was restored as a museum in 1977, commemorating the important contributions by Chinese immigrants to Oregon history.[4]

Simply amazed, I put the Kam Wah Chung Museum at the top of my list of places to visit once I arrived in my new home state. On a sunny morning in June, during my first summer in Oregon, I made the six-hour trip to John Day. It turned out to be an eye-opening experience for me in several ways.

First, the life stories of "Doc Hay" and Lung On, or "Leon," as his white friends called him, were uniquely fresh and inspiring. They were not the stereotypical faceless Orientals, but two remarkably vivid and successful individuals with real personal identities. They broke the racial barriers of the mining frontier and became respected citizens in Eastern Oregon. Even today they are warmly remembered by some of the old-timers in John Day and Canyon City. Doctor Ing Hay's fame and legend as an herbal doctor represents one of the most successful stories in Chinese immigration history. Patients, many of them white, would travel more than a hundred miles to see "Doc" Hay, even though there were two practicing Western doctors in the immediate area. According to the map, "The China Doctor's Medical Territory," drawn by Jeffrey Barlow and Christine Richardson, Doctor Hay's service extended from the Walla Walla, Washington area in the north all the way to the Nevada border in the south, and from Portland in the west to Payette, Idaho in the east. His patients also came from Seattle, Astoria, Klamath Falls, and as far away as Terry, South Dakota. One local resident told me that Dr. Hay once saved thousands of lives when influenza plagued eastern Oregon around 1918 and 1919. It was even more interesting to learn how his reputation and local support helped him fight prejudice and discrimination. For example, in 1905 he was charged by local white doctors with practicing medicine illegally; yet, according to the local lore, there was no jury in Grant County that would convict him. "They'd never convict him anyway . . . they tried him, but he never done anything wrong," said Hay's nephew. "They couldn't get any man to stand up against him, so he had no fear."[5] Another fascinating anecdote I learned during my visit was that following his death, while cleaning out his old room, friends and relatives found over $23,000 dollars in uncashed checks from his patients under his bed. According to his nephew, when asked why he did not cash all his patients' checks, Doc Hay replied, "I don't need the money, I no cahee. They need it."

Doc Hay's friend, Lung On, was a remarkable individual in his own right. Mrs. Carolyn Micnhimer, the caretaker of the Kam Wah Chung Museum, said that Doc Hay wouldn't have been nearly as successful as he was without the help of Lung On ("They were a perfect pair"). Handsome, well-educated and English-speaking, Lung On had the reputation of being a macho Chinese young man who enjoyed various intimate relations with local white women. For example, as described by Barlow and Richardson in their book, a series of letters between Lung On and his Chinese friend Markee Tom, written between 1905 and 1907, suggested both simple friendships and illicit liaisons. In the Kam Wah Chung documents collection, there is a letter to Lung On, dated October 1905, that mentions a girl who "wants Leo [Lung On] to come over [because] she is alone, her parents have left." Indeed, Lung On presents a sharply different Chinese image, one that goes directly against the long-time racist stereotype of Chinese males as effeminate, asexual or sinister. Both Doctor Hay and Long On were buried in the Rest Lawn Cemetery in John Day. Both are celebrated as folk heroes by the locals today.

What is more, the story of this 19th-century Kam Wah Chung structure is a pleasant surprise by itself. Unlike the fate of many Chinatowns in the frontier West, that were vandalized, burned to the ground or simply died from neglect, this one-of-a-kind facility, the center of John Day's little Chinatown, survived and became a treasure box holding one of the finest and most complete records of pioneer Chinese life and culture in the West. The small and unglamorous building (with a total 1,250 square feet of exhibit space) is filled with thousands of historical relics, including tools, furniture, clothing, account books, personal papers, store merchandize and household items, some of which date as far back as the 1800s.[6] The wealth of business and financial records, letters, orders, invoices and personal papers are all gems for historians. Since opening its door in 1977, 5,000 people visit the Museum each year to learn the history and pay tribute to the significant contributions made by Chinese pioneers in both the economic development and the cultural heritage of Oregon for over 100 years. In June every year, John Day holds a Chinese festival in memory of Doctor Hay and the Chinese miners.

Finally, I was also inspired by Mrs. Carolyn Micnhimer, the curator and caretaker of the building for 25 years. Looking a bit frail, it was Carolyn who made my tour of the facility a memorable one. I was extremely impressed by her in-depth knowledge of the area's history, her anecdotal stories about Doctor Hay, her humor and, most of all, her commitment and devotion to preserving this rare piece of local history. Born and raised in Brooklyn, New York, she moved to John Day in 1951. Unrelated to the Chinese community, she came to appreciate Doctor Hay, whom she called "an old-fashioned doctor," and has been guiding the museum tours tirelessly for 25 years. I leafed through the visitor book and found numerous letters from people who credited her with giving them "the best history lesson" of their lives.

Mrs. Micnhimer told me that she was currently writing a book about Doctor Hay and the Kam Wah Chung Museum, "to pay tribute to the Chinese men." Lately, she felt that she had been trying to beat the biological clock. Many people who had known Doctor Hay have already passed away, taking their memories with them. In my follow-up phone interviews with her, Mrs. Micnhimer made a passionate appeal to the scholar community to help translate Doctor

Hay's papers. There are 13 boxes of Chinese-language papers from the museum that needed to be identified and translated. Those papers were stored in John Day's city hall for years and now have been transferred to the State Parks office. According to Mrs. Micnhimer, when translated into English, Hay's history will come alive, along with the real names of his patients and the details of thousands of his prescriptions.

Coming back from the visit, I decided to honor the heritage of Kam Wah Chung and Ing "Doc" Hay by gathering materials about Chinese immigrants in Oregon. In the process, I have learned about many other fascinating historical sites in the state, such as the Nikkei Legacy Center in downtown Portland, the Colegio César Chavez in Mount Angel and the Museum of Warm Springs. To me, there was no better way to learn about Oregon and teach about ethnic minorities in the state than telling the stories of the local communities. With this goal in mind, I designed a new ethnic studies course (ES351 "Ethnic Minorities in Oregon") as part of the Baccalaureate Core at Oregon State University. Reading and gathering sources for the course, I came across some works dealing with ethnic groups in Oregon, but I found no textbook that provided a comprehensive coverage of the different groups. Obviously, there was a gap in the existing literature that needed to be filled. In 2003, I had some very productive discussions about the book project with my colleagues in Ethnic Studies. They all expressed an interest in working with me. In view of their credentials and respective expertise on Oregon's different ethnic groups, I decided to turn it into a collaborative project for the department. Now, as we celebrate the happy occasion of the project's completion, I want to credit Ing "Doc" Hay's legacy that taught me at least three important lessons about ethnicity in Oregon.

I. OREGON WAS MORE THAN "WHITE"

Needless to say, Kam Wah Chung represents just one piece of the racial fabric in Oregon. While it is true that Oregon is predominantly a "white" society, racialized minorities have been present in the state from its beginning. Native Americans, the "first Oregonians," had been living in the area for thousands of years before the arrival of European immigrants. Black people were among the first explorers of the territory (before York). Hispanics, under the auspices of the Spanish crown, played an important role in exploring and naming portions of the Oregon Coast in the late 16th and early 17th centuries. Mexican migrant labor passed through Oregon as early as the second and third decades of the 20th century, making their presence felt in the beet fields of eastern Oregon. Asian laborers, both Chinese miners in mid-19th-century and Japanese farmers in early 20th-century, made significant contributions to the state's economic development.

Racialized minorities, like other Oregonians, have left their legacy on our state's history and helped shape our future, even as they continue to struggle with racial prejudice, environmental pressures, shrinking state revenues, the effects of globalization and the changing dynamics of the state economy. Today, U.S. immigration policy changes and the forces of globalization have played a critical role in what David Peterson del Mar called the "browning of Oregon" in his new book *Oregon's Promise: An Interpretive History*. Oregon's population jumped by 20% between 1990 and 2000, led by a surge of Hispanics, Asians and African Americans. In 2000, people of color constituted over 15% of the state population. Another 100,000 people, or 3% of the population, identify themselves as multiracial.[7] It is also interesting to note that one out of every seven babies born in the state was of more than one race. And, multiracial children were more common than single-race children when a parent was Asian, Native or African American. Of course, compared to most other parts of the U.S., Oregon is still homogeneous and Portland is the nation's whitest metropolis. But things are changing more rapidly in the state's ethnic composition. Between 2000 and 2003, according to the new U.S. Census data, Oregon's ethnic minorities made up 60% of the state's added population. With a growth rate of 18.5%, Hispanics now make up 9% of the state's residents and 23 out of 37 Oregon counties had double-digit percentage increases in the Hispanic population. Asian Pacific American communities grew by more than 16%. The increase in the number of African Americans in Oregon was most dramatic in Portland-area suburbs. Oregonians of two or more races are the third-fastest growing minority group.

Until very recently, there was little scholarly publication on Native Americans and ethnic minorities in our state history. The only influential work was Luther S. Cressman's *The Sandal and the Cave: The Indians of Oregon*, published in Portland in 1962 and reprinted by Oregon State University (OSU) Press in 1981. However, since the 1980s and 1990s, we have seen several monographs and edited volumes on specific native communities and ethnic or racial groups in Oregon. For example, 1980 saw the publication of Elizabeth McLagan's *A Peculiar Paradise: A History of Blacks in Oregon, 1788–1940*. In 1993, Linda Tamura, a professor at Willamette University and a Sansei (third-generation) native of Hood River, after conducting extensive interviews with the original Japanese American farmers and merchants, published *The Hood River Issei: An Oral History of Japanese Settlers in Oregon's Hood River Valley*. In 2004, University of Washington Press released Marie Rose Wong's *Sweet Cakes, Long Journey: The Chinatowns of Portland, Oregon*. What is more, in the 1990s, the Oregon Council for the Humanities published two landmark works on Native Americans and Hispanics in the state's history: *The First Oregonians: An Illustrated Collection of Essays on Traditional Lifeways, Federal-Indian Relations, and the State's Native People Today* (1991), and *Nosotros: The Hispanic People of Oregon, Essays and Recollections* (1995). In addition, some recent titles with a regional focus in the Pacific Northwest included significant articles on Oregon's immigrant groups, such as Erasmo Gamboa's *Mexican Labor and World War II: Braceros in the Pacific Northwest, 1942–1947* (2000) and *Memory, Community and Activism: Mexican Migration and Labor in the Pacific Northwest* (2005) by Jerry Garcia and Gilberto Garcia.

Although these are significant publications about specific Native Americans and ethnic communities and their histories in Oregon and the Pacific Northwest, there has yet to be a widely published work bringing together the rich and varied historical experiences of Oregon's native communities and racialized minorities in a single volume. I hope this book will help fill this gap with an emphasis on a multiethnic, cross-disciplinary and comparative approach. In addition, this anthology represents an earnest attempt to help the general public, especially young Oregonians, understand that people of various cultural traditions have lived and thrived in the area we now call Oregon for centuries.

II. OREGON WAS "A VERY PREJUDICED STATE"[8]

Oregon has often been studied as part of the Pacific Northwest. While sharing similarities in terms of geographical landscape with Washington and Idaho, Oregon is unique in many ways. The regional identity of the Pacific Northwest has long been questioned by scholars. For example, historian John Findlay challenged the concept by calling it a "dubious, artificial, and ever-shifting" proposition. He wrote, "until recently, the peoples who have lived in Oregon, Idaho, and Washington have generally neither defined themselves as belonging to the same region nor, naturally, agreed on the meaning of that region." According to him, this "regional" mentality often turns out to be a product of commercial interests.[9] Social historians have verified that regions are oftentimes much less relevant to people's lives than locality. Based on this insight, this book focuses on Oregon instead of the much-hyped regionalism.

Indeed, in the realm of racial politics, Oregon, to quote from Elizabeth McLagan, is "a very prejudiced state." In 1859, Oregon held the distinction of being the only free state admitted to the Union with a Black exclusion clause in its constitution. The state legislature in 1866 passed the anti-miscegenation law, prohibiting intermarriage between whites and anyone with "one fourth or more of Negro, Chinese or Hawaiian blood, or any person having more than one-half of Indian blood." The law was not repealed until 1951.[10] In 1870, Oregon was one of six states to reject the 15th Amendment. After the end of WWII, Portland had the reputation as the most discriminatory city north of the Mason-Dixon line. If we compare the three Pacific coast states of Oregon, California and Washington, both California and Washington passed legislations in the 20th century preventing KKK members from wearing hoods to conceal their identity. Oregon had no such law. African American representatives were elected in California and Washington much earlier than in the state of Oregon. Clearly, Oregon lagged behind its Pacific coast neighbors in civil rights legislations before 1940.

Drawing close to our time, race as a social construct still matters in people's daily lives in Oregon. Under a mandate from the legislature, every two years, the Oregon Progress Board assesses how well Oregon racial and ethnic minorities are doing in regard to a range of Oregon benchmarks.[11] Each report looks at racial and ethnic parity between Oregon's population and minority groups in education, health care and economic profiles.[12] In a sense, those benchmarks present a picture of the issues and challenges faced by ethnic minorities. For example, a 2000 study found that Oregon's minorities were about twice as likely to live in poverty as their white counterparts.[13] Poverty in Oregon varies dramatically by race and ethnicity. Almost one African American in three, 30%, was living in poverty, while 27% of Hispanics and 22% of Native Americans were below the poverty line. Education is another area that shows serious disparities. Almost 44% of African American children drop out of high school. In health care, African Americans, Native Americans and Hispanics are uninsured at rates significantly higher than state average, at 15%, 18% and 22% respectively. Whites and Asians are at or near the state average. African American children in Oregon are nearly three times more likely to die in infancy than white children. AIDS is the fourth-largest cause of death for the state's Latino population, making it much more deadly for Latinos than for any other group. In politics, at the city and county level, whites make up a far greater proportion of elected and appointed officials than they represent in the state's overall population, accounting for 98% of all local-level officials. We see clear gaps along racial lines in many other ways. For instance, the distribution of arrests by racial and ethnic categories, one of the most controversial issues in the state, is tracked by the police department. Between 1990 and 1998, the percentage of white Oregonians arrested dropped significantly, from 85% of all arrests to 77%, while the percentage of African Americans arrested increased substantially from 6% to 12%.

Before reading this book, many of our readers may believe that the state of Oregon is, and has been, progressive in many ways, such as those renowned environmental policies. But, after reading the book, we hope they can also acknowledge and reflect on the dark side of our history, especially with regard to race and racial politics. The racial tolerance "success stories" of Ing "Doc" Hay and Lung On in Eastern Oregon are perhaps the exception instead of the rule for racial relations in the state. That is why their stories are so moving and inspiring at the same time.

III. OREGON'S PEOPLE OF COLOR WERE AGENTS OF HISTORY

Historian Patricia Nelson Limerick once wrote pointedly, "Power—sometimes subtly expressed, sometimes openly wielded—has structured most cross-cultural interactions, with those in power directing land, resources, labor, markets, and laws toward their own benefit."[14] Power relations among different cultural groups, as suggested by Limerick, lay the foundation of any local history. Even with relatively little power, ethnic minorities in Oregon have been active players in this process, engaged in both constructing cultural meanings and modifying their social environments. They have been powerful agents of our state history.

History books have too often depicted ethnic minorities as victims of prejudice and discrimination. The approach taken by our contributors differs from those old paradigms by interpreting Oregon history in a new way. On the one hand, we recognize the weight that social privilege and power have on the range of choices available for Oregon's native and marginalized ethnic minorities, while, on the other, we acknowledge and celebrate the diverse strategies employed by ethnic Oregonians which enabled them to achieve a larger measure of control over their daily lives. Reading through the book's chapters, you will notice our writers have often emphasized the historical process of struggle more than their immediate results, thereby affirming the significance of their lives, of decisions made and of consequences accepted. Put differently, we hope our readers will come away with a sense of historicity and agency in the past and current battles for equality and social justice.

In the meantime, this power-relations approach also differs from the so-called "contributions" model that focuses single-mindedly on the roles played by women and minority groups in the building of the state. This contributions paradigm, however noble it seems, overlooks the deeper meaning of a multi-ethnic history, that is, people's resistance against racism, their struggles for equal rights, and their fight against the dominant power structure in the society. Again, the dominant theme running throughout the book is that people of color in Oregon are key historical actors who have been continually engaged in the historical process of creating social power and social relationships. Some of the key questions explored in the following pages include how people have shaped their lives and gained control over their circumstances within the limits of their situations; what the various strategies communities employed for survival and resistance; and, although present-day Oregon has come a long way towards becoming a more ethnically diverse state, what some of the major challenges are that native and ethnic minorities still face today.

Anchored in this "power relations" perspective, the book has been organized around several major historical themes, such as the history and legacy of racialization, the formation of ethnic communities, race and labor, collective memory and communal history, and political and civil rights issues, rather than by chronology or racial groups. Such a theme-based organization will not only highlight the distinctive experiences of communities and individuals, but also inform us of the broader interlocking categories of social identities, such as race, gender, religion and economic class.

Robert Thompson's article in Part I gives us an idea of the current demographic spread of indigenous and ethnic communities across the state and posits the notion that demographics represent "a contested socio-historical political, social, cultural, and economic terrain." The sections that follow indeed bear out this notion. In Part II: A Legacy of Racialization, for example, Peggy Pascoe's article examines Oregon's 1866 miscegenation law and its impact on multiple communities. Her article also makes clear ways in which race and gender were simultaneously mobilized in the intent and enforcement of such laws, men of color with white women and white men with women of color hardly being viewed in the same light by most legislators of the time. Janet Nishihara's article in the same section gives a brief sketch of the convergence of political, economic and social concerns of the WWII era, which resulted in the growth of a significant and prosperous Japanese American settlement in the area of Ontario in Eastern Oregon, the only "free zone" in the state. Voluntary evacuees were joined by new settlers released from internment camps after the war and together they created a vibrant community with a Buddhist Temple and scores of businesses. Both articles highlight historical moments at which racial categories were mobilized against particular communities of color as well as ways individuals found to resist and challenge such constraints.

The work of Sarah Griffith in Part III: Indigenous Peoples and Early Communities of Color offers an in-depth exploration of the contributions of Chinese laborers in two distinct settings. In John Day, Oregon and its vicinity,

Chinese immigrants played an important role in the development of this mining region in the late 18th century. Portland, with its reputation for being a
safe haven, attracted immigrants fleeing anti-Chinese sentiment, violence and
exclusion in other regions. In the essay that follows, Elizabeth McLagan
draws heavily on the African American press to tease out stories that contain
a deeply ingrained history of prejudice, discrimination, and civil rights abuses
against the African American community of Portland and other locations in
the state. The third essay in the section, by Erlinda Gonzales-Berry with
Dwaine Plaza, gives a broad overview of the presence of *mexicanos* in Oregon: early settlers in Eastern Oregon in the 1930s, guest workers (*braceros*)
during World War II, *Tejanos* (Mexican Americans from Texas) in the fifties
and sixties—a circuitous and seasonal stream of Mexican nationals. These articles offer important documentation of these communities' histories and per-
severance.

The fact that race and labor have been inextricably tied in the history of the
U.S. becomes even more apparent in Part IV. In the first article in this section,
Patti Sakurai looks at some of the history of Asian and Pacific Islander American labor in Oregon. She also questions the legitimacy of the contemporary
"model minority" stereotype by showing that while Asian and Pacific Islander
Americans in Oregon are more likely to hold professional and managerial positions than white Oregonians, they are also more likely to live below the
poverty line than White Oregonians. The article by Lynn Stephen clearly shows
that indigenous workers from Mexico, a relatively recent group to settle in Oregon, are concentrated around low paying agricultural and nursery work. She
points out, however, that they have addressed unfavorable labor conditions by
joining the Pineros y Campesinos Unidos (PCUN), a dynamic labor union that
advocates for the rights of agricultural and nursery workers in the Northwest.
They also band together through the formation of hometown associations
through which they engage in activities that solidify their transborder identities.
Together, these two articles bear witness to the lasting presence of racialized
ethnic minorities in Oregon's labor force and give a strong sense of the challenges they have and continue to face, as well as of their deployment of organized social agency in response to those challenges.

In Part V: History and Memory, Linc Kesler's article and that of Ed Edmo
and Lani Roberts, as disparate as they are in topics and style, help highlight
some important points about "Oregon." First, our state history begins with
Native Americans, the original inhabitants of Oregon, long before Euro-
American settlement in the 19th century—the traditional framework of "pioneer" history. Two, diversity is an important feature within Native American
communities, and, for that matter, within any racialized communities in Oregon. Three, Native people are noted for their cultural resilience, having

lodged successful forms of persistence, transformation and creativity during their life experiences in Oregon. In that same section, Kera Abraham draws on a number of individual stories, including her own, to help illuminate Arab American experiences in Oregon and counter misconceptions and stereotypes, particularly in the post-9-11 era of increased anti-Arab sentiment and discrimination.

Finally, in the last part on politics and social control, Robert Dash offers a revision to the view of Oregon as a bastion of progressive politics, and fills an important gap in political discussion when it comes to race and ethnicity. As his essay demonstrates, barriers to participation in electoral politics have run far and wide in Oregon history. Communities of color have found different ways of countering this history with various strategies for participation in electoral politics—from increasing political campaign contributions, to lobbying efforts, to running for office, to increasing voter turnout. While barriers to voter participation and representation continue to be a concern, especially for immigrant groups in the state, the shifting demographics and trends toward increased political participation in general mark an exciting development on the state's political landscape. Turning to the prison industrial complex, David Leonard and Jessica Hulst bring this critical issue home to Oregon by looking at Oregon legislation, political trends, and prison labor practices. The disproportionate impact of public policy surrounding the Oregon prison system on communities of color raises crucial questions about our justice system and how race and racism continue to factor into how we view crime and punishment in Oregon.

In closing, my intent in this introduction is to provide some general information about the conceptualization and methodology of the book. I also want to acknowledge my co-editors for their collaborative work in putting the book together.[15] I would reserve my final comments for the authors. As represented by the co-editors themselves, the contributors selected are an interdisciplinary group, established scholars from the fields of ethnic studies, women studies, English, literature, history, anthropology, philosophy, sociology, journalism and political science. In addition, some of our contributors have also served the role of community leaders and social workers. Because of its multiethnic, cross-disciplinary and comparative nature, this book should make a unique contribution to the field of racial relations. It both reflects national trends and is distinctive given the State's past and present demographics and its unique place in the context of Western expansionism, the "frontier" and the Pacific Northwest. On the surface, you may find the collections of essays vary widely in style and substance, ranging from oral history to autobiographical reflections. But, together, they combine to create a portrait of Oregon that allows us to appreciate the multifaceted experiences of its communities of color.

NOTES

1. CNN.com, "Oregon: Town guards, Chinese herbalist's legacy," 2 Oct. 2002.

2. Hundreds of Chinese immigrated to this area during the gold rush to work in the mines. The 1879 Census lists 960 whites and 2,468 Chinese miners in the gold fields of Eastern Oregon.

3. There are books and a recent NPR radio documentary program on Ing "Doc" Hay. For a book, see Jeffrey Barlow and Christine Richardson, *China Doctor of John Day* (Portland: Binford & Mort, 1979). For a video, see "The Story of Ing 'Doc' Hay" a one-hour radio documentary by Dame Roberts from MediaRites Productions. For information about the program that aired on Tuesday, June 16, 2005 on NPR, see www.NPR.org.

4. The building was restored by the Oregon Historical Society, National Historic Trust and the American Revolution Bicentennial Committee. Currently, there is a restoration campaign that was launched by a public-private partnership to raise funds of $800,000 for building repairs, collection restoration and visitor service.

5. See Barlow and Richardson, 66.

6. The apothecary stands as the most fascinating part of the collection. Protected by iron window bars, it contains more than 500 different medical herbs, most of which were imported directly from China, such as wild asparagus, tortoise shell, bat wings and brown bear paws. The shrines in every room are also some of the museum's most exquisite exhibits. Looking at them when I visited, it was hard to believe that those dried and dehydrated fruits on display were the original ones from the 1940s. Many of the objects were covered with smoke from decades of incense burning. It was obvious the shrines served the purpose of divination and fortune telling. Before the shrines remained several sets of divining sticks, or "fortune sticks," traditionally used to consult the Buddha figure about future events.

7. See "Oregon's Racial/Ethnic Demographics, 2001, U.S. Census, 2001, Supplementary Survey Profile."

8. See Chapter 8, "A Very Prejudiced State, Discrimination in Oregon, 1900–1940," in Elizabeth McLagan's *A Peculiar Paradise: a History of Blacks in Oregon, 1788–1940* (Portland, Oregon: The Oregon Black History Project, 1980).

9. See "A Fishy Proposition," in *Many Wests: Pace, Culture, and Regional Identity*, ed. by David M. Wrobel and Michael C. Steiner (Lawrence: University Press of Kansas, 1997).

10. For more information, please see Peggy Pascoe's chapter in this book.

11. The word "minority" in the report is defined as African American, Native American, Asian or Hispanic.

12. See Bradley Basson, "Elected and Appointed Officials in Oregon: A Report on Race, Ethnicity and Gender Parity." Oregon Progress Board, July 2002. <http://www .econ.state.or.us/opb/parity/offic02.htm>.

13. See "Oregon Update: Oregon Minorities, A Summary of Changes in Oregon Benchmarks by Race and Ethnicity 1990–1998," prepared by Sigmund Research Associates for Oregon Progress Board, July 2000. For more information, see the bian-

nual report by the Oregon Progress Board. The Oregon Progress Board is an independent state planning and oversight agency responsible for developing and monitoring the implementation of Oregon's twenty-year strategic vision, *Oregon Shines*. Created by the Oregon Legislature in 1989, the Board is chaired by the governor and made up of citizen leaders reflecting Oregon's social, ethnic and political diversity.

14. See "The New Significance of the American West," *A New Significance: Reenvisioning the History of the American West*, ed. Clyde A. Milner II (New York: Oxford University Press, 1996), 64.

15. In writing the final section of the introduction, I have incorporated some editorial comments from the co-editors, initially written as section introductions, especially those brief synopses of the individual chapters. Without giving individual credits to each of the co-editors, I want to acknowledge their contributions together here.

16. See Ronald Takaki, *A Different Mirror: A History of Multicultural America* (Boston: Little, Brown and Company, 1993), 14.

Part I

DEMOGRAPHICS

Chapter One

Racialized Minority Demographics of Oregon

Robert D. Thompson, Jr.

The history of indigenous peoples in what is now called Oregon began long before the state's founding one hundred and forty seven years ago (1859) and millennia before Lewis and Clark were commissioned by President Thomas Jefferson to explore and assay the territory purchased from Imperial France (529,911,681 acres for 15 million dollars), which in turn created a hunger and thirst in explorers and eventually settlers to expand to the territory further west of the Louisiana Purchase, the Pacific Northwest: Idaho, Oregon, Washington, and the western portions of Montana and Wyoming.

The Pacific Northwest and specifically the area known as Oregon was populated with various indigenous ethnic groups who had traveled through the land, settled the land, cultivated the land, traded, fished, inter-married, and hunted on the land for thousands of years.

Before the Euro-American settlers, people were living on the land, which some called Ooligan, "common in Chinook jargon."[1] Scott Byram and David Lewis' research suggest that the name Oregon may derive from the "place name Ourigan [which] may reflect Western Cree interaction with indigenous people west of the Rockies and awareness of the astounding wealth of the Northwest Coast."[2] The official history of Oregon—the master narrative—"the grand story" which overlooks indigenous peoples' histories and claims to tell the story of everyone whether they know it or not[3] is rooted in a particular kind of society that emerged in both the European Enlightenment and industrialization eras. Both were tightly bound to the myth of progress, and the notion of a "linear narrative imposed on nonlinear plural experiences."[4] The construction of this master, settler narrative of history is raised as a "major barrier" which, "makes individual, [collective] and local consciousness so insignificant."[5] Thus, the marginalization and erasure of indigenous place names, not to mention peoples, in Oregon require that we carefully read histories, but more importantly that we pay even closer attention to the erasure marks that represent other historical perspectives that can give rise to the counter-memory of Oregon, Ooligan/Ourigan.

Counter-memory according to George Lipsitz "looks to the past for the hidden histories excluded from the dominant narratives. But unlike myths that seek to detach events and actions from the fabric of any larger history, counter-memory forces revision of existing histories by supplying new perspectives about the past."[6] Demography tells a story. The story is not a neutral natural occurrence but it represents a contested socio-historical political, social, cultural, and economic terrain. People of color have a long but often overlooked history in what is now Oregon.

This chapter on the demographics of Oregon's racialized minorities and indigenous peoples is not a history of these various groups of people though I will use some historical events to contextualize the numbers that make an implied claim to tell the story of people. Demography tells a story, and this story does not have to be static like a stratification graph—the pyramid shaped chart with a small wealthy powerful elite at the top; then a professional and less powerful but influential group below; below this group a large middle-class group; and at the base of the pyramid a vast majority of working-class, working-poor, and the dispossessed (underclass). The stratification chart tells us how society is organized at a given moment but it does not tell us how people came to be situated in the social structure the way we see them at a given moment. Like a stratification chart, demographics of a given people at a particular time can tell us the size of a group, educational attainment of a group, median income and poverty levels of a group and more; but the numbers alone do not tell us how the group came to be the size that it is or how it came to be situated, fixed in society where it is. Minority demographics of Oregon can either tell a story that affirms the official historical myth/s—thus maintaining the status quo, or it can look at the erasure marks and the silences in the historical texts to evoke a counter-memory revealing and taking into account other historical perspectives that speak to rich diverse histories of interconnected peoples living in Oregon. The reality has been and still is to a certain degree that the movements, migrations, and places of residence have been historically managed if not outright policed—influenced by economic, social, and political conditions.

INDIGENOUS PEOPLES

The official historical record of settler contact with the indigenous peoples in Oregon estimates that between 50,000 and 100,000 indigenous peoples lived in Oregon at the time of "contact." Years of war and disease decimated the cohesion of the indigenous societies and, by 1870, the remnant of peoples left were forced to live on a few reservations. For nearly eight decades the population of indigenous peoples declined until the 1950s when the population began a gradual incline—by approximately three tenths of the total population (1,521,341).

In 1954 the United States government passed the Termination Act. One hundred and nine indigenous tribes were terminated, with sixty-two of those tribes in Oregon alone. Over the course of nearly three decades a number of tribes in Oregon were restored to their tribal government status: Confederated Tribes of the Siletz (1977), Cow Creek Band of Umpqua Indians (1982), Confederated Tribes of the Grand Ronde (1983), Confederated Tribes of Coos, Lower Umpqua, and Siuslaw Indians (1984), Klamath Indian Tribe (1986), and Coqualiie Indian Tribe (1989).

Today, the state of Oregon has a formal relationship with nine federally recognized tribal governments. Of the 49,138 Native Americans (Census 2004) counted in Oregon, 42, 686 (86 percent) live in 16 of Oregon's 36 counties. Sixty seven percent of the total Native American population lives in nine Oregon counties. Thirty eight percent (18,849) Native Americans are concentrated in five counties (Clackamas, Lane, Marion, Multnomah, and Washington) that are either located in or surround major metropolitan areas in Oregon. Most of the Native American/Indigenous populations in Oregon are dispersed over 31 counties, and in five of these counties (13.8 percent) there are 100 or less Indigenous peoples living there.

ASIAN AMERICAN AND PACIFIC ISLANDERS

Chinese were the first of many Asian groups to come to Oregon seeking work and to eventually settle in Oregon. The popular cultural view of Asians, no matter how long they have lived in the United States and Oregon, is that they are the perennial foreigner within. There is a general myth about Asian and Pacific Islanders' presence in the Pacific Northwest that their arrival here is fairly recent, usually seen as beginning about 156 years ago with the establishment of the state of Oregon. There are reports and some recent historical and archaeological evidence that the Kanaka (Native Hawaiians) and Chinese had visited and even traded with indigenous inhabitants of the Pacific Northwest about a thousand years or more before Europeans and Euro-Americans arrived on the scene (Dmae Roberts Crossing East radio documentary). John Henrik Clarke reports that it, even, had "become routine for English fishermen to travel across the Atlantic to fish the outer banks where they often caught sight of the mainland to the west."[7] It seems reasonable to me that if English fishermen could sail west to fish off the east coast of North America and that even the Vikings, "according to physical evidence,"[8] had established settlements in North America 1000 years ago, then it would seem well within the realm of possibility that the Kanaka, as well as the Chinese, sailed their long boats and ships east across the Pacific Ocean to the Pacific Northwest.

As Oregon was being established as a state, Chinese began arriving in the 1850s as contract workers who found employment in the construction of railroads, mining and the canning industry on the Columbia River. In the 1870s and 1880s the Chinese population reached it historical peak of 5 percent of the total population. After the early 1880s the Chinese population declined, and continued to decline until the 1930s when it reached its low point through the World War II years. By the mid 1950s the Chinese population began a gradual increase and continued to increase to 20,930 in the year 2000, or six tenths of one percent (.6 percent) of the total population, which makes Chinese the largest Asian group in Oregon.

Before the end of the 19th Century, Japanese presence began to grow rapidly. This growth continued until 1900 when it leveled off and slumped before 1925 when the federal government passed immigration laws designed to reduce Japanese immigration. The Japanese population reached nadir during the Second World War and did not begin to increase until the 1960s when the Japanese population began a shallow but gradual increase until the early 1990s, and then a slight decline to the census year 2000 when the population was recorded at 12,131, or .35 percent of the total Oregon population.

Vietnamese are the second largest Asian group living in Oregon, having migrated as refugees to Oregon during and after the war in Vietnam. In the 2000 census the Vietnamese population was 18,890 (.55 percent). A later group to enter Oregon after the Vietnam War was the Hmong. These were people who lived in the highlands of Vietnam and who had been allies of the Americans during the war. After the war ended and facing reprisals from the Vietnam government, the Hmong were brought to the United States by the State Department. In 2000, 2,100 Hmong were living in Oregon. During the mid- to late 1980s and the 1990s, with the growth in the technology industry and globalization in other sectors of the economy, other Asian groups, including Koreans (12,387; 2000 census) and Filipinos (10,627; 2000 census) among others were drawn to the state.

The majority of Asian Americans and Asian immigrants (89 percent) are concentrated in six of Oregon's thirty-six counties. The areas of concentration seen today in counties of residence bear testimony to past as well as present racial conditions, not only for Asians and Asian Americans but also for other racialized minority groups and indigenous peoples in Oregon. Seventy five percent of the Asian population lives in three counties that intersect and over-lap the city of Portland. In the two counties that are home to Oregon's two Flagship Universities, Oregon State University and the University of Oregon, Asian Americans and Asian immigrants represent nearly ten percent (12,107) of the total Asian American and Asian immigrant population. In eleven Oregon counties, Asian Americans and Asian immigrants have one hundred or fewer persons of Asian ancestry living in them. Of the 9,630 Native Hawaiians and other Pacific Islanders, 7,945 (82 percent) live in eight of Oregon's thirty-six counties. One hundred or fewer Native Hawaiians and other Pacific Islanders live in half (18) of Oregon's 36 counties.

AFRICAN AMERICANS

African Americans or black people were present before the Oregon territory and the state of Oregon were established. Historically, the black/African American population has always been small. For instance, today the black population in Oregon ranks forty-first (1.7 percent; 2004) of the fifty states in terms of percentage of the total state population. In 1850 the black population in Oregon was about 1.5 percent of the total population.

After 1857 the Oregon Constitution barred any "free Negro or Mulattoes" from owning land or even settling in the state. The census of 1860 documented 124 "blacks and mulattoes" living in Oregon. African Americans/ Blacks came to Oregon for many of the same reasons that the Chinese came to the state, to find work and for freedom. Most of the Blacks that came to Oregon during the 1880s lived in Portland. During the years between the 1880s and the war years of the early to mid-1940s, the African American population grew gradually.

In 1942, 3,000 African Americans moved to Portland with nearly 20,000 other workers seeking employment in the Kaiser shipbuilding yards. With the infusion of the 3,000 black workers into the Portland area, African Americans became the largest racialized minority group, surpassing Chinese Americans. By 1946, 15,000 African Americans were living in Portland. From the late 1940s to the end of the twentieth century, the population of African Americans has steadily grown, reaching 1.8% (64,117; 2004 census data) of the total population. The black presence in Oregon since the 1880s has been concentrated in the Northeast part of Portland, the Albina district. To be sure, since the Vanport flood of May 30, 1948, there has been a concerted public policy attempt to contain black people in the Northeast area of the city of Portland. Today 61.1% of the 64,117 black people who live in Oregon live in Northeast Portland. In the three counties that make up the Portland Metropolitan area, 77% of the black population in Oregon lives those three counties.

LATINOS

By the 1970 census, Latinos had become the largest minority group in Oregon. Latinos entered Oregon in large numbers at the beginning of the 20th century. Mexicans initially represented the largest number of the Latinos in Oregon. The attraction to Oregon in the early decades of the 20th century for Mexicans and other Latino groups was the abundance of low paying agricultural work available. Latinos through six or more decades of the 20th century were largely itinerant migrants from Texas, California and Mexico who came with the crops, and who lived and worked in harsh conditions in rural Oregon. In about 1976 there was a sharp increase in Latino immigration to Oregon as well as to other parts of the United States. The Latino population in Oregon more than doubled (112,707 to 275,314) in the decade from 1990 to 2000.

As of the 2000 census, 89 percent of the Latino population live in fourteen of Oregon's thirty-six counties. Forty four percent of the Oregon Latino population lives in three counties that comprise the greater metropolitan area around the city of Portland: Washington, Multnomah, and Clackamas. Sixty eight percent of the Latino population resides in five counties that are home to three of Oregon's largest urban centers: Portland, Salem, and Eugene. At the end of the 20th and the beginning of the 21st centuries the majority of the Latino workers now lives and works in urban settings. They are employed in small businesses, retail, and various owner-operated businesses. According to census 2000, Mexicans make up seventy seven percent (214, 662) of the total Latino population in Oregon. Of the remaining thirty three percent of the Latino population who were not Mexican, there were 5,092 Puerto Ricans, 3,091 Cubans, 7,955 Central Americans, and 3, 975 South Americans and other Latino groups lived in the state.

ARAB AMERICANS

A less visible racialized minority group living in Oregon is the Arab population. Some of the invisibility of the group can be accounted for by the fact that in the U.S. Census, Arabs are counted as Whites (as are Latinos). Possibly another facet of the perceived invisibility of Arab peoples is due to their relatively small numbers—9,316, or .27 percent of the total Oregon population of

3,421,399 (2000 census). Arabs began immigrating to the United States in the 1860s. These first Arab immigrants were primarily Christians. A second wave of Arab immigrants came to the United States after World War II. The religious background of the second wave of Arab immigrants was primarily Muslim. There are over three million Arabs who live in the United States, and three tenths of one percent (.3 percent) of the Arab population live in Oregon. Sixty one percent of Arab Oregonians come from Lebanon, Syria, and Egypt, and like other minority groups in Oregon, live in urban areas. Lebanese Oregonians represent the largest Arab group in Oregon. For instance, sixty nine percent of Arabs living in Oregon live in the three counties that make up the greater Portland metropolitan area: Multnomah, Clackamas, and Washington counties.

The story that demography tells is not a natural phenomenon. It is a socio-historical construction mediated by power and dominant group interests and subsequent resistance to domination. In the next four or five decades of the Twenty First Century it is projected that the population of racialized minority groups in Oregon will continue to grow (along with resistance and struggle). With this growth, the histories that make up the cultural, political, and social fabric of Oregon, though hidden and muted in the past, will undoubtedly change our understanding of what it means to be an "Oregonian."

NOTES

1. S. Byram and D.Lewis, "Ourigan: Wealth of the Northwest Coast," *Oregon Historical Quarterly* 102, no. 2 (summer 2001): 132–33.

2. Byram and Lewis, "Ourigan," 132–133.

3. G. Lipsitz, *Time Passages: Collective Memory and American Popular Culture* (Minneapolis, Oxford: University of Minnesota Press, 1991), 216.

4. Lipsitz, *Time Passages*, 216.

5. Lipsitz, *Time Passages*, 216.

6. Lipsitz, *Time Passages*, 227.

7. John Henrik Clarke, *Christopher Columbus and the Afrikan Holocaust: Slavery and the Rise of European Capitalism* (Brooklyn, New York: A&B Publishers Group 1993), 14.

8. Clarke, Christopher Columbus, 14.

Part II

A LEGACY OF RACIALIZATION

Chapter Two

"A Mistake to Simmer the Question Down to Black and White": The History of Oregon's Miscegenation Law

Peggy Pascoe

"[I]t shall not be lawful within this state for any white person, male or female, to intermarry with any negro, Chinese, or any person having one fourth or more negro, Chinese, or kanaka blood, or any person having more than one half Indian blood; and all such marriages, or attempted marriages, shall be absolutely null and void."

—*Oregon Laws, 1866*

In October 1866, when representative James Gingles asked the Oregon legislature to prohibit whites from marrying "negroes, Chinese, Kanaka [or Native Hawaiians], and Indians," he stood at a turning point in the history of the American racial state.[1] At the very same moment—the end of slavery and the U.S. Civil War—when freed blacks and radical republicans pushed the federal government to grant civil rights to African Americans, lawmakers like Gingles pulled in the opposite direction. Eager to build a new, and even more expansive, structure of white supremacy from the tumbling bricks of older racial hierarchies, they stretched pre-Civil War bans on marriage between whites and blacks to cover additional "races." As historian Nancy F. Cott has argued, marriage bridged the public-private divide in a manner that made it an especially potent political icon, and legislators made miscegenation laws a key element of their attempts to fashion the post-Civil War "body politic."[2]

Over the past two decades, scholars have written a great deal about the history of American laws against interracial marriage, especially as they applied to whites and blacks in southern states.[3] The laws date back to 1664, when the first prohibition on marriage between whites and blacks was enacted in the colony of Maryland; thereafter, they gradually spread through the South and into the Midwest and West as well. Until 1860, they served primarily to prop up the racial regime of slavery, but during and after the Civil War, they took on new importance. When the U.S. Congress enacted the 13th, 14th, and 15th Amendments to the U.S. constitution, ending slavery, making African Americans citizens, and promising all persons "equal protection of the laws," it embarked on a fundamental reformation of the American nation state. Yet what would eventually emerge from this reformation was a new racial regime, one that found its highest justification—and its most common-sense support—in the supposed need to prohibit marriage between blacks and whites.

James Gingles was, however, proposing more than a prohibition on black/white marriages. Oregon already had a law, enacted four years earlier, that prohibited "negroes" from marrying "whites."[4] Rather, the list of races featured in Gingles' bill ("negro, Chinese, kanaka or Indian") marked a multiracial expansion of prohibitions on marriage, a pattern that surfaced in other western states and territories, too. During the 1860s, Nevada prohibited whites from marrying "any black person, mulatto, Indian, or Chinese" and Arizona passed a similar law naming "negroes, mulattoes, Indians, or Mongolians."[5] Idaho forbade any white person to marry "any person of African descent, Indian or Chinese" and Wyoming targeted any person of "negro, asiatic, or mongolian blood."[6]

Laws like these, which passed by overwhelming votes and remained in effect throughout the first half of the 20th century, deserve more attention than they have so far received.[7] In this essay, I will use the history of Oregon's 1866 miscegenation law—the story of its passage, its enforcement, and its eventual repeal—to show why. It is impossible to understand the history of miscegenation law without examining the antiblack racism that was its taproot, but it is also impossible to understand the history of miscegenation law, or the history of the American racial state, without taking a close look at the use of marriage as the legal ground for a multiracial hierarchy of white supremacy.

Like post-Civil War Southern politicians, who passed a rash of laws designed to prohibit whites from marrying blacks, western politicians considered access to marriage and family formation an index of American liberty and citizenship rights.[8] The list of races featured in the Gingles bill—"negro, Chinese, kanaka or Indian"—was, in fact, a distillation of Oregon's previous attempts to limit the legal privileges of citizenship to white men. In 1857, for example, the Oregon Constitutional Convention had directed its legislature to find a way to deny every "Negro, Chinaman, or Mulatto" the right to vote.[9] The legislature responded by enacting a poll tax that applied to every "negro, chinaman, kanaka, or mulatto."[10] In 1864, legislators discussed, but eventually declined to pass, a bill that would have prohibited any "African, Chinese, Indian, or Kanaka" from testifying in court.[11]

In October 1866, when Oregon legislators debated Gingles' miscegenation bill, a few raised the possibility that post-Civil War changes in the legal status of African Americans might doom Oregon's emergent racial state. They pointed out that prohibiting interracial marriage might contradict two new pieces of federal legislation: the U.S. Civil Rights Act of 1866 and the 14th Amendment to the U.S. Constitution, which sought to protect freed blacks by promising equal protection of the laws. Their concerns were quickly overridden by legislators who insisted that these laws surely could not allow the legalization of interracial marriage. When one representative told the assembly that interracial marriage must be a legal right because under the civil rights bill, "You can make no distinction [on] account of race or color," the room erupted in laughter.[12]

By pushing aside the newly enacted constitutional guarantee of equal protection, Oregon lawmakers cleared the ground for the enactment of a multiracial miscegenation law. Building on the prohibitions on marriage between whites and blacks that were already part of Oregon law, legislators reached easy agreement on adding Chinese and "kanakas" to the list. They seem to have regarded the need to do this as too obvious to require any discussion at all. One reason for this "taken-for-granted" quality was their implicit emphasis on a particular race-and-gender combination: because men accounted for the vast majority of Oregon's Chinese and Native Hawaiian populations, Oregon lawmakers tended to envision Chinese and Hawaiian men paired with white women. By prohibiting such marriages, legislators hoped to protect white women from the sexual threats supposedly posed by non-white men and to prevent non-white men from forming the marriages that would have been an integral part of establishing their claims to political and legal citizenship.

When it came to adding American Indians to the law, Oregon legislators were noticeably more hesitant. Here, though, their reluctance focused on a different race-and-gender combination, that of white men and Indian women. During the settlement of far western territories like Oregon, white men's relationships with Indian women had created cross-cultural networks that facilitated land acquisition and economic development. Some intermarried men had become respected community "pioneers" and a few were even honored as community founders.[13] In 1854, when Oregon's Territorial Supreme Court considered a case involving one such marriage, it had posed the rhetorical question "Is not an Indian woman, married to a white male citizen of the United States, 'a wife in every sense of the law?'" and answered it with a resounding "Yes," justifying its decision in terms of the traditional legal rights of white husbands.[14] During the 1860s, however, the white settlers who continued to pour into the state disparaged "squaw men" as riff-raff who needed to be shunted aside in order for a truly respectable (read "white") polity to form.

During consideration of the Gingles bill, both groups of settlers—those who honored intermarried "pioneers" and those who criticized "squaw men"—wrapped themselves in the rhetoric of white male property rights and citizenship privileges. Lawmakers found these claims difficult to dismiss, especially when they overlapped with their traditional reluctance to tread on the marital rights of white men. James Gingles' original proposal had listed American Indians in exactly the same way as African Americans, Chinese, or Native Hawaiians, measuring the "race" of all these groups by a standard of "one-fourth or more of negro, Chinese, kanaka or Indian blood."[15] But the committee that considered his bill recommended loosening this standard to be "more liberal to that class of our citizens who, coming here at an early day, married Indian women and have raised families by them."[16] A few legislators would have gone even further. One explained that he objected to "making the law apply to persons of light Indian blood." "There are," he declared, "a great many people in the State of this class, who are persons of talent and respectability—some of them educated and highly accomplished. This would be a direct insult to them."[17] In the end, lawmakers compromised by amending the bill to include a special "one-half" blood standard for Indians.

Once this compromise had been reached, however, the Gingles bill received strong support from both of the leading political parties of the day, the Democrats and the Union party. Before approving the measure, Oregon Democrats briefly tried to embarrass their opponents by suggesting that Union men like James Gingles, who had favored the North in the Civil War and supported the 14th amendment, should logically *favor* rather than oppose interracial marriage. But Oregon's Union party leader, W.W. Upton, left no room for doubt about his party's position. The very idea, Upton proclaimed, "that there is any party in the State which favors amalgamation of the races" was simply "too absurd to demand attention."[18] The bill passed the House by a vote of 32 to 4, the Senate by a vote of 15 to 4, and was signed into law by Governor George Woods one week later.[19]

Once in place, Oregon's miscegenation law proved remarkably durable. In 1893, a black minister from Portland persuaded a state legislator to introduce a repeal measure, but the bill faltered in the House, and the legislature seized the occasion to pass a new law voiding the marriages of whites and "Mongolians."[20] In 1917 a second attempt at repeal, also introduced on behalf of "colored" constituents, died before it even had a chance to emerge from committee.[21] All told, Oregon's miscegenation law would shape the state's regulation of marriage for 85 years, from its passage in 1866 until its repeal in 1951.

The provisions of the law reached well beyond the simple statement that interracial marriages were "absolutely null and void." Marriage license clerks were required to "inquire into the facts" to see if license applicants came "within the above forbidden degrees." The law also set criminal penalties. Interracial couples who attempted a prohibited marriage were subject to sentences of 3 months to 1 year "in the penitentiary or county jail." Clerks, ministers, and justices of the peace who "knowingly" allowed such couples to marry were subject to similar sentences, with additional fines of $100 to $1,000.[22] These sanctions were especially important, because the threat of criminal prosecution gave state and local bureaucrats a personal stake in serving as the gatekeepers of white supremacy.

Like the debates over its passage, enforcement of the law combined multiracial coverage with an emphasis on particular race-and-gender pairings. In practice, enforcement depended on formal and informal networks that stretched from judges, prosecutors, and marriage license clerks to neighbors and newspaper reporters. Public and press attention focused mostly on couples involving white women and non-white men. One example is the case of Helen Emery and Gunjiro Aoki, which was splashed across the pages of newspapers up and down the West Coast in 1909. The incident started in San Francisco, when Helen Emery, the daughter of California's Episcopal archdeacon John A. Emery, announced her engagement to Gunjiro Aoki, a Japanese student. San Francisco newspapers gleefully reported that Bishop Emery, who opposed the marriage, quarreled with his wife, who supported her daughter.[23] Reporters tracked down Aoki's elder brother, a businessman, who described Gunjiro as an uneducated farm boy and "trouble maker among women, Japanese and white."[24] These intimations of sexual danger provoked a group of young white men to threaten to give Aoki "an involuntary ride on a rail to the edge of the town."[25] Friends and associates of both families soon joined the chorus of disapproval. Aoki's mother was "bitterly opposed" to the marriage, and his "relatives and Japanese friends" were said to have offered him $1000 to give up his fiancée.[26] Pressure from parishioners forced Bishop Emery to tender his resignation and Mrs. Emery to step down as president of the Episcopal Ladies Guild.[27]

Appalled by this reaction, Helen Emery and Gunjiro Aoki left California in search of a less poisonous venue. Their first stop was in Oregon, where they seem to have hoped that the state's 1893 prohibition on marriage between whites and "Mongolians," enacted with the Chinese in mind, might not apply to a Japanese immigrant like Gunjiro Aoki.[28] Oregon officials were quick to cut off any such possibility. The *Oregonian* assured its readers that such a "foolish and unnatural" wedding would never take place in Oregon, whatever the language of the law might be.[29] As one reporter explained, "the County Clerk and District Attorney will place their own construction on that law, and they are agreed that a Jap and a Mongolian are one and the same." Portland's county clerk issued orders to his staff to "[n]ot only refuse them a [marriage] license, but if they attempt to argue the matter, throw them out of the office." Portland's district attorney threatened to have them arrested as a "public nuisance." "If they think," he declared, "that the people of Portland will accord them any better treatment than they got in San Francisco they are mistaken."[30]

Unable to marry in Oregon or California, the couple crossed the border into Washington state. Here they found themselves on firmer legal ground, for Washington's miscegenation law, enacted in 1855, had never named Chinese, Japanese, or Mongolians, and it had, in any case, been repealed in 1868. Its repeal left Washington officials, who were also eager to prevent the match, with an awkward problem. The Vancouver city attorney tried to hold the line anyway. "[W]hile there is no legal impediment to such a marriage in this state," he said, "I should do all I can to prevent such a union."[31] Not until the procession reached Tacoma was a public official, the mayor, willing to concede the couple's legal right to marry in Washington state.[32] Much to their relief, Emery and Aoki were finally married in Seattle on March 27, 1909. "I am tired of this fleeing from place to place," Helen Emery told a reporter just before the wedding. "I have done nothing to deserve it, and because I love Mr. Aoki and am willing to marry him, is no reason why I should be hunted by everybody."[33]

The Emery scandal drew on a deep popular reservoir of rhetoric about the protection of white womanhood that had, among other things, often been used to justify the lynching of African American men. Sensational dramas involving white women and non-white men sold newspapers, so reporters continued to "hunt" interracial couples. During the 1920s, for example, Portland papers tracked interracial couples who slipped over the border between Portland and Vancouver, Washington, to apply for marriage licenses. As in the case of Helen Emery, these stories generally featured white women and "Hindu," Filipino, or "negro" men. One such story, entitled "Hindu's Fiancee Weeps: White Woman Collapses at License Counter," reported on a match between Helen Burnick, "who said she was a white woman," and Rale Ram, a "Hindu." According to the story, the couple received their marriage license but then "tried in vain to get married . . . as Vancouver ministers have ruled against mixed marriages and refuse to perform them."[34] Another story featured "Miss Lois Kendall," a "white woman," and Sam Morgan, described as "negro, single, deaf and unable to write." "[S]eeing the bride-to-be was a white woman," the minister approached by the couple "said that he was not in favor of performing a marriage ceremony for a negro and a white woman." Only the recognition "that if he did not perform the ceremony, someone else would" persuaded the minister to agree to officiate. In a move that must have struck fear in the heart of the couple, the story ended by giving the number and street address of the couple's Portland home.[35]

While newspapers played on the sexual fears and fascinations that surrounded white women and non-white men, courts pondered another aspect of the question of interracial marriage, its effect on property and inheritance. In cases involving white men and non-white women, another justification for miscegenation law—the desire to protect "white" property—came to the fore. Take, for example, the case of *In re Paquet's Estate*, heard by the Oregon Supreme Court in 1921.[36] Like many other American court cases involving interracial couples, this one centered on a white man who had been married to an Indian woman.

Fred Paquet died in 1919, survived by his 63-year-old Tillamook wife, Ophelia. Fred and Ophelia's life together had begun in the 1880s, when Fred began visiting Ophelia so frequently that he was targeted by a local grand jury, which periodically threatened to indict white men who lived with Indian women. Seeking to protect his relationship, Fred consulted a lawyer, who advised him to hold a wedding ceremony that would meet the legal requirements for an "Indian custom" marriage. Accordingly, in 1889, Fred not only reached the customary agreement with Ophelia's Tillamook relatives, paying them $50 in gifts, but also sought the formal sanction of Tillamook tribal chief Betsy Fuller (who was herself married to a white man); Fuller arranged for a tribal council to consider and confirm the marriage. Afterwards Fred and Ophelia lived together until his death, for more than thirty years. Over the course of their relationship, then, Fred and Ophelia had managed to ignore the Oregon miscegenation law of 1866, elude grand jury crackdowns in the 1880s, and win recognition as a couple from many of their neighbors.

They would not, however, ultimately escape the power miscegenation law held to connect white supremacy to the transmission of property. Fred Paquet clearly considered Ophelia his wife, but because Fred died without leaving a formal will, administration of the estate was subject to state laws that provided for the distribution of property to surviving family members. The county court recognized Ophelia as Fred's widow and promptly appointed her administrator of his estate, which included 22 acres of land, some farm animals, tools, and a buggy, altogether worth perhaps $2500. The couple had no children, so all the property, including the land and the house Ophelia lived in, would ordinarily have gone to the surviving widow. Two days later, though, Fred's brother John came forward to contest Ophelia's inheritance. John Paquet had little to recommend him to the court. Some of his neighbors accused him of raping native women, and he had such an unsavory reputation in the community that at one point the county judge declared him "a man of immoral habits . . . incompetent to transact ordinary business affairs and generally untrustworthy."[37] John Paquet was, however, a "white" man, and when the case reached the Oregon Supreme Court, that was enough to ensure his victory over Ophelia, an Indian woman.

In making its decision, the Oregon Supreme Court focused on the question of whether or not to recognize Fred and Ophelia's marriage. If the court recognized Ophelia Paquet as the legitimate wife of Fred Paquet, she would inherit his estate; if it did not, Ophelia would, in effect, be moved out of the category of legitimate wife into the category of illicit sexual partner, and she would no longer be entitled to inherit anything at all from her "alleged" husband. Ophelia's lawyers insisted that Fred and Ophelia had formed an "Indian custom" marriage, which should have been recognized as valid out of routine courtesy to the authority of another, "foreign," jurisdiction (that of the Tillamook tribe). The Oregon Supreme Court, however, rejected this claim. Deciding that Fred and Ophelia's marriage must be declared void because it violated Oregon's miscegenation law, the Court ordered that the estate and all its land and property should be transferred to "the only relative in the state," John Paquet, to be distributed among him, his siblings and their heirs.[38] In this manner, miscegenation law kept the Paquet property within "white" racial boundaries by invalidating the marriage of a white man to a woman of color at the request of an ancillary white relative.

But the Oregon Supreme Court did not stop there. Its decision reached beyond the Paquets themselves to refute the charge, made by Ophelia's lawyer, that Oregon's miscegenation law was an unconstitutional discrimination against Indians. Forty years earlier, in a case involving an Alabama criminal law prohibiting interracial sex and marriage between whites and blacks, the U.S. Supreme Court had ruled that Alabama's law did not discriminate against blacks because "[t]he punishment of each offending person, whether white or black, is the same."[39] In *Paquet*, the Oregon Supreme Court set this argument on a multiracial base. Oregon's law, the judges ruled, did not discriminate against Indians because it "applies alike to all persons, either white, negroes, Chinese, Kanaka, or Indians."[40]

Buttressed by decisions like *Paquet*, the racial categories of miscegenation law continued to multiply, especially, but not only, in western states. Altogether, twelve states passed laws prohibiting whites from marrying "Indians." Eleven states made use of the category "Mongolian," which generally covered both Chinese and Japanese. Three states used the more specific term "Japanese" and six used "Chinese" (including a few like Oregon, which used both "Mongolian" and "Chinese"). After Filipino immigrants began arriving on the West Coast, nine states passed laws prohibiting marriages between whites and "Malays." And even this didn't exhaust the list. South Dakota's law targeted "Coreans," Arizona named "Hindus," and, as we have seen, Oregon named "Kanakas."[41] By the 1920s, the multiracial pattern of white supremacy devised in western states had become the model for new laws passed in Southern states. In 1927, for example, the state of Georgia passed a law forbidding "a white person to marry anyone except a white person," then defined white" people as only those having "no ascertainable trace of either Negro, African, West Indian, Asiatic Indian, Mongolian, Japanese, or Chinese blood in their veins."[42]

Yet the sheer racial expansiveness of this multiracial framework of white supremacy eventually contributed to the downfall of miscegenation law, for the naming of multiple races gave multiple groups a stake in challenging the system of race classification embedded in the laws.[43] In 1947, for example, the Catholic Interracial Council of Los Angeles, a small but determined multiracial pressure group, decided to mount a frontal attack on California's miscegenation law. Taking their case to the California Supreme Court, they offered an innovative, if also counterintuitive, argument that miscegenation laws were a violation of the religious freedom of Catholic parishioners. In 1948, in a decision that subsumed the claim of religious freedom under renewed demands for equal protection and an assertion that the racial categories of California miscegenation law (which named "negroes, Mongolians, and Malays") were "too vague and uncertain to constitute a valid regulation" on the "fundamental right" to marry, the California Supreme Court declared the law unconstitutional by a razor-thin, 4-3 margin.[44]

Three years later, in a debate that emphasized the marriage of whites to Indians and Asians, Oregon became the first state legislature to repeal a miscegenation law in more than half a century. The repeal campaign had been inadvertently set in motion in 1950, when Oregon's Republican governor, Douglas McKay, scheduled a state Conference on Indian Affairs. In the context of discussions of the impending "termination" of government responsibility for tribal affairs, delegates demanded progress on a number of civil rights issues, including the repeal of the state's miscegenation law, which Boyd Jackson of the Klamath tribe described as a particularly humiliating example of Oregon's entrenched history of racial discrimination. After the conference, McKay asked the state's attorney general to take a look at the law. The attorney general predicted that if Oregon's miscegenation law were ever challenged in court, Oregon judges were likely to follow the California Supreme Court's recent example and declare it unconstitutional.[45]

With the Council on Indian Affairs, the governor, and the attorney general all in agreement that Oregon's miscegenation law had to go, a bill to repeal it was submitted to the state legislature. Its primary supporter was Senator Philip Hitchcock, of Klamath Falls, who called the law "an insult to the other races" and "a disgrace to the state of Oregon."[46] Building on the California

Supreme Court's example, Hitchcock insisted that Oregon's miscegenation law "violates the constitution and the laws of God."[47] It soon became clear, though, that legislators were more worried about insulting some "races" than others. Democratic Senator Thomas R. Mahoney, who hailed from Portland, the home of Oregon's largest African American population, immediately objected to the bill, telling reporters that "he is not opposed to marriage between whites and Indians, but objects to Negro and white marriages," which he described as a "crime to unborn children."[48] Insisting that Oregon's miscegenation law was "just as discriminatory against whites as against colored persons," Mahoney claimed that repeal was "the kind of legislation Negroes do not want" and that it would "set civil rights back 20 years."[49] There is some reason to believe that a majority of white Oregonians would have agreed with Mahoney, for only six months earlier, Portland voters had rejected a civil rights ordinance by a vote of 77,084 to 60,969.[50] Building on this base, Mahoney initially managed to persuade the Senate law committee to kill the repeal bill by a one-vote margin.[51]

Then, however, supporters of repeal forced the committee to reconsider. Unlike Mahoney, who framed his comments in black-and-white racial terms, the senators who urged repeal used examples of whites married to Indians or Asians. Warren Gill, of Lebanon, expressed "sympathy for the stand of Oregon Indians," whose complaint that the law was racially discriminatory became the *leit-motif* of newspaper coverage of the repeal.[52] The example of white men married to Indian women was, of course, already a familiar one. In the years just after World War II, Oregon legislators had begun to focus on another example—white soldiers who had served in Japan and Korea and now wished to bring their "war brides" to the U.S. As legislator Marie Wilcox explained to reporters, "several veterans, who have married girls overseas who belong to races other than white, had asked her to support the [repeal] bill so they could bring their wives home."[53] In the end, it was supporters like Wilcox, who insisted that it was a "mistake to simmer the question down to white and black," that carried the day.[54] The Oregon Senate voted for repeal 21 to 7, the Oregon House agreed by an even larger margin, and Governor Douglas MacKay signed the bill on May 8, 1951.[55]

After the Oregon repeal got the ball rolling, a dozen other state legislatures followed suit, in campaigns that gradually widened the repeal coalition to include the Japanese American Citizens League (JACL), the American Civil Liberties Union (ACLU), western state chapters of the National Association for the Advancement of Colored People (NAACP), a variety of local church groups, and a sprinkling of anti-racist white officials. This same coalition was in evidence in 1967, when the ACLU took the case of *Loving v. Virginia* all the way to the U.S. Supreme Court, backed by *amicus curiae* briefs from the JACL, the NAACP, and two clusters of Catholic laypeople and bishops. The fact that so many western state legislatures had recently repealed their laws helped the U.S. Supreme Court, which had been avoiding the subject of interracial marriage for more than two decades, to decide that the time had finally come to declare miscegenation laws unconstitutional.

Over the past decade, historians have spent a considerable amount of time and energy trying to understand the tortured history of miscegenation law, a project that has taken on ever-greater importance as the number of mixed-race couples increases, and as the current debate over same-sex marriage demonstrates that marriage license clerks are now required to enforce legal categories of sex in much the same way they once enforced legal categories of race. Yet it is still commonplace for Americans, in Oregon as elsewhere, to assume that anti-black racism was the sole source of laws prohibiting interracial marriage. As I hope this study has demonstrated, we need to widen our angle of vision. Before we can come to terms with the history of Oregon's miscegenation law, we need to plumb the depths of Oregon's anti-black racism, measure the multiracial breadth of Oregon's vision of white supremacy, and pinpoint the particular race-and-gender formations that preoccupied both its supporters and its opponents.

NOTES

1. I would like to thank Camille Walsh for her excellent research assistance in the final stages of this article. For more information on the concept of the "racial state," see Michael Omi and Howard Winant, *Racial Formation in the United States from the 1960s to the 1990s*, 2nd ed. (New York: Routledge, 1994), 77–91; María Lugones, "Hablando cara a cara/Speaking Face to Face: An Exploration of Ethnocentric Racism," in *Making Face, Making Soul: Haciendo Caras*, ed. Gloria Anzaldúa (San Francisco: Aunt Lute Foundation, 1990), 49 footnote; and David Theo Goldberg, *The Racial State* (Malden, Mass.: Blackwell, 2001).

2. Nancy F. Cott, "Giving Character to Our Whole Civil Polity: Marriage and the Public Order in the Late Nineteenth Century," in *U.S. History as Women's History: New Feminist Essays*, ed. Linda K. Kerber, Alice Kessler-Harris, and Kathryn Kish Sklar (Chapel Hill: University of North Carolina Press, 1995), 109–115, 119.

3. See, for example, Jane Dailey, "Sex, Segregation and the Sacred after *Brown*," *Journal of American History* 91 (2004): 119–144; David A. Hollinger, "Amalgamation and Hypodescent: The Question of Ethnoracial Mixture in the History of the United States," *American Historical Review* 108 (2003): 1363–1390; Randall Kennedy, *Interracial Intimacies: Sex, Marriage, Identity, and Adoption* (New York: Pantheon, 2003); Julie Novkov, "The Legal Regulation of Miscegenation in Alabama," *Law and History*

Review 20 (2002): 225–277; Charles F. Robinson, *Dangerous Liaisons: Sex and Love in the Segregated South* (Fayetteville: University of Arkansas Press, 2003); Renee C. Romano, *Black-White Marriage in Postwar America* (Cambridge: Harvard University Press, 2003); Eva Saks, "Representing Miscegenation Law," *Raritan* 8.2 (1988): 39–69; Emily Field Van Tassell, "'Only the Law Would Rule Between Us': Antimiscegenation, the Moral Economy of Dependency, and the Debate over Rights after the Civil War," *Chicago-Kent Law Review* 70 (1995): 873–926; and Peter Wallenstein, *Tell the Court I Love My Wife: Race, Marriage, and Law—An American History* (New York: Palgrave, 2002). This essay builds gratefully on all of this work, but takes its inspiration from Rachel Moran's comment that "[a]ny history of antimiscegenation laws must begin with the regulation of black-white intimacy, but it must not end there." Rachel F. Moran, *Interracial Intimacy: The Regulation of Race and Romance* (Chicago: University of Chicago Press, 2001), 17. My hope is to encourage more work on the multiple (and multiply complex) racializations embedded in miscegenation law. For exemplary recent examples of this sort of scholarship, see Leti Volpp, "American Mestizo: Filipinos and Antimiscegenation Laws in California," *U.C. Davis Law Review* 33 (1999–2000): 795–835; and Dara Orenstein, "Void for Vagueness: Mexicans and the Collapse of Miscegenation Law in California," *Pacific Historical Review* 74 (2005): 367–407.

4. An Act to Regulate Marriages, sec. 3, 1862 Or. Gen. Laws 85.

5. An Act to Prohibit Marriages and Cohabitation of Whites with Indians, Chinese, Mulattoes and Negroes, ch. 32, 1861 Nev. Terr. Stat. 93; An Act Amendatory of Chapter Thirty, Thirty-one, and Thirty-two, Howell Code, ch. 30, 1865 Ariz. Sess. Laws 58.

6. An Act to Prohibit Marriages and Cohabitation of Whites with Indians, Chinese and Persons of African Descent, 1864 Idaho Terr. Laws 604; An Act to Prevent Intermarriage between White Persons and Those of Negro, or Mongolian Blood," ch. 83, 1869 Wyo. Terr. Laws 706.

7. With the exception of a brief paragraph in Wallenstein, *Tell the Court I Love My Wife*, 144, the only accounts of these measures are three scattered articles, one each on Arizona, Nevada, and Wyoming. Two of these articles date back to the 1980s, as does the first attempt to analyze the effect of miscegenation laws on Asian Americans in California. See Phillip I. Earl, "Nevada's Miscegenation Laws and the Marriage of Mr. and Mrs. Harry Bridges," *Nevada Historical Society Quarterly* 37.1 (1994): 1–17; Roger D. Hardaway, "Prohibiting Interracial Marriage: Miscegenation Law in Wyoming," *Annals of Wyoming* 52.1 (1980): 55–60; Hardaway, "Unlawful Love: A History of Arizona's Miscegenation Law," *Journal of Arizona History* 27 (1986): 377–390; and Megumi Dick Osumi, "Asians and California's Anti-Miscegenation Laws," in *Asian and Pacific American Experiences: Women's Perspectives*, ed. Nobuya Tsuchida (Minneapolis: University of Minnesota Asian/Pacific American Learning Resource Center, 1982), 2–8.

8. Karen Leong, "A Distinct and Antagonistic Race: Constructions of Chinese Manhood in the Exclusionist Debates, 1869–1878," in *Across the Great Divide: Cultures of Manhood in the American West*, ed. Matthew Basso, Laura McCall, and Dee Garceau (New York: Routledge, 2001), 131–35.

9. Or. Const. Art. 2, sec. 6.

10. Of Poll-Tax on Negroes, Chinamen, Kanakas and Mulattoes, enacted 15 October 1862, ch. 35, 815, in *Organic and Other General Laws of Oregon, 1845–1864*, ed. M. P. Deady (Portland: Henry L. Pittock, State Printer, 1866).

11. *Journal of the Proceedings of the House of the Legislative Assembly of Oregon 1864* (Portland: Henry L. Pittock, State Printer, 1864), 57.

12. "Oregon Legislature," *Oregonian*, 6 Oct. 1866, 2.

13. For overviews of the initial frequency, and later condemnation, of sexual relationships and marriages between white men and Indian women in early Pacific Northwest history, see David Peterson del-Mar, "Intermarriage and Agency: A Chinookan Case Study," *Ethnohistory* 42 (1995), 6–8; and Brad Asher, *Beyond the Reservation: Indians, Settlers, and the Law in Washington Territory, 1853–1889* (Norman: University of Oklahoma Press, 1999), 62–68.

14. *Vandolf v. Otis*, 1 Or. 153, 155 (1854).

15. A Bill to Prohibit Amalgamation and the Intermarriage of Races, H.B. No. 1, "House Bills no. 1–111," Box 13, 1866 Legislature, 4th Session, Record Group 61–117, Secretary of State, Oregon State Archives, Salem, Oregon.

16. "Oregon Legislature," *Oregonian*, 5 Oct. 1866, 2.

17. "Oregon Legislature," *Oregonian*, 6 Oct. 1866, 2.

18. "Oregon Legislature," *Oregonian*, 6 Oct. 1866, 2.

19. Journal *of the Proceedings of the House of the Legislative Assembly of Oregon 1866* (Salem: W.A. McPherson, State Printer, 1866), 286; *Journal of the Senate Proceedings of the Legislative Assembly of Oregon 1866* (Salem: Wm. McPherson, State Printer, 1866), 236; An Act to Prohibit Amalgamation and the Intermarriage of Races, 1866 Or. Gen. Laws 10.

20. "Bill Favors Negroes," *Oregonian*, 11 Jan. 1917, 6; "House Is Opposed to Any Changes in the Intermarriage Law," *Oregonian*, 17 Jan. 1917, 5; Act to Amend Section 2853 of Hill's Annotated Laws of Oregon, Relating to Marriages, H.B. 41, 1893 Or. Laws 41.

21. Elizabeth McLagan, *A Peculiar Paradise: A History of Blacks in Oregon, 1788–1940* (Portland: Georgian Press, 1980), 164.

22. An Act to Prohibit Amalgamation and the Intermarriage of Races, 1866 Or. Gen. Laws 10.

23. "Archdeacon Does Not Approve Alliance," *San Francisco Chronicle*, 11 March 1909, 9.

24. "Brother of Aoki Frowns on the Match," *San Francisco Chronicle*, 12 March 1909, 1.

25. "Kissing is Barred," *Morning Oregonian*, 15 Mar. 1909, 2.

26. "Emery Girl Ready to Marry the Japanese," *San Francisco Chronicle*, 19 March 1909, 1; "Both Families Are Divided," *Oregonian*, 25 Mar. 1909, 4.

27. "Law Will Block Mesalliance Here," *Oregonian*, 26 Mar. 1909, 3; "Don't Want Aoki in Their Town," *San Francisco Chronicle*, 15 Mar. 1909, 16.

28. Aoki had first considered making this argument in California, where the state miscegenation law also used the category "Mongolians." On this point, see "Emery Girl Ready," 1.

29. "A Disgusting Spectacle," *Oregonian*, 26 Mar. 1909, 10.

30. "Law Will Block Mesalliance," 1, 3.

31. "Stapleton Would Object," *Oregonian,* 26 Mar. 1909, 3.

32. "Tacoma Will Not Say Nay," *Oregonian*, 26 Mar. 1909, 3.

33. "Aoki and Bride to Live on Farm," *Oregonian*, 28 Mar. 1909, 8.

34. "Hindu's Fiancee Weeps: White Woman Collapses at License Counter," *Oregonian*, 22 Mar. 1923, 12.

35. "Deaf Negro Weds White," *Oregonian*, 22 Apr. 1921, 7.

36. For a much fuller account of the *Paquet* case, see Peggy Pascoe, "Race, Gender, and the Privileges of Property: On the Significance of Miscegenation Law in the American West," in *Over the Edge: Remapping the American West*, ed. Valerie J. Matsumoto and Blake Allmendinger (Berkeley: University of California Press, 1999), 215–230. This discussion rests on two legal case files in the Oregon State Archives in Salem, Oregon: 1) Oregon Supreme Court File No. 4268, *Paquet v. Paquet*, and 2) Tillamook County Probate File #605.

37. "Findings of Fact and Conclusions of Law," 3 Feb. 1920, in Tillamook County Probate File #605.

38. *In re Paquet's Estate*, 200 P. 911, 914 (Oregon 1921).

39. *Pace v. Alabama*, 106 U.S. 583, 585 (1882).

40. *Paquet*, 200 P. at 913.

41. Peggy Pascoe, "Miscegenation Law, Court Cases and Ideologies of 'Race' in Twentieth-Century America," *Journal of American History* 83 (1996): 49.

42. Persons of Color, Marriage, Registry, Pub. L. 317, 1927 Ga. Laws 272.

43. For more on this point, see Pascoe, "Miscegenation Law"; for more on the *Perez* case in particular, see Orenstein, "Void for Vagueness", and Mark Brilliant, "Color Lines: Civil Rights Struggles on America's Racial Frontier, 1945–75," (Ph.D. Diss., Stanford University, 2002), 128–53.

44. *Perez v. Sharp*, 32 Cal. 2d 711, 728 (1948).

45. Matthew Aeldun Charles Smith," Wedding Bands and Marriage Bans: A History of Oregon's Racial Intermarriage Statutes and the Impact on Indian Interracial Nuptials" (M.A. Thesis, Portland State University, 1977), 150–57.

46. "Senate OKs Inter-Racial Marriages," *Klamath Falls Herald and News*, Mar. 21, 1951, 2.

47. "Senate Okehs Removal of Miscegenation Ban," *Oregonian*, 21Mar. 1951, 1.

48. "Mixed-Marriage Proposal Beaten," *Oregonian*, 1 Feb. 1951, 1.

49. "Senate Okehs Removal," 1; "Senate Votes to Permit Inter-Race Marriages," *Salem Statesman Journal,* 21 March 1951, 5.

50. "Senate Okehs Removal," 1.

51. "Mixed-Marriage Proposal," 1

52. "Marriage Law Clears Hurdle," *Oregonian*, 13 March 1951, 8.

53. "Senate OKs Inter-Racial Marriages," 2.

54. "Senate Okehs Removal," 1.

55. Smith, "Wedding Bands," 158–65; An Act Relating to Marriages, ch. 455, 1951 Or. Laws 792.

BIBLIOGRAPHY

Asher, Brad. *Beyond the Reservation: Indians, Settlers, and the Law in Washington Territory, 1853–1889.* Norman: University of Oklahoma Press, 1999.

Brilliant, Mark. "Color Lines: Civil Rights Struggles on America's Racial Frontier, 1945–75." Ph.D. Diss., Stanford University, 2002.

Cott, Nancy F. "Giving Character to Our Whole Civil Polity: Marriage and the Public Order in the Late Nineteenth Century." In *U.S. History as Women's History: New Feminist Essays*, ed. Linda K. Kerber, Alice Kessler-Harris, and Kathryn Kish Sklar, 107–121. Chapel Hill: University of North Carolina Press, 1995.

Dailey, Jane. "Sex, Segregation, and the Sacred after *Brown.*" *Journal of American History* 91 (2004): 119–144.

Earl, Phillip I. "Nevada's Miscegenation Laws and the Marriage of Mr. and Mrs. Harry Bridges." *Nevada Historical Society Quarterly* 37.1 (1994): 1–17.

Goldberg, David Theo. *The Racial State.* Malden, Mass.: Blackwell, 2001.

Hardaway, Roger D. "Prohibiting Interracial Marriage: Miscegenation Law in Wyoming." *Annals of Wyoming* 52.1 (1980): 55–60.

———. "Unlawful Love: A History of Arizona's Miscegenation Law." *Journal of Arizona History* 27 (1986): 377–390.

Hollinger, David A. "Amalgamation and Hypodescent: The Question of Ethnoracial Mixture in the History of the United States." *American Historical Review* 108 (2003): 1363–1390.

Kennedy, Randall. *Interracial Intimacies: Sex, Marriage, Identity, and Adoption.* New York: Pantheon, 2003.

Leong, Karen. "A Distinct and Antagonistic Race: Constructions of Chinese Manhood in the Exclusionist Debates, 1869–1878." In *Across the Great Divide: Cultures of Manhood in the American West,* ed. Matthew Basso, Laura McCall, and Dee Garceau, 131–48. New York: Routledge, 2001.

Lugones, María. "Hablando cara a cara/Speaking Face to Face: An Exploration of Ethnocentric Racism." In *Making Face, Making Soul: Haciendo Caras*, ed. Gloria Anzaldúa, 46–54. San Francisco: Aunt Lute Foundation, 1990.

McLagan, Elizabeth. *A Peculiar Paradise: A History of Blacks in Oregon, 1788–1940.* Portland: Georgian Press, 1980.

Moran, Rachel F. *Interracial Intimacy: The Regulation of Race and Romance.* Chicago: University of Chicago Press, 2001.

Novkov, Julie. "The Legal Regulation of Miscegenation in Alabama." *Law and History Review* 20 (2002): 225–277.

Omi, Michael, and Howard Winant. *Racial Formation in the United States from the 1960s to the 1990s.* 2d ed. New York: Routledge, 1994.

Orenstein, Dara. "Void for Vagueness: Mexicans and the Collapse of Miscegenation Law in California." *Pacific Historical Review* 74 (2005): 367–407.

Osumi, Megumi Dick. "Asians and California's Anti-Miscegenation Laws." In *Asian and Pacific American Experiences: Women's Perspectives*, ed. Nobuya Tsuchida, 2–8. Minneapolis: University of Minnesota, Asian/Pacific American Learning Resource Center, 1982.

Pascoe, Peggy. "Race, Gender, and the Privileges of Property: On the Significance of Miscegenation Law in the American West." In *Over the Edge: Remapping the American West,* ed. Valerie J. Matsumoto and Blake Allmendinger, 215–30. Berkeley: University of California Press, 1999.

———. "Miscegenation Law, Court Cases, and Ideologies of 'Race' in Twentieth-Century America." *Journal of American History* 83 (1996): 44–69.

Peterson-del Mar, David. "Intermarriage and Agency: A Chinookan Case Study." *Ethnohistory* 42 (1995): 1–30.

Robinson, Charles F. *Dangerous Liaisons: Sex and Love in the Segregated South.* Fayetteville: University of Arkansas Press, 2003.

Romano, Renee C. *Black-White Marriage in Postwar America.* Cambridge: Harvard University Press, 2003.

Saks, Eva. "Representing Miscegenation Law." *Raritan* 8.2 (1988): 39–69.

Smith, Matthew Aeldun Charles. "Wedding Bands and Marriage Bans: A History of Oregon's Racial Intermarriage Statutes and the Impact on Indian Interracial Nuptials." M.A. Thesis, Portland State University, 1997.

Van Tassell, Emily Field. "'Only the Law Would Rule Between Us': Antimiscegenation, the Moral Economy of Dependency, and the Debate over Rights after the Civil War." *Chicago-Kent Law Review* 70 (1995): 873–926.

Volpp, Leti. "American Mestizo: Filipinos and Antimiscegenation Laws in California." *U.C. Davis Law Review* 33 (1999–2000): 795–835.

Wallenstein, Peter. Tell the Court I Love My Wife: Race, Marriage and Law—An American History. New York: Palgrave, 2002.

Laws

Act Amendatory of Chapters Thirty, Thirty-one, and Thirty-two, Howell Code, of Marriages, of the Rights of Married Women, of Divorce, and Repealing Chapter Twenty-seven of Estates in Dower. 30 Dec. 1865. 1865 Ariz. Sess. Laws 58.

Act to Amend Section 2853 of Hill's Annotated Laws of Oregon, Relating to Marriages. H.B. 41. Ch. 30. 20 Feb. 1893. 1893 Or. Laws 41.

An Act Relating to Marriages. Ch. 455. 4 May 1951. 1951 Or. Laws 792.

An Act to Prevent Intermarriage between White Persons and Those of Negro, or Mongolian Blood. Ch. 83. 7 Dec. 1869. 1869 Wyo. Sess. Laws 706.

An Act to Prohibit Amalgamation and Intermarriage of Races. 24 Oct. 1866. 1866 Or. Laws 10.

An Act to Prohibit Marriages and Cohabitation of Whites with Indians, Chinese and Persons of African Descent. 6 Jan. 1864. 1864 Idaho Sess. Laws 604.

An Act to Prohibit Marriages and Cohabitation of Whites with Indians, Chinese, Mulattoes and Negroes. Ch. 32. 28 Nov. 1861. 1861 Nev. Stat. 93.

An Act to Regulate Marriages. 15 Oct. 1862. 1862 Or. Laws 85.

A Bill to Prohibit Amalgamation and the Intermarriage of Races. H.B. 1. 1866. Record Group 61–117, Box 18, House Bills no. 1–111. Oregon State Archives, Salem.

Of Poll-Tax on Negroes, Chinamen, Kanakas and Mulattoes. Ch. 35. 15 Oct. 1862. In *Organic and Other General Laws of Oregon, 1845–1864*, ed. M.P. Deady (Portland: Henry L. Pittock, State Printer, 1866).
Or. Const. Art. 2, sec. 6.
Persons of Color; Marriages; Registry. Pub. L. 317. 20 Aug. 1927. 1927 Ga. Laws 272.

Legislative Proceedings

Journal of the Proceedings of the House of the Legislative Assembly of Oregon 1864. Portland: Henry L. Pittock, State Printer, 1864.
Journal of the Proceedings of the House of the Legislative Assembly of Oregon 1866. Salem: W.A. McPherson, State Printer, 1866.
Journal of the Senate Proceedings of the Legislative Assembly of Oregon 1866. Salem: Wm. A. McPherson, State Printer, 1866.

Court Cases

In re Paquet's Estate. 200 P. 911 (Oregon 1921)
Loving v. Virginia. 388 U.S. 1 (1967)
Pace v. Alabama. 106 U.S. 583 (1882)
Perez v. Sharp. 32 Cal. 2d 711 (1948)
Vandolf v. Otis. 1 Or. 153 (1854)

Manuscripts

Oregon Supreme Court File No. 4268. Paquet v. Paquet. Oregon State Archives, Salem.
Tillamook County Probate File #605. Oregon State Archives, Salem.

Chapter Three

Japanese Americans in Eastern Oregon: The Wartime Roots of an Unexpected Community

Janet Seiko Nishihara

"Town opened doors for war's outcasts" proclaims a dramatic headline from a February 17, 2002, issue of the *Seattle Times*. The limited number of such articles, written about the growth of a small but thriving Japanese American community on the edge of the Oregon desert, tends to convey the same spirit—that this small farming community defied the prevailing anti-Japanese hysteria immediately after Pearl Harbor by offering a warm welcome to Japanese Americans. This small town of Ontario, Oregon, has been recognized occasionally for its unexpectedly large concentration of Japanese Americans, with most authors tying the community's growth to the welcoming nature of the community during a time when other communities reacted with fear and panic. The *Seattle Times* article describes Ontario as "just a speck on the Oregon-Idaho border," which "chose to snub fear and gamble on strangers."[1] How did this small farming community, in an area of the state known far more for its conservatism than for its appreciation of outsiders, become home to this pocket of Japanese Americans, complete with Buddhist Temple and grocery stores devoted to Japanese food? Like much of our history, the image of a community offering a warm welcome with open arms turns out to be a combination of equal parts of truth mixed with romanticized hindsight.

The history of the Japanese presence in Oregon has been occasionally gathered and recorded, decades ago by Marjorie Stearns,[2] later by Marvin Pursinger[3] and, more recently, by Linda Tamura[4]. The pre-World War II Japanese American communities in Hood River and Portland have been the subject of a number of articles, documentaries, and monographs. More recently, Cox recounted the story of an ill-fated attempt to bring Japanese laborers to the coastal Oregon mill town of Toledo in 1925 and the resulting riot.[5] However, aside from a recent piece which touches on the movement of

44

Nikkei (persons of Japanese descent living outside Japan) in a "Free Zone" during World War II,[6] little has been written about a small but thriving Japanese American community built from dust and sagebrush in the Treasure Valley of Eastern Oregon during, and just after, World War II. This chapter focuses on the creation of this Japanese American community, in and around the town of Ontario, Oregon.

The history of the treatment of the Japanese in America began long before their arrival in any noticeable numbers in the United States. The first large waves of movement from Asia consisted of Chinese laborers escaping famine and a disrupted political system in the Fujian and Guangdong provinces of southeast China. According to Chan, "after Great Britain stopped participating in the African slave trade in 1807, and especially after slavery was abolished in the British Empire in 1833, Indians and Chinese became the two main groups of nonwhite international migrant workers."[7] The Gold Rush of 1849 brought another large influx of Chinese to the west coast of the United States in search of the fabled Gold Mountain. This rush was short-lived for the Chinese, however. In 1852 alone, "more than 20,000 Chinese passed through the San Francisco Customs House enroute to the gold fields in the Sierra Nevada foothills. Fewer than 5,000 stepped ashore in 1853, partly because California had imposed a Foreign Miners' Tax . . . but also partly because news of the gold discovery in Australia had by then reached Guangdong province."[8] The Chinese were immediate targets of bigotry and nativism.

An essay titled "The Chinese Must Go," by the Reverend E. Trumbull Lee in the *Portland Daily News*, February 13, 1886, clearly laid out the arguments of anti-Asian agitators in three major points:

Why must the Chinese go?

1st. Because they never can become a part of our Nation. The cry against Chinese is not that that they are foreigners, but that they are a race that cannot be taken up and assimilated into our body politic. They have no ambition to become citizens except in very rare instances, and they hug pagan traditions and customs with a tenacity which our better civilization cannot break. . . .

2nd. The Chinese are unclean and immoral to an extent unapproached by our lowest classes, except where individuals of these low classes have been overcome by the unclean and immoral stench of Chinese corruption, and have fallen into the sink of pagan abominations. . . .

The Rev. William B. Lee, of Olympia, who has made a study of this question, says: "These beings (Chinese) are leprous, extremely filthy, and loaded with loathsome diseases. They are grossly immoral, and rotten in their corruption. And they also inveigle into their dens, large numbers of boys and men, who share their habits of opium smoking and prostitution. . . ."

3rd. Chinese laborers live on these shores at the expense of white laborers. . . . A Chinaman has no family to support, no home to adorn, no pantries to fill, no free schools to support, no churches to sustain, no government here which he will supply with brain and muscle in time of war. . . .Very nearly all that constitutes our political strength is unknown, unnoticed and despised by the Chinaman. Not so the white laborer. He must live. He has responsibilities and duties which he feels he must meet. He cannot live on a dollar a day. The employer who would ask him to, should be kicked out of the country, or converted.[9]

The vitriol clearly expressed in this essay, and others like it in newspapers up and down the west coast, represented the sentiment facing Asian immigrants at the time. This level of sentiment was not limited to the editorial pages. Beginning in California in 1855, many state legislatures, and ultimately the U.S. Congress, passed laws to first control and then completely halt immigration from China. The 1882 Chinese Exclusion Act suspended the entry of Chinese laborers for ten years, but then was renewed at every possible point. The Scott Act, passed in 1888, made it impossible for Chinese laborers to return to the U.S. if they ever left the country. The quick passage and enforcement of this act denied 20,000 Chinese laborers, who were at that time outside the U.S., the right of re-entry, including 600 who were already on board ships returning to the U.S.

As the immigration of laborers from China ended, the anti-Asian agitation which had been vented in literal tar-and-feathering as well as numerous Chinatown fires and other assaults, was transferred without pause to Japanese laborers who, to non-Asian eyes, seemed to be mere replicas of the "heathen Chinese." Certainly, most anti-Asian organizations wasted little time in transferring their hatred to "the Japanese peril." Where the Chinese, however, were scorned for being standoffish and clannish, presumably freely choosing to live "among their own" and not intermingle with the general population, the Japanese were feared because their "partial adoption of American customs" was interpreted as a sign of their superior cunning, making them much more dangerous than the more conspicuous Chinese. Numerous examples exist, throughout the history of the Chinese and Japanese in the U.S., of attempts to compare and contrast immigrants from the two groups, all the while declaring that they could not be distinguished because "they all looked alike."

During the first half of the 20th century, anti-Japanese sentiment continued to grow as part of the general anti-Asian emotional and political landscape that had been developing along the West Coast. After the passage of the Chinese Exclusion Act in 1882, demand for agricultural workers in Hawaii and all along the West Coast created a market for the importation of laborers from Japan.

By 1920, enough attention had shifted to Japanese immigrants to cause Oregon's Governor Olcott to commission a "Report on the Japanese Situation in Oregon."[10] Frank Davey, researcher and author of the report, noted that his "sole aim has been to get the facts as they exist and to obtain a knowledge of the sentiment of the several communities where Japanese form any noticeable part of the population."[11] Davey went on to note that he had "visited only such places in the state as I understood there was an appreciable element of Japanese and have made no effort to trace out the number or the activities of those who are scattered through other parts."[12] Consequently, although he visited numerous farming communities near Portland, in the fertile Willamette Valley, and, most notably, the Hood River Valley, he ventured no further east than the town of Bend in Central Oregon. For the most part, Davey ignored the sparsely populated counties on the eastern side of the state.

Through his travels and discussions with local farmers, Davey discovered that the concern about "the Japanese problem" was most prevalent where Japanese were in direct economic competition with white farmers. In those communities, talk was widespread that there was a Japanese conspiracy to acquire all of the good farmland in Oregon. The inaccuracy of this concern can be seen in Davey's own statistics which note that, at the time of his report, nearly half of the Japanese residents of Oregon were employed by railroads or lumber mills. Farming came in a distant 5th on the list of occupations of Japanese men.[13] Any notable presence of Japanese who were employed in agriculture was limited to small pockets in isolated communities. The main areas of contention were the Hood River valley and small communities to the east and west of Portland.

Notwithstanding the limited presence of Japanese farmers in the state, Oregon passed its own Alien Land Law in 1923, restricting the ability of Japanese immigrants (who were denied, by law, the right to naturalization) to own or lease land. After repeated attempts to close this traditional route to self-sufficiency, California became the first state to pass an alien land law in 1913. These alien land laws had gained in popularity throughout the western states during the 1920s, so much so that even states where virtually no Asians resided insisted on passing their own homegrown versions. Like many other laws designed to exclude or force out Chinese and Japanese immigrants, this law did not identify its true target by name, rather falling back on the expedient euphemism of "aliens ineligible to citizenship." By that time, all any law had to do was refer to "aliens ineligible to citizenship" and it would soon be implemented against its true primary target—immigrants from Asia.

These were unsettling times for Japanese immigrants who, unlike their Chinese predecessors, had wives and growing families. In contrast to the harsher restrictions placed on the immigration of Chinese women, the U.S. government's restriction on the immigration of Japanese women was implemented in stages. The cost of traveling to Japan, added to easier immigration for betrothed or already-married spouses (sometimes by proxy), fostered the development of the picture bride system that brought Japanese women to America to their husbands, sometimes on the mere basis of a picture and the work of a marriage broker. Even though the picture bride system was highly controlled, it did allow Japanese immigrants to form families, and consequently communities, much more easily and quickly than the Chinese before them. As Japanese families became more commonplace in America (compared to the largely "bachelor society" which Chinese immigration restraints had created) so did anti-Japanese sentiment, resulting in the cessation of the picture bride system. However, in the minds of the anti-Japanese campaigners, the damage had already been done. "By the time that the immigration of picture brides was cut off [in 1920], there were almost 30,000 American-born children of Japanese ancestry (Nisei) in the continental United States, compared to only 4,500 ten years earlier. They [the Nisei] comprised almost 27 percent of the total population of Japanese ancestry."[14] Although the Immigration Act of 1924 subsequently ended immigration from Japan, by 1930, there were 68,000 Nisei on the mainland and 91,000 in Hawaii—"49 and 65 percent, respectively of the Japanese-ancestry population."[15] Clearly, this small immigrant group had gained a foothold as this American-born generation, possessing all the rights and privileges of citizenship, began to flourish and multiply.

With the vast majority of Japanese immigrants residing in Hawaii and California, the state of Oregon was not developing as a primary home to Japanese Americans. By the 1940 census, there were only 4,071 persons identified as Japanese living in Oregon. Although, of that small number, only 137 were living in Malheur County on the far eastern side of the state, their small percentage in that county (.6%) was approximately double the average percentage of the state as a whole. Even though the total numbers were low, the Japanese American community surrounding Ontario, the largest town in Malheur County, was cohesive and "robust and successful enough to build a Japanese Hall for community functions."[16] Church meetings were held there as well as "dances, parties and occasional Japanese movies or plays."[17]

In counties adjacent to Malheur County, the numbers of Japanese were so low as to be virtually zero. In contrast, Japanese constituted 4% of the population in Hood River County.[18] According to the 1940 Census, there were only 25 "farm operators" in Malheur county at the same time that there were 68 identified farm operators in Hood River County and 91 in Multnomah County, which included areas of Gresham and Troutdale, directly east of Portland, where anti-Japanese agitation ran high.[19]

Marking the point at which the Oregon Trail enters the state, Malheur County occupies the far southeast corner of Oregon. Legend has it that French trappers and traders were in the area searching for furs when they were attacked by Indians. Several members of the party were killed and many others were wounded. Because of the misfortunes of their trip, the French named the river Malheur, literally meaning "bad hour," or, loosely translated, "unhappy river."[20]

By the time of the attack on Pearl Harbor in December of 1941, and the ensuing entrance of the U.S. into World War II, previous rumblings about a Japanese "takeover" exploded. All of the fears surrounding Japanese farming success, the increase in the numbers of native-born Nisei, and the newly-declared war came to a head when President Roosevelt signed Executive Order 9066, on February 19, 1942. This presidential decree created a pathway to, and a nominal legitimization for, the incarceration of over 120,000 Nikkei (two-thirds of them American citizens by birth) in concentration camps located in desolate and isolated locations of the western and southern regions of the United States. The president, and those who worked to carry out his wishes, used the rampant fear in the face of entering a world war as justification for this unprecedented abridgement of constitutional rights. One major goal of internment was to limit the risk of sabotage around areas of military importance on the west coast.

In order to designate the areas which were at highest risk of sabotage, "Lieutenant General John L. DeWitt, commander of the Western Defense command, issued a public eviction notice on March 2, 1942, which outlined two military zones."[21] In Oregon, boundaries of the two zones ran roughly north and south through the state, with some notable exceptions:

Zone Number 1 in Oregon ran from the coastline inland to U.S. Highway 99-W plus the entirety of Portland, Hermiston, La Grande, and Pendleton. Zone Number 2 was roughly all the area between U.S. Highway 99-W and U. S. Highway 97 plus the Bonneville Dam region and the Bull Run water reserve which furnished Portland's drinking water supply. Thus Zone Number 2 ran through the centers of such cities as Redmond, Bend, and Klamath Falls. Zone Number 3, the Oregon area not needing to be evacuated, comprised the remainder of the state.[22]

The government decided the boundaries of the various zones based upon the pockets of Japanese American communities, with the boundary of Zone 1 being pulled awkwardly inland in order to be sure to include not only the relatively large and beleaguered Nikkei community in Hood River, but also those isolated Japanese Americans living in the vicinity of the very small farming communities of Hermiston, Pendleton and La Grande.

"Nikkei residents were encouraged to leave the coastal areas defined by Military Area 1 and to relocate eastward into Military Area 2 or beyond.

There, they were led to believe, they might find employment on farms."[23] Because the Nikkei were allowed to remain in Oregon as long as they were outside Zones 1 and 2, those who were already living in Zone 3, and in particular the far eastern part of the state, were allowed to stay. This area came to be called the "free zone."[24]

Meanwhile, the U.S. Army was busy converting the Pacific International Livestock Exhibition buildings in North Portland to serve as temporary assembly centers for the soon-to-be-interned Japanese Americans. They were to report to this new Portland Assembly Center as an intermediate step until the more permanent internment camps were ready.

Even before President Roosevelt signed Executive Order 9066, the Federal Security Agency had decided that a period of "voluntary relocation" would be allowed during which Japanese Americans could move to lower priority zones as long as they could provide proof of private employment or sponsorship by relatives or friends.[25] Federal representatives were not unaware of the danger that individual Japanese Americans would be facing were they to go unprotected into communities which did not want them. Paul McNutt, administrator of the Federal Security Agency, informed Oregon's governor Sprague that

> Insofar as possible, we hope to help alien enemies and their dependents move to places that are either within the restricted, but not prohibited, areas or in unrestricted areas, on an individual basis and in accordance with their own desires. It is our hope also that work can be found for the adults of such families where their productive labor can be best utilized. Above all, it is our hope that we can allay alarm, hysteria, and prejudice, so that these people may continue to work and live among us in an orderly manner, and be given the opportunity to demonstrate their loyalty to the country by their own self-discipline, as well as by the surveillance of the Department of Justice.[26]

Even after learning that all Japanese Americans would be forced out of Zones 1 and 2, many "concerned citizens" went so far as to advocate that, rather than merely being imprisoned, any person of Japanese ancestry should be "returned" to Japan, even those who had been born and raised in the U.S. and had never left American soil. Governor Clark of Idaho gave political voice to ideas that many had had before him when he famously announced: "a good solution to the Jap problem in Idaho—and the Nation—would be to send them all back to Japan, then sink the island. They live like rats, breed like rats, and act like rats."[27]

In contrast to the sentiments of their governor, however, the Commercial Club of Weiser, Idaho, (located across the Snake River from Oregon's Malheur County) had already wired Oregon's Governor Sprague in March of

1942 about a Nikkei community that was growing just across the river in Oregon. The Club asked if the Oregon governor had any objections to the Japanese staying in the area to work as long as the local farmers and the War Department and farmers did not object.[28] Sprague's terse reply was, "I have no objection."[29]

While local growers cried out for help in topping, thinning, and harvesting their sugar beet crops, the Chambers of Commerce of Vale and Nyssa, two other small towns in Malheur County were reflecting the increasing concern pervading their communities over the possibility of Japanese settling permanently in the area. In a sternly worded telegram to Governor Sprague, also in March of 1942, the Vale Chamber said,

> We desire and will cooperate 100 per cent in national defense, but four large irrigation dams and canal systems rended [sic] us extremely vulnerable to sabotage that could destroy our entire territory in a few hours.
> We will not tolerate these people locating in our community unless they are colonized . . . and unless the United States Army provides ample supervision and keeps them under surveillance at all times, unless they will not be permitted to buy or lease lands and unless they be taken from this area at the end of the national emergency.[30]

Resistance to the possible influx of Japanese Americans who might volunteer to leave the Portland Assembly Center to relocate to eastern Oregon resulted in the rapid withdrawal of the offer for voluntary exclusion. The opportunity for voluntary relocation ended on March 29, 1942.[31]

The mounting panic was clearly centered not only on the possibility of wartime sabotage but also the recurring fear that the Japanese would settle permanently in the area after the end of the war. The old fears which had spurred several western states to enact Alien Land Laws had re-emerged even stronger than before, fueled by the shock of Pearl Harbor and the fear of Japanese military might in the Pacific. It is no surprise that some of those who, earlier in the century, had been the strongest proponents for the exclusion and deportation of Japanese Americans found avid audiences ready to hear their message anew.

During that same spring, while forces were gathering to solve the "Japanese problem" through forced relocation or deportation, other forces were at work to mobilize any labor that could be located, including the thousands of Americans of Japanese descent who were soon bound for internment camps in the desert west. With so many men away at war or working in the war industry, those farmers and businessmen involved with the sugar beet crop already in the ground in Eastern Oregon and Western Idaho were very concerned about the clear possibility that there would not be enough labor available to top, thin, and harvest their beets. A variety of other important crops had been planted in the area, most notably potatoes and onions, but none garnered the fervent political support that the sugar beet crop did.

The sugar industry, in fact, was so strong that concessions were obtained from the federal government to exempt Japanese American workers, consisting of existing residents, voluntary evacuees and internees, from internment. The Oregon Historical Society documented this phenomenon:

> The Amalgamated Sugar Company and state officials convinced President Franklin D. Roosevelt to allow an evacuation exception, providing Japanese internees the choice of working in Malheur County. In early May, 1942, several hundred Japanese families moved into a former Farm Security Administration (FSA) camp located near Nyssa. The Amalgamated Sugar Company, which owned a sugar beet factory in Nyssa, paid their wages and living expenses. Before the war ended, many of the Japanese moved to the farms where they worked.[32]

Why was the Amalgamated Sugar Company in particular lobbying so strongly for the utilization of the new internees to work on their crops? And why did representatives of the state and federal governments feel the need to respond to the pleas of sugar producers while other requests went unheeded? The answer, at the time seen as so obvious that few explanations were given, was written about explicitly by Pursinger: "the [sugar-producing] companies were being called upon for almost unlimited quantities of sugar by two great consumers whose supplies were not to be severely rationed by the government. One of these was the producers of beverage alcohol; the other was for sugar alcohol to be converted into explosives for munitions."[33] Fiset adds that huge quantities of industrial alcohol were needed to manufacture synthetic rubber for the war effort. Federal restrictions on acreage planted to sugar beets were lifted, resulting in 25% more acres planted to sugar beets in 1942 than had been in 1941.[34] The U.S. involvement in the war and further Japanese incursions cut off access to sugar supplies from the Philippines and Java. The Amalgamated Sugar Company, which had plants in Nyssa, Oregon, and nearby Nampa, Idaho, wanted to plant 30,000 acres of sugar beets in 1942 in the eastern Oregon-western Idaho district and wanted Malheur County alone to produce 12,000 acres.[35] This huge increase in acreage meant a parallel increase in a demand for seasonal farmhands to cultivate and harvest the beets, just at a time when farm laborers were enlisting in the military or being drawn to more lucrative jobs in the military-industrial complex. Japanese American labor was more crucial than ever for the success of this ambitious plan.

Although it would not become law until March of 1943, the groundwork for the Emergency Farm Labor Act was laid in early April of 1942 in what was called "The Oregon Plan." The Oregon Plan was a fortuitous coming together of the labor needs of the sugar producers, the need to "do something" about the Japanese Americans gathering in the temporary Assembly Centers, and concerns about the underutilization of the unoccupied Civilian Conservation Corps camps and the Federal Security Agency.

Milton Eisenhower, Director of the War Relocation Authority and Karl Bendetson, DeWitt's assistant Chief of Staff in charge of Civil Affairs, called for a meeting of governors and other state officials of the western states (excluding California). At this momentous conference, held in Salt Lake City on April 7, 1942, Eisenhower presented the plan to forcibly evacuate and relocate all people of Japanese descent in the shortest amount of time possible. The added benefit was the sudden availability of an idle yet hard-working labor force. Thus, Eisenhower already had a plan in place which would not only remove Japanese Americans from the west coast, but would also move toward meeting, and therefore silencing, the demands of the sugar industry and the sugar beet growers.

By the end of the Salt Lake City conference, Eisenhower had concluded that "states were prepared to neither provide . . . protection for seasonal workers nor to deal fairly with them, despite the acute shortage of labor facing the states' farmers."[36] Soon, however, pressure from the sugar industry and the farmers brought about a change in attitude, at least at the executive level of state governments. In Oregon, Governor Sprague, who had earlier demonstrated a moderate stand toward the issues surrounding Japanese Americans, began to swing toward those who saw all Japanese as potential enemies and not to be trusted beyond the barbed wire and guards of the concentration camps. Malheur County beet growers, however, were very insistent.[37]

On May 20, 1942, DeWitt issued Civilian Restrictive Order 2, which gave authorization for 400 evacuees to leave the Portland Assembly Center for private employment in Malheur County. As a result of well-publicized anti-Japanese invectives by such prominent persons as the Governor of Idaho (his "rat speech" having seen wide distribution in regional media), very few in the Assembly Center took DeWitt up on his offer of manual stoop labor in what appeared to be a much-less-than-welcoming environment. "Only 15 inmates from the Portland center could be mustered for the first train that pulled out for Vale, Oregon, on May 21."[38] Fortunately, those 15 were not harassed in their new jobs and earned $5 their first day. They shared their experiences with friends still at the center with the result that 50 more signed up to be part of the second group and 190 for the third.[39]

Once word spread that it was safe to volunteer on Eastern Oregon farms, volunteerism spread to other assembly centers, and subsequently to the "relocation centers," which were planned to be much less temporary homes than

the assembly centers had been. Unfortunately, the Malheur County experience was not the norm and the "reactions of townspeople ranged from luke-
warm acceptance in Rupert, Idaho, to outright hostility in small Montana
communities."[40] In fact, in Hamilton, Montana,

> [N]o restaurants would serve Japanese Americans, nor would barbers cut their
> hair. Under pressure from farmers, the one movie theater in town agreed to hold
> special matinees on Sundays "for Japs only." But merchants refused to sell pro-
> visions to workers unaccompanied by their employers. More than 250 Nikkei in
> this immediate area eventually harvested 25 percent of the total sugar beet crop.
> Many vowed not to return the next season.[41]

While documentation of harsher treatment exists, including violence, discrimination and exploitation, "Japanese Americans received praise from
nearly all quarters and were credited with saving the beet crops in Idaho,
Montana, Wyoming, and Utah."[42] The end of the 1944 growing season
marked the end of the work furlough program. In Fiset's evaluation, "in its
two and a half years, work release had permitted 33,000 evacuees to trade imprisonment for meaningful, paid labor experiences."[43]

As a result of the convergence of these security, economic, and societal
concerns, a prosperous and unexpectedly large Japanese American community grew in and around the Ontario area. The tiny pre-war population of
Japanese American farmers around the Ontario area, combined with voluntary evacuees who came to the only "free zone" in Oregon, went a long way
toward creating a critical mass which in turn led others to relocate to the area
after they had been released from the concentration camps. Restaurants, grocery stores and other Japanese-American owned businesses found success in
catering to the growing Japanese American population, while also serving
many from the larger community. In addition, Japanese American-owned
businesses that directly served local farmers slowly built on the trade they received from their Japanese American peers, ultimately developing long-last-
ing and widely-respected businesses. The Idaho-Oregon Buddhist Temple
and nearby Methodist Church both served predominantly Japanese American
congregations.

The population of Japanese Americans in Malheur County reached a high
of approximately 5,000 in the 1960s.[44] In recent years, the impetus behind
that growth has been attributed directly to the acceptance of those who voluntarily relocated during and after the war, adding to the town's reputation for
welcoming Japanese Americans with open arms. In 1988, then-Representa-
tive Ron Wyden called Ontario "the largest community of voluntarily relocated Japanese-Americans in the United States" during hearings on proposed
Plans for a Japanese-American Cultural Center in Ontario.[45] During these

hearings, the co-chair of the steering committee argued that, while places like "the State of Utah legislatively barred the relocation of coastal Japanese-Americans into their State . . . the Malheur Valley of eastern Oregon was different. There was already an established community of Japanese-Americans here. More came and were put to work in the fields, homes, and businesses of the eastern Oregon county."[46]

While hindsight has accentuated the rosy picture of Ontario, Oregon, as a warm and welcoming community, gratefully accepting those Japanese Americans who had voluntarily come to help Malheur County in the war effort, the real story is much more complex. A 1988 article written about the move to create the Japanese-American Cultural Center quoted local resident Mary Wakasugi in a statement which at first may seem unequivocally positive, but which, at second glance, clearly reveals her ambivalent view of the welcome that Japanese Americans received in this valley: "The community was so good to us,' Mary Wakasugi said. 'They accepted us, made us feel . . . not like dogs."[47]

NOTES

1. Florangela Davila, "Town Opened Doors for War's Outcasts," *Seattle Times* 17 Feb. 2002, <http://seattletimes.nwsource.com>. Retrieved 21 Aug. 2006.

2. Marjorie R Stearns, *The History of the Japanese People in Oregon*. MA Thesis. University of Oregon, 1937.

3. Marvin G. Pursinger, *Oregon's Japanese in World War II, A History of Compulsory Relocation*. PhD Dissertation. University of Southern California, 1961.

4. Linda Tamura, *The Hood River Issei: An Oral History of Japanese Settlers in Oregon's Hood River Valley* (Urbana: University of Illinois Press, 1993).

5. Ted W. Cox, *The Toledo Incident of 1925: Three Days That Made History in Toledo, Oregon: The True Story of an Angry Mob, the Japanese/Asians They Forced Out of Town, and the Lawsuit that Followed* (Corvallis, Oreg.: Old World Publications, 2005).

6. Robert C. Sims, "The 'Free Zone' Nikkei: Japanese Americans in Idaho and Eastern Oregon in World War II," *Nikkei in the Pacific Northwest: Japanese Americans & Japanese Canadians in the Twentieth Century* (Seattle: University of Washington Press, 2005).

7. Sucheng Chan, *Asian Americans: An Interpretive History* (New York: Twayn Publishers, 1991), 4.

8. Chan, *Asian Americans*, 28.

9. E. Trumball Lee, "Anti-Chinese." *Portland Daily News*, 13 Feb. 1886. <http://www.ohs.org/education/focus_on_oregon_history/APH-Document-Lee-Article-1886.cfm> Retrieved 21 Aug. 2006.

10. Frank Davey, "Report on the Japanese Situation in Oregon: Investigated for Governor Ben W. Olcott, Aug. 1920" (Salem, Oreg.: State Print. Dept., 1920), 20.

11. Davey, "Japanese Situation in Oregon," 3.

12. Davey, Frank. "Japanese Situation in Oregon," 3.

13. Davey, Frank. "Japanese Situation in Oregon," 13.

14. Chan, *Asian Americans*, 109.

15. Chan, *Asian Americans*, 109.

16. Sims, "The 'Free Zone' Nikkei ," 239.

17. Sims, "The 'Free Zone' Nikkei," 239.

18. United States. Department of Commerce, Bureau of the Census. Sixteenth Census of the United States: 1940. *Japanese Population of the United States and its Territories and Possessions*. Series P-3, No. 23. Washington, D. C.: GPO, 1941.

19. U.S. Census, *Japanese Population of the United States,* 4–5.

20. "Welcome to Malheur County," <http://www.malheurco.org/> Retrieved 5 Aug. 2006.

21. Louis Fiset, "Thinning, Topping, and Loading: Japanese Americans and Beet Sugar in World War II." *Pacific Northwest Quarterly* 90, no. 3 (summer 1999): 124.

22. Pursinger, *Oregon's Japanese,* 131.

23. Fiset, "Thinning, Topping, and Loading," 124.

244. Sims, "The 'Free Zone' Nikkei ," 236.

25. Pursinger, *Oregon's Japanese,* 95.

26. Quoted in Pursinger, *Oregon's Japanese,* 96.

27. Clark, 22 May 1942, quoted in Pursinger, *Oregon's Japanese,* 135.

28. Weiser Commercial Club, 14 Mar. 1942, in Pursinger, *Oregon's Japanese,* 136.

29. Pursinger, *Oregon's Japanese,* 136.

30. Quoted in Pursinger, *Oregon's Japanese,* 136.

31. Sims, "The 'Free Zone' Nikkei ," 236.

32. Kathy Tucker, "Japanese Evacuee Tops Sugar Beets," Oregon Historical Society, <http://www.ohs.org/education/oregonhistory/historical_records/dspDocument.cfm?doc_ID=000ABD16-BEFF-1E52-BEFF80B05272FE9F>. Retrieved 21 July 2006.

33. Pursinger, *Oregon's Japanese,* 224.

34. Fiset, "Thinning, Topping, and Loading," 123.

35. Pursinger, *Oregon's Japanese* 224.

36. Fiset, "Thinning, Topping, and Loading," 126.

37. Fiset, "Thinning, Topping, and Loading," 126.

38. Fiset, "Thinning, Topping, and Loading," 129.

39. Fiset, "Thinning, Topping, and Loading," 128.

40. Fiset, "Thinning, Topping, and Loading," 131.

41. Fiset, "Thinning, Topping, and Loading," 131.

42. Fiset, "Thinning, Topping, and Loading," 134.

43. Fiset, "Thinning, Topping, and Loading," 136.

44. United States. Congress. House. Committee on Small Business. Subcommittee on Regulation and Business Opportunities. "Plans for a Japanese-American Cultural Center in the Northwest," Hearing before the Subcommittee on Regulation and Business Opportunities of the Committee on Small Business, House of Representatives, One Hundredth Congress, second session, Ontario, OR, 17 Aug. 1988.

45. "Plans for a Japanese-American Cultural Center in the Northwest." Hearing before the Subcommittee on Regulation and Business Opportunities of the Committee on Small Business, House of Representatives, One Hundredth Congress, Second Session. Ontario, Oreg., 17 Aug. 1988. Serial No. 100–70. Washington, D. C.: U.S. Government Printing Office, 1989, 2.

46. Kirby in "Plans for a Japanese-American Cultural Center in the Northwest," 5.

47. Alan R. Hayakawa, "Ontario Pushes Japanese-American Center." *The Oregonian,* 26 May 19881.

BIBLIOGRAPHY

Chan, Sucheng. *Asian Americans: An Interpretive History.* New York: Twayn Publishers, 1991.

Cockle, Richard. "Free Zone: From the Seeds of War, a Japanese-American Community Grows in Ontario." *The Sunday Oregonian* 16 Feb. 1992.

Cox, Ted W. *The Toledo Incident of 1925: Three Days that Made History in Toledo, Oregon: The True Story of an Angry Mob, the Japanese/Asians they Forced out of Town, and the Lawsuit that Followed.* Corvallis, Oreg.: Old World Publications, 2005.

Davila, Florangela. "Town Opened Doors for War's Outcasts." *Seattle Times,* 17 Feb 2002. http://seattletimes.nwsource.com. Retrieved 21 Aug. 2006.

Davey, Frank. "Report on the Japanese Situation in Oregon: Investigated for Governor Ben W. Olcott, August 1920." Salem, Oreg.: State Print. Dept., 1920.

Fiset, Louis. "Thinning, Topping, and Loading: Japanese Americans and Beet Sugar in World War II." *Pacific Northwest Quarterly* 90, no. 3 (summer 1999): 123–139.

Hayakawa, Alan R. "Ontario Pushes Japanese-American Center." *The Oregonian* 26 May 1988.

"The Japanese Problem in Oregon: Report of a Committee Appointed by the President of the Multnomah Bar Association to Report on the Japanese Problem in Oregon." Reprinted in *Japanese Immigrants and American Law: The Alien Land Laws and Other Issues.* Ed. Charles McClain. New York: Garland Publishing, Inc., 1994.

Lee, E. Trumball. "Anti-Chinese." *Portland Daily News*, 13 Feb. 1886. <http://www .ohs.org/education/focus_on_oregon_history/APH-Document-Lee-Article-1886.cfm>. Retrieved 21 Aug. 2006.

Pursinger, Marvin G. *Oregon's Japanese in World War II, A History of Compulsory Relocation.* PhD Dissertation. University of Southern California, 1961.

Sims, Robert C. "The 'Free Zone' Nikkei: Japanese Americans in Idaho and Eastern Oregon in World War II." *Nikkei in the Pacific Northwest: Japanese Americans & Japanese Canadians in the Twentieth Century.* Seattle: University of Washington Press, 2005.

Stearns, Marjorie R. *The History of the Japanese People in Oregon.* MA Thesis. University of Oregon, 1937.

Tamura, Linda. *The Hood River Issei: an Oral History of Japanese Settlers in Oregon's Hood River Valley.* Urbana: University of Illinois Press, 1993.

Tucker, Kathy, "Japanese Evacuee Tops Sugar Beets," Oregon Historical Society, <http://www.ohs.org/education/oregonhistory/historical_records/dspDocument .cfm?doc_ID=000ABD16-BEFF-1E52-BEFF80B05272FE9F>. Retrieved 21 July 2006.

United States. Congress. House. Committee on Small Business. Subcommittee on Regulation and Business Opportunities. "Plans for a Japanese-American Cultural Center in the Northwest," Hearing before the Subcommittee on Regulation and Business Opportunities of the Committee on Small Business, House of Representatives, One Hundredth Congress, second session, Ontario, Oreg., 17 Aug. 1988, Serial No. 100-70. Washington, D. C.: U.S. Government Printing Office, 1989.

United States. Department of Commerce, Bureau of the Census. Sixteenth Census of the United States: 1940. *Japanese Population of the United States and its Territories and Possessions.* Series P-3, No. 23. Washington, D. C.: GPO, 1941.

"Welcome to Malheur County," <http://www.malheurco.org/>. Retrieved 5 Aug 2006.

Part III

INDIGENOUS PEOPLES AND EARLY COMMUNITIES OF COLOR

Chapter Four

Ethnicity, Solidarity and Tradition: A Study into the Dynamics and Complexities of the Chinese Immigrant Community in John Day

Sarah M. Griffith

The Chinese immigrant experience in Oregon began in 1851 and turned into a powerful ethnic, political, and social feature in the decades to come. Though Chinese immigrants and Chinese Americans still compose a notable population in the state, the nature of Chinese America in the twenty-first century is remarkably different than in the early immigration period. For instance, in the 1850s, Oregon's Chinese population was dominated by men who came to Oregon primarily as sojourners. They sought to turn quick profits off rich natural resources, send savings home to family in China and then return to their country. This early history was dominated by transnational ties that connected families (and other laborers and merchants seeking new opportunities) in China to sojourners in the United States.[1] Over time, a variety of opportunities pulled Chinese from their homeland—mining, agricultural, railroad development and entrepreneurial enterprises—encouraging the settlement, both temporary and permanent, of thousands of Chinese throughout Oregon, as can be seen in Table 4.1.

Oregon's Chinese immigrants first settled north of the California border in the Rogue River Valley, around Jacksonville, Oregon. Gold strikes in the region encouraged early migration and, by the 1860s, opportunities in other regions of the state pulled Chinese, and a variety of other groups, to wider regions in Oregon. Chinese established enclaves specific to their community's needs that included social and labor services and commissaries that catered to the immigrant population. The 1860s brought new discoveries of gold in Eastern Oregon and opportunities in urban areas like Portland, further spreading Chinese immigrants in the state. Along the north coast of Oregon, Chinese settled and played a significant role in the salmon-canning industry in Astoria.[2] The Columbia River Basin lured many hundreds of Chinese laborers who worked for railroad developers. Chinese immigrants also worked in

Table 4.1. Chinese in Oregon, 1860–1950. Adapted from Roger Daniels, Asian America: Chinese and Japanese in the United States since 1850, (Seattle: University of Washington Press, 1988), 60; and Marie Rose Wong, Sweet Cakes, Long Journey: The Chinatowns of Portland, Oregon (Seattle: University of Washington Press, 2004), 158.

Year	Chinese State Population	Chinese as Percentage of State Population
1860	425	0.81
1870	3,330	3.6
1880	9,510	5.5
1890	9,540*	3.0
1900	10,397**	2.5
1910	7,363***	1.09
1920	3,090	0.39
1930	2,075	0.22
1940	2,086	0.19
1950	2,102	0.14

*3,421 of this total are rural Chinese
**1,319 of this total are rural Chinese
**719 of this total are rural Chinese

quartz mining operations and land reclamation projects in towns outlying Portland. While the majority of Chinese immigrants served as laborers for white-owned companies, a handful of immigrants were successful, independent merchants and labor contractors. Merchants served as middlemen between the white and Chinese communities and often as unofficial leaders among the local Chinese population.

To better understand Chinese immigration history in Oregon, this chapter looks through two lenses: the first highlights two regions, John Day, in rural Eastern Oregon, which established itself as a small mining community in what would become Grant County; and, Portland, which became the state's urban center of development and commerce. The former flowered as a labor center and served as home to many hundreds of Chinese immigrants between 1855 and 1885. John Day's Chinese merchants opened stores in the city center and laborers looked to John Day as a hub for labor contracting services, entertainment and an outpost for Chinese culture set among a predominantly Anglo-American society. Portland operated as an urban parallel to rural Oregon, and, by the 1880s, gained a reputation among Chinese as a center for culture and newfound labor opportunities in and around the city. As a port city, Portland was a bustling hub of commerce, labor and eventually international trade. Portland's immigrant community maintained a lasting presence in the city while John Day's died out with downturns in mining, logging and agricultural opportunities.

In addition to these two vignettes, this chapter explores the longer-term effects of anti-Chinese immigration laws on Chinese laborers, families, and first-generation Chinese American youth in Oregon. Racial discrimination at the local level plagued early immigrants, but it was the 1882 Chinese Exclusion Act that federally mandated discriminatory policies against all Chinese immigrants. Despite discrimination, Chinese in Oregon fought back against exclusion by utilizing loopholes in the American legal system. They used both legal and illegal means to continue entering the state and some Chinese eventually brought their families to Oregon.

JOHN DAY

John Day's Chinese community is illustrative of many early immigrant communities in the mining-boom west. As the immigrant population grew, so did merchant and social centers. Laborers fanned out through Grant County to find independent and contracted work, and, in John Day, immigrants cultivated traditional and adapted social and political systems in order to navigate immigrant life.

John Day's rise to prominence came slowly—prior to 1885, most newcomers to the area settled in Canyon City, a mining town just ten miles south of John Day. Canyon City was founded in 1863 when white miners, en route to mining fields in Idaho, found gold in Canyon Creek. Once word of the discovery was out, miners flocked to the area, and Chinese were among those who saw potential opportunities. Grant County's Chinese population grew rapidly, with 940 immigrants recorded in census records in 1870. In 1885, Canyon City's Chinese population alone was around 900 inhabitants and included merchants, laborers and independent miners. Almost all recorded immigrants were men and Canyon City never had a notable female Chinese population.

Despite relatively peaceful relations between whites and Chinese in Canyon City, resentment and occasional violence did erupt. Reports of abuses against Chinese were periodically listed in the *Grant County News* and tensions culminated in 1885 when a fire—thought to be arson by whites—burned most of Canyon City's Chinese enclave to the ground. Not permitted to rebuild by city ordinance, a majority of immigrants relocated to John Day, where they established a new community. This second enclave provides the best-documented history of rural Chinese in nineteenth-century Oregon and serves as a guide for understanding the organization of Chinese life in the region.[3]

With an influx of Chinese from Canyon City, John Day's Chinese population quickly swelled to around 600 inhabitants in 1887, with many more immigrants coming in and out of the town depending on seasonal labor cycles. Infrastructure included a joss house, or religious temple, at least three stores, small shanty houses, and communal fishponds and vegetable gardens. The community was composed of sojourning miners, who worked claims both independently and for whites, general laborers, merchants, launderers and even physicians. With the growth of infrastructure and the maintenance of social organizations brought from China, John Day became a centralized meeting place for Chinese throughout northeastern Oregon.

IMMIGRANT SOCIETY: CLANS, CAPITAL
AND COMMUNITY RESPONSIBILITIES

Like many Chinese enclaves in the West, John Day's Chinese population relied heavily on traditional and adapted social institutions. Three general classes of traditional social affiliations existed in John Day. First among these was the family association. These fairly well-defined, lineage-based organizations were common in southern China and were marked by members who shared a common surname. The association functioned as an aid to the immigrant's settlement process, settled disputes among members and provided protective and financial assistance to immigrants. Another traditional association brought to John Day were village associations, or *hui guan*. Membership in village associations required a shared provincial origin (most immigrants came from a variety of Toisan provinces but other village associations were also represented in John Day) and a common spoken dialect.[4] While less well-defined than family associations, village associations enrolled and counted new members as they arrived in John Day, or, in some cases, upon arrival in port cities where village associations often had headquarters. Similar to family associations, village associations served benevolent functions, such as providing social and financial aid to new immigrants and protection to members. The third traditional association was the tong, often referred to by the white community as a "secret society." Tongs were perhaps the most misunderstood institution to whites, and historians continue to struggle with the fundamental characteristics of tongs. Some suggest that tongs were Americanized forms of old Chinese organizations that had served as semi-political/religious organizations, and which would later be most commonly associated with protest, banditry and rebellion in southern China.[5] In John Day, records show that tongs were most often formed when companies of immigrants that dominated a particular industry such as import and distribution stores or labor contracting came together. In some cases, these local tongs had connections to urban groups that focused on import/export trade in opium, prostitution rings and, in the early twentieth century, more illicit and violent activity. It was not uncommon for members of various institutions to overlap with others. Overall, the network of traditional associations created a well-developed, sociopolitical fabric in John Day's Chinatown.[6]

By looking at the specifics of these organizations, we can gain a better sense of *how* John Day's community functioned. One of the better documented family associations in the region is recorded in the history of the Kam Wah Chung Company (KWCCo.). The KWCCo. began as a merchant operation and later fused into the center of a vibrant Chinese social and business center in John Day. It was founded in the 1880s by two Chinese immigrants: Ing Hay, who came to the United States with his father in 1883, and Lung On who arrived alone in John Day in 1882 after first working in and around San Francisco and northern California. The Ing family association, located primarily in Walla Walla, Washington, served as a catalyst for Ing Hay and his father's move—the family association there encouraged the two men's immigration to the United States and facilitated the move financially and through business opportunities once they arrived. When Ing Hay's father returned to China a few years later, the extended Ing clan offered up money for the younger Ing Hay to start his new business with partner Lung On. Money would be repaid once the business in John Day was established and Ing Hay would be expected to repay his financial debt, as well as serve as an association sponsor when other clan members arrived in the United States.[7]

Traditions from China permeated other areas of John Day's community. The primarily male population was expected to support family through transnational networks while sojourning in the United States. The majority of men sent money home on a monthly basis for basic family needs such as food, clothing and building costs. More financially stable merchants were expected to provide greater assistance to family when grave sites needed repair or outstanding debts plagued family back in China. Merchants, in particular, were asked to help with greater travel expenses for immigrants wishing to travel to John Day. While most Chinese immigrants fulfilled their familial duties, some Chinese in John Day chose to disregard these responsibilities, remaining in the United States with little contact with family in China. Still others simply did not have the funds to support both themselves and their families. Overall, however, the transnational nature of Chinese immigration was strong and served as a unifying force among immigrants in the United States and their families back home.

Life in the white-dominated society encouraged an internalization of social networks among Chinese that included religious affiliations, annual festivals and central gathering places unique to Chinese. As a religious and social center, John Day stood at the center of Grant County's Chinese population and encompassed outlying towns like Auburn, Monument and Enterprise—each of which had substantial Chinese populations between the 1870s and 1890s. Chinese living in outlying regions viewed John Day's Chinatown as a place to gather with fellow immigrants, purchase needed supplies and congregate during the off-season. For many years, the KWCCo. supported annual festivals traditional in China, and a post office located within the store gave Chinese the opportunity to stay connected to fellow immigrants in the country and with family in China. Ing Hay regularly scribed letters for non-literate immigrants and Lung On's business notoriety in Portland, San Francisco and Seattle's Chinese communities helped to assure some laborers work when opportunities slowed in Grant County. In addition, John Day contained provisions stores, lodging facilities for sojourning Chinese and rooms where Chinese congregated to hear about local news from home.

Almost entirely missing from the Eastern Oregon landscape were Chinese women. Although a few Chinese women lived in the region, primarily working as prostitutes forced into service, the John Day region did not have an extensive female population. In fact, the absence of Chinese women, wives and prostitutes alike, led some immigrant men to carry on relationships with white women, as testified in photographs taken in John Day in the nineteenth and twentieth centuries. Letters written between Chinese men and white women also testify to long-term relationships between the two groups.[8]

LABORERS AND MINERS

John Day's Chinatown flourished in large part because of the sheer number of laborers and independent miners who migrated to the region after its founding. Chinese laborers flocked to Grant County for work in mining operations run by whites, to pursue work as ranch hands on farms and to work on railroad tracks being laid between eastern Oregon and other western states. In addition, Chinese miners leased land from hydraulic miners—generally whites—who no longer profited from working claims with the higher-technology tools.[9] Although some local mining laws restricted the sale of land to Chinese, and state law prohibited them from owning land entirely, some whites nonetheless sold their claims illegally to Chinese. In these cases, groups of five or six immigrants combined their money to purchase claims previously owned by whites. Usually, the remnants of hydraulic mining operations paid well for Chinese companies who used lower technology and labor-intensive placer mining techniques to work old claims.

In addition to placer mining, many Chinese in Eastern Oregon worked as laborers on railroad construction and for white timber operators; they were also found on ranches and as domestic servants in the homes of whites. While family association members already in the United States often helped new Chinese immigrants find work, Chinese labor contractors were much more influential in this regard. The Chinese labor contractors in John Day performed three specific functions. First, they were in contact with members of the white community that required laborers (and because these contractors spoke English, they had an edge over laborers who generally did not). Second, labor contractors located individual laborers or large gangs of Chinese laborers and helped place them in jobs throughout Eastern Oregon. Finally, as middle men, labor contractors managed contractual matters with white employers, often maintaining close business and personal associations with whites in the region. In cases where whites refused to pay for labor services, Chinese contractors stepped in to ensure timely payment. Over many years, a sort of loose, symbiotic relationship developed between Chinese laborers, labor contractors and whites. Chinese laborers relied on fellow Chinese contractors to locate work and whites, who demanded a steady supply of laborers, relied on contractors to find them cheap labor.[10]

VIOLENCE IN EASTERN OREGON

The symbiosis that existed between whites and Chinese contractors and laborers did not necessarily mean that the Chinese immigrant-white experience was conflict free. As was the case in so many western towns, ethnic minorities like the Chinese felt the brunt of discrimination and racism. Early on, local mining districts passed foreign miners taxes that targeted Chinese placer miners. In later years, the attributes that first brought praise to Chinese were the same that brought them disdain from whites, who claimed Chinese competed unfairly for jobs. Frugality, hard work and an ability to squeeze benefits from the most frugal gold claims increased nativist sentiment by the late 1880s. While John Day and the northeastern region of the state did not see the level of violence against Chinese that occurred in Nevada, Idaho and California, the threat was always present. Newspaper stories joked of young (white) boys throwing rocks at passing Chinese, and police in Grant County regularly turned a blind eye to violence against the immigrants. Because state and federal laws forbade Chinese from testifying against whites in court, most acts of violence against them went entirely unpunished. Perhaps one of the most violent cases occurred not far from Grant County in the Hell's Canyon region along the Oregon-Idaho border. In this case, at least thirty-one Chinese miners were murdered by white bandits on horse back—one of the perpetrators was barely fifteen years of age.[11]

Other more random acts of violence included claim jumping and robbery by whites, and merchants were regularly prosecuted in the courts for selling alcohol, opium and other goods without licenses. In addition, newspaper editorials criticized Chinese, and especially laborers, for their "decrepit" living standards and perceived "moral depravity." Opium smoking and prostitution were two of the more common reasons behind the criticism, even though white themselves engaged in these pastimes, frequently among Chinese in the Chinese section of town. Merchants seemed to receive fewer discriminatory attacks and were even praised for their willingness to adopt American dress, business practices and the English language. Perhaps the most ironic insult to Chinese immigrants in Eastern Oregon came from whites who complained that sojourners sent the majority of their earnings home to China and never intended to remain in the country long-term. Of course, these critics were very often the same people who pushed for local, state and federal laws that forbade Chinese from gaining citizenship in the United States or from bringing family to the country.[12]

Although Chinese in John Day certainly felt the brunt of discrimination and racism, fewer acts of organized violence, prevalent in urban hubs like Seattle, Tacoma, and San Francisco, occurred in Eastern Oregon. Chinese in John Day likely managed to avoid this by working in professions not highly desired by whites. Furthermore, immigrant miners rarely engaged in white-dominated hydraulic mining in John Day and opted instead for placer mining, an industry not often sought by whites. When Chinese did work for white-owned hydraulic mining operations, they generally did jobs that whites did not desire, like hauling heavy hoses used to dislodge gold from steep hillsides. In the railroad industry, Chinese in Eastern Oregon also performed dangerous jobs that whites would not do, including dynamiting mountains and tunnels and climbing steep ravines to lay track. Finally, although both Chinese and whites served as cooks and hired hands in the abundant lumber camps, the jobs numbered enough that competition was not great enough to cause deep-seeded resentment.

By the late 1880s, gold mining and railroad development in and around John Day had slowed, and so had the influx of immigrants to the region. Yet throughout the 1880s, when white miners in Eastern Oregon were on the decline, the number of Chinese miners remained steady. Totaled together, white and Chinese miners numbered somewhere around 2,171; of those, 73.9 percent were Chinese. Statewide, the census reported a decrease in the total number of miners by 1890 but an actual increase in the percentage of Chinese miners during the same period.

The Chinese population in Eastern Oregon eventually fell to such lows that communities were no longer able to sustain merchant shops or religious sites.

As mining claims played out, Chinese migration to Eastern Oregon ended and immigrants began to settle in predominantly urban enclaves like Portland, where there were more opportunities for work. The urbanization of Chinese immigrants led to the development of more complex immigrant communities that lasted much longer than the once-bustling rural communities.[13]

PORTLAND

Portland did not necessarily begin with a reputation for great economic potential. Early on, the small town on the banks of the Willamette River was called Stumptown for its slow rise from a logging town to a trade, merchandising and shipping center. In fact, in the 1860s and 1870s, Astoria, located at the mouth of the Columbia River, was the pearl of Oregon's shipping and manufacturing businesses. New canneries were regularly built and shipping boomed. It was not until the middle 1870s that Portland gained a reputation for shipping and business and garnered its urban environment. With aggressive promotion campaigns that capitalized on its location—river access to Eastern Oregon on the one side, the Willamette Valley to the South and the Pacific Ocean to the West—Portland became the state's center of shipping and urbanized industry by 1880. When the city was connected to San Francisco via the Northern Pacific rail line in 1881, the city became the Pacific Northwest's largest. By 1880, it had eclipsed Astoria in terms of growth, economic development and population.

For Chinese immigrants, Portland's appeal was unmistakable. Chinese merchants, who projected rapid growth in the region, began establishing businesses in the city center as early as 1851. These earliest merchants catered their businesses to sojourning immigrants who passed through the city on their way to destinations further inland and to the white industrialists who desired cheap labor. When direct steamer travel between China and Portland was permanently established in 1871, Portland's population of Chinese laborers increased dramatically, as did a community infrastructure that far surpassed that of rural John Day. In 1870, Portland's Chinese enclave boasted thirty-one Chinese-owned businesses, including four merchant companies, three doctors and twenty-three laundries. This development occurred despite the fact that the majority of Chinese immigrants at the time lived in rural regions like Grant and Jackson Counties. In fact, it was not until the late 1870s that an urbanization of Chinese immigrants, and Portland's reputation as a center for Chinese life, encouraged immigrant life to blossom.

New urban opportunities alone did not account for Portland's appeal among Chinese immigrants. Portland also had a reputation for being a safe haven for immigrants who had been tormented, and, in some cases, run out of other Western and Pacific Coast cities. This was certainly true following particularly heated anti-Chinese demonstrations in Seattle and Tacoma, Washington, in 1885 and 1886. Chinese were run out of these towns and the anti-Chinese sentiment spread south to target Chinese woodcutters in Albina, East Portland and Mount Tabor on the outskirts of Portland. Immigrants in these camps were beaten and their camps torn apart. On another occasion, 150 Chinese in Oregon City were driven from their jobs in a woolen mill located on the Willamette River.[14] Many of the Chinese involved in these attacks quickly relocated to Portland. Similar acts of violence in Washington and California also encouraged migration to Portland throughout the 1880s and 1890s, driving the population to some of its highest levels on record (surpassing five thousand residents in 1900).[15]

Despite its reputation as a safe haven, anti-Chinese editorials were a fairly common site in Portland's newspapers. As early as 1865, the *Daily Oregonian* editorialized Chinese women, particularly prostitutes, as "disgusting specimens of decrepi[t] humanity" who were given police whistles to call on officers while "decent Americans" had to hunt for protection against violent Chinese men. Laborers who came in and out of Portland with seasonal labor cycles were also stereotyped in the same editorial as "drunken loafers" who threatened the moral well-being of whites in the city.[16] Furthermore, discriminatory ordinances passed by the city council followed the lead of cities like San Francisco, which had also passed laws targeting Chinese immigrant's livelihoods. For instance, in June 1873, the Portland city council passed the "cubic air" ordinance that required the chief of police to arrest all persons living in a building that contained less than 550 cubic feet of air for each occupant. Fifty-two Chinese violators were arrested on June 26 and 27, 1873, and all but two paid a five-dollar fine. In February 1874, the city council prohibited the cutting of wood on sidewalks. In April 1874, it prohibited the carrying of swill or other "offensive material" without being properly covered. Attempts were also made to impose a prejudicial tax on Chinese washhouses in 1863 and 1865. However, Mayor Henry Failing, who would later become an advocate of many of the city's most wealthy merchants, vetoed this act because of its discriminatory nature.[17]

IMMIGRANT LIFE IN THE RIVER CITY

The experience of Chinese in Portland paralleled that of other immigrants in ways other than discriminatory laws. Intricate socio-political networks of clan and village associations existed in Portland and functioned in a similar fashion to those in John Day. These associations welcomed newly arriving immigrants and provided housing, financial assistance and job connections to hundreds of laborers and new businessmen. Tongs functioned as business entities and later as foundations for illicit trade in opium and prostitution. Additionally, Portland's Chinese enclave was isolated from the majority white population by geographic lines including the Willamette River to the South and Fourth Street to the North. Burnside and Southwest Clay Streets enclosed the community on the east and west sides respectively.[18] In addition to the bustling urban center of Chinatown, a second Chinese enclave developed many city blocks southwest of the center at the base of the West Hills. Composed primarily of Chinese vegetable gardeners and agriculturalists, a collection of wooden shanty houses were built along terraced hills that butted up against some of Portland's wealthiest white homes. The vegetable garden community flourished between 1879 and 1910 and independent Chinese vegetable peddlers eventually expanded their gardens to more than 20 acres.[19]

The central Chinese enclave offered everything immigrants needed whether they were permanent residents in the city or passing through town on their way to inland regions. Services included labor contracting, religious and social centers, merchant shops that sold Chinese goods and supplies, laundries, butchers and fish markets. Although the community developed independently from the white majority, cross-cultural relationships certainly developed over time, and this was particularly the case with Chinese and white businessmen. Key in this development were Chinese merchants whose businesses flourished in Portland's central Chinese enclave. Merchants had many functions serving as general import/export businessmen, labor contractors and mediators between the white and Chinese communities. Most labor contractors had experience serving as supervisors in labor camps and mining and railroad operations prior to establishing businesses in Portland. The men were generally skilled in the English language and they placed laborers in a diverse array of jobs, including railroad development, land reclamation and cannery and textile work.[20] Because labor contractors often maintained personal relationships with Portland's white elite, they also lined general laborers up with jobs as cooks and caretakers in the homes of whites. Finally, although Chinese could not testify against whites in court, it was not uncommon for Chinese contractors to bring civil action against white employers who failed to pay laborers or otherwise broke contractual agreements.[21] This service, in practice, met with unexpected success for Chinese laborers who otherwise lacked the money, position or language skills to bring their employers to court.[22]

CLASS AND STATUS AMONG
PORTLAND'S CHINESE COMMUNITY

By the late 1870s, Portland Chinatown included three fairly well-defined groups of immigrants: women, who made up a very small portion of the community; laborers, who worked for whites on jobs in the urban center and in outlying regions; and, merchants, who were the bedrock of Portland's Chinatown. Although merchants traditionally held little power in southern China, in the United States they became the most powerful and well connected among the Chinese population. Whites and Chinese alike relied on the merchant class for supplies of cheap laborers. Because of their wealthy status, specialization in services not desired by whites and more assimilated positions among American society, merchants were somewhat protected from the anti-Chinese resentment that increased in the 1880s. Over time, the distinction between Portland's Chinese laborers and merchants became abundantly clear through anti-Chinese immigration and exclusion laws.

In addition to their adaptability to American standards of business, dress and language, merchants were known for their organization and support of charitable causes among Chinese, having the means to provide assistance to new immigrants. Chinese merchants also regularly challenged discriminatory laws passed at the local level to thwart the success of everyday Chinese in the city—merchants often wrote editorials in defense of their community and attended meetings with white officials to defend Portland's Chinese residents when discrimination occurred. For instance, when city officials passed laws against piling firewood on streets or against the carrying of buckets of water on poles, merchants were the first to protest. In these ways, merchants both protected and unified the Chinese community, while positioning themselves as a distinct and powerful class separated from their laboring counterparts. During the Exclusion Era, beginning in 1882, some of Portland's most prominent Chinese merchants took further advantage of their position in the Chinese and white community by funding clandestine immigration rings that undercut the authority of anti-immigration officials.

CHINESE WOMEN

An area of Oregon's Chinese immigrant history that remains less studied by historians concerns Chinese women. Not until the 1940s did Chinese women make up a notable population in Oregon, and most of these women were wives of merchants or first-generation Chinese American youth. Furthermore, because Chinese women during the early immigration period left few written records, and archival documentation of their presence is limited, historians of their experience must rely on the few official documents that do remain. Perhaps the most immediate way to build a profile of Chinese women in Oregon in the nineteenth century—their origins, age, family relationships, work—is through census records. Although flawed by under- and over-counting of immigrant populations—this was especially the case for Chinese women, many of whom arrived as prostitutes through illicit tong networks—federal and state censuses do provide a beginning approach to reconstructing the presence of Chinese women in Oregon.

Census records and official reports allow for certain estimates of the numbers of women living in different areas. For instance, as early as 1865, a Portland City Assessor conducting population counts in the city's Chinese enclave noted that, in one boarding house alone, "150 Chinamen, and 80 women were booked."[23] In Portland, as well as outlying areas like The Dalles, local politicians began passing laws to suppress Chinese prostitution as early as 1865. In that year, The Dalles City Council passed an ordinance prohibiting Chinese bawdy houses within city limits. The penalty for running a bawdy house in the city was a fine ranging from $50–$250 or, in lieu of payment, one day in jail for every $2 of the fine.[24] Portland passed a similar ordinance in 1871, long after Chinese prostitution was firmly established in the city. In that year, the Portland Common Council passed a law fining operators of "houses of ill fame," and a decade later furthered its mandate with a revised "Ordinance to Suppress Bawdy Houses" which held owners and operators of bawdy houses responsible for fines that could total as much as $100 and twenty days in jail.[25]

Laws seeking to suppress Chinese prostitution, however, seemed to have had little effect on the number of Chinese prostitutes in Oregon.[26] The Chinese Exclusion Act of 1882, and subsequent anti-Chinese immigration laws, certainly curbed the tide of women entering the state, but did not entirely end the trade. In 1900, fifty-six "female boarding houses" were listed in Portland alone, with a handful of these being owned and operated by Chinese men. Census enumerators throughout the state documented the presence of Chinese prostitutes but also cited numerous Chinese women working in trades other than forced prostitution. Female cooks, laundresses and even merchants in later years appeared in census reports. However, the fact that most Chinese women were brought to the state for the purpose of prostitution remains a sad truth, and it is equally clear that Chinatown tongs remained the main coordinators of Chinese prostitution through the nineteen-teens when Chinese prostitution saw a slight downturn.

The overall effect of Chinese Exclusion laws on the population of immigrant women in the state was wide ranging. In the 1880s and 1890s federal legislation prevented the wives of laborers from entering the country, most likely out of a desire to limit the permanent settlement of Chinese families

Table 4.2.   Chinese Populon, Sex, and Sex Ratios in Oregon

Year	Male	Female	Ratio
1880	9,346	164	57.0:1
1890	9,270	270	34.3:1
1900	10,032	365	27.5:1
1910	7,043	320	22.0:1
1920	2,629	461	5.7:1
1930	1,525	550	2.8:1
1940	1,459	627	2.3:1
1950	1,351	751	1.8:1

Marie Rose Wong, *Sweet Cakes, Long Journey: The Chinatowns of Portland, Oregon* (Seattle: University of Washington Press, 2004).

and the rise of a second generation, Chinese American population in the country. And as with Chinese men, between 1890 and 1910, those women who arrived as prostitutes, or wives of merchants, became part of the growing urban Chinese population.

The proportion of women to men increased steadily after the turn of the twentieth century as shown in Table 4.2, despite restrictions barring the wives of laborers entry to the country and a later 1924 law that restricted the immigration of merchant's wives into the country. The more balanced sex ratio of the Chinese population in the twentieth century was due in part to an increase in births among first-generation Chinese immigrants.[27]

CONCLUSION

Long after the first generation of Chinese immigrants came to Oregon, their effects on Oregon history is still clear. "Chinese walls" still exist where rural laboring communities cleared land and made irrigation and mining systems. Railroads, constructed in large part by Chinese laborers, are still in use, and in John Day, the Kam Wah Chung Company was recently designated a historic landmark, thereby symbolizing the important cultural heritage Chinese left behind in rural Oregon.

NOTES

1. For discussion and debate on transnational history in the Asian and Asian American communities see Wanni W. Anderson and Robert G. Lee, eds., *Displacements and Diasporas: Asians in the Americas* (New Brunswick, N.J.: Rutgers University

Press, 2005), esp. chps. 1, 2, 3; see also John Y. Okamura, "Asian American Studies in the Age of Transnationalism: Diaspora, Race, Community," *Amerasia*, 29 (2): 171–193. On first generation Chinese immigrants in the West and transnational ties therein see Chen, Yong, *Chinese San Francisco, 1850–1943: A Trans-Pacific Community* (Stanford, CA: Stanford University Press, 2000). For a comparative analysis of nineteenth century ethnic groups and transnational identity, see Gunther Peck, *Reinventing Free Labor: Padrones and Immigrant Workers in the North American West, 1880–1930* (Cambridge, U.K.; Cambridge University Press, 2000); see also Madeline Hsu, *Dreaming of Gold, Dreaming of Home: Transnationalism and Migration between the United States and South China, 1882–1943* (Stanford: Stanford University Press, 2000).

2. Chris Friday, *Organizing Asian American Labor: The Pacific Coast Canned-Salmon Industry, 1870–1942* (Philadelphia: Temple University Press, 1994).

3. Sarah Griffith, "Ethnicity, Solidarity and Tradition: A Study into the Dynamics and Complexities of the Chinese Immigrant Community in John Day, Oregon, 1860–1906," (B.A. thesis, Lewis & Clark College, 2000); Jeffrey Barlow and Christine Richardson, *China Doctor of John Day* (Portland: Binford & Mort, 1979).

4. In 1854, the majority of Chinese arriving in the United States came from one of about fifteen Kwangtung provinces. Eventually, Chinese immigrants represented twenty-one districts out of the seventy-two districts that existed in southern China. Each of these districts or provinces would have likely had a village association affiliation in the United States. See Arlif Dirlik, ed. *Chinese on the American Frontier* (New York: Rowman & Littlefield Publishers, Inc., 2001), 4.

5. See Roger Daniels, *Asian America: Chinese and Japanese in the United States since 1850* (Seattle: University of Washington Press, 1988).

6. Stanford M. Lyman, *The Asian in North America* (Santa Barbara: ABC-Clio, Inc., 1977), 190–192; Melford S. Weiss, *Valley City: A Chinese Community in America* (Cambridge, Mass.: Schenkman Publishing Company, 1974).

7. In addition to family associations like the Ing clan, a more widely-cast network of village associations existed. The *Sam Yup* association was transplanted to Eastern Oregon from California as immigrants migrated north from that state. The second, and less developed *Sze Yup* association, also included immigrants from southern China's Toisan County in particular. The two associations maintained a certain competition for members and socioeconomic power throughout the early immigration period and into the twentieth century. For more on Chinese associations over time in the United States see Chan, Sucheng, *Asian Americans: An Interpretive History* (Boston: Twayne Publishers, 1991), 63–72.

8. Letters are held in the *Kam Wah Chung Company Papers, John Day, Oregon*, translated and compiled by Chia-lin Chen, Vault 325.251 K15p, Oregon Historical Society; Photographs are held in the *Kam Wah Chung Photographic Collection*, Org Lot 676, Oregon Historical Society; Oregon passed its first anti-miscegenation law in 1862 and, although, relationships between Chinese men and white women were not illegal, many whites frowned upon mixed-race relationships. See Peggy Pascoe, "Miscegenation Law, Court Cases, and Ideologies of 'Race' in Twentieth-Century America," *Journal of American History* 83 (June 1996), 44–69.

9. For more on Chinese in the West and labor opportunities see Sucheng Chan, *This Bittersweet Soil: The Chinese in California Agriculture, 1860–1910* (Berkeley: University of California Press, 1986).

10. For more on Chinese labor in Oregon see Gunther Barth, *Bitter Strength: A History of the Chinese in the United States, 1850–1870* (Cambridge, Mass.: Harvard University Press, 1964); see also Alexander Saxton, *The Indispensable Enemy: Labor and the Anti-Chinese Movement in California* (Berkeley: University of California Press, 1971).

11. David H. Stratton, "The Snake River Massacre of Chinese Miners, 1887," in *A Taste of the West: Essays in Honor of Robert G. Athearn*, edited by Duane Smith (Boulder, Colo.: Pruett Publishing Co., 1983), 109–129.

12. See Rodman Wilson Paul for more on the issues and psychologies of the anti-Chinese movement in the West, *Mining Frontiers of the Far West, 1848–1880* (Albuquerque: University of New Mexico Press, 2001 revised).

13. Urbanization by Chinese immigrants occurred throughout Western states by the nineteenth century. Ronald Takaki notes that by 1920, Chinese had virtually vanished from the agriculture, mining, manufacturing and transportation industries that they had once dominated. By 1920, less than one percent of harvesters in California agriculture were Chinese and the 17,000 Chinese documented in mining in 1870 had dwindled to less than 150. Of the 10,000 Chinese railroad workers employed by the Central Pacific Railroad in the late 1860s, only 500 Chinese remained employed by the railroads in 1920. Ronald Takaki, *Ethnic Islands: The Emergence of Urban Chinese America* (New York: Chelsea House Publishers, 1989), 40. For comparative assessment on other ethnic labor in the West see Gunther Peck, *Reinventing Free Labor: Padrones and Immigrant Workers in the North American West, 1880–1930* (New York: Cambridge University Press, 2000); see also Walker Nugent and Martin Ridge, *The American West: The Reader* (Bloomington: Indiana University Press, 1999), esp. chps. 4, 7, 11, 12.

14. Marie Rose Wong, *Sweet Cakes, Long Journey: The Chinatowns of Portland, Oregon* (Seattle: University of Washington Press, 2004), 44–45; see also Nelson Chiachi Ho, "Portland's Chinatown: The History of and Urban Ethnic District," (Portland, Oreg.: Bureau of Planning, City of Portland, 1978).

15. For more on anti-Chinese violence see Clayton D. Laurie, "'The Chinese Must Go': The United States Army and the Anti-Chinese Riots in Washington Territory, 1885–1886," *Pacific Northwest Quarterly* 81 (1): 22–29.

16. *Daily Oregonian*, 22 Nov. 1865.

17. Charles A. Tracy, "Race, Crime and Social Policy: The Chinese In Oregon, 1871–1885," *Crime and Social Justice*, (1980), 11–25; see also Sarah Griffith, "The Courts and the Making of a Chinese Immigrant Community in Portland, Oregon, 1850–1910," (M.A. thesis, Portland State University, 2003), 10–12.

18. Rose Marie Wong's thorough research on the changing shape of Portland's Chinatown can be found in *Sweet Cakes, Long Journey*, esp. 239–262. Maps of old Chinatown and the new Chinatown of Portland are included; so, too, is an analysis of conflicts between whites and Chinese, and between Chinese organizations who battled one another over moving Chinatown from the Southwest of Portland to the Northwest where it is currently located.

19. Wong, *Sweet* Cakes, 204–220.

20. Peck, *Reinventing Labor,* for comparative analysis of Greek, Italian and Mexican labor contractors, or padrones.

21. John Wunder's work on trans-Mississippi West Chinese presence in the court reveals similar instances of Chinese ability to access the legal forum against whites despite the legal limitations imposed against them. See John Wunder, "Law and the Chinese on the Southwest Frontier: 1850–1902," *Western Legal History* 2 (2): 139–158; Wunder, "Chinese in Trouble: Criminal Law and Race on the Trans-Mississippi Frontier," *Western Historical Quarterly* 17 (1): 25–41; Wunder, "The Chinese and the Courts in the Pacific Northwest: Justice Denied?" *Pacific Historical Review,* 191–211; Wunder, "Law and Chinese in Frontier Montana," *Montana* 30 (3): 18–31.

22. For more on Chinese laborers and contractors see Todd Stevens, "Brokers Between Worlds: Chinese Merchants and Legal Culture in the Pacific Northwest, 1852–1925," (PhD. diss., Princeton University, 2003); see also Peter J. Lewty, *Across the Columbia Plain: Railroad Expansion in the Interior Northwest, 1885–1893* (Pullman: Washington State University Press, 1995); Lewty, *To the Columbia Gateway: The Oregon Railway and the Northern Pacific, 1879–1884* (Pullman: University of Washington Press, 1987).

23. Wong, *Sweet Cakes,* 164.

24. Wong, *Sweet Cakes,* 229.

25. Wong, *Sweet Cakes,* 229.

26. To understand the myriad legal restrictions against female immigration from China prior to the Exclusion Era, see George Anthony Peffer, *If They Don't Bring Their Women Here: Chinese Female Immigration before Exclusion* (Urbana: University of Illinois Press, 1999), esp. chaps. 1, 5, 7.

27. For more on Chinese families and the changes in demographics among these groups between World War I and II see Sucheng Chan, "Women, Families, and the Second-Generation Dilemma," in *Asian Americans*, 103–118. Also see Jan Lin's work on the changing nature of U.S. Chinatowns from primarily bachelor societies to contemporary youth culture, family life and generational divides in, *Reconstructing Chinatown: Ethnic Enclave, Global Change* (Minneapolis: University of Minnesota Press, 1998), esp. 23–55.

Chapter Five

A Very Prejudiced State: Discrimination in Oregon from 1900–1940

Elizabeth McLagan

In the first four decades of the 20th century, African American Oregonians, who were never more than .4 percent of the population of the state, lived under discriminatory conditions. Social discrimination was common (black people were regularly refused admission to restaurants, theaters and hotels), medical care was difficult to obtain, unions barred blacks from membership, employment practices restricted them to certain job categories and integrated housing was resisted. Passing a state public accommodations law to make discrimination illegal was a long and difficult struggle that began in 1919, and, despite persistent efforts, was not successful until 1953. According to an African American Portlander,

> Oregon was a Klan state . . . a southern state transplanted to the North . . . a hell-hole when I grew up. It has always been a very prejudiced state. It is today, believe it or not. There's a lot of prejudice even now, as far as that's concerned, but nothing like it used to be.[1]

Portland's black press informed, educated, and supported the African American community through difficult times. A.D. Griffin, editor of the *New Age*, which was published in Portland from 1896 to 1907, consistently argued that the race problem would be solved when African Americans proved, by their industry and good character, they were the equals of whites. While Griffin's paper urged black Portlanders to be "sober, industrious and honest."[2] The *Advocate,* Portland's other African American owned newspaper, took a more activist position, focusing the blame on white attitudes:

> Reading history back three hundred years ago, we are constrained to believe the white man has the biggest side to solve . . . [T]his white man is not willing to concede manhood, nor even human rights, to the colored man. When that indi-

vidual becomes willing to deal justfully and manfully with his colored neighbor, then and only then will the race problem begin to be solved.[3]

Whether urging the community to improve its behavior, or shining the journalistic light on instances of prejudice, Portland's African American press was an invaluable record of the social discrimination that existed and persisted in Oregon.

African American Portlanders recalled that many theaters practiced discrimination: "I can remember my children going to the Egyptian Theater on Union Avenue for years before we realized that the only place they could sit was in the balcony."[4] This type of discrimination was sanctioned by the force of local law as early as 1905, when a decision by Judge Frazier allowed theaters to draw the color line. Oliver Taylor, an African American Pullman car conductor, purchased tickets for a performance at the Star Theatre but was refused seating by an usher who informed him that it was against the policy of the theater to seat persons of color in box seats. The usher offered to exchange the tickets, but Mr. Taylor refused to accept inferior seats and brought suit for *$500* in damages. Judge Frazer ruled that a theater ticket was a revocable license and that anyone could be refused admittance; the theater's only obligation was to refund the ticket price. The court declared that this ruling applied to all people, and the fact that Mr. Taylor was African American did not in any way influence the decision. The *Oregonian* editorialized the next day, arguing that theaters have the right to respect the known prejudices of its patrons:

If one person—a Chinaman, for example—has a right to buy any seat in the house, and sit in it, so may any other person—a Hottentot, or a woman of notorious reputation—do the same thing? It is not a question as to whether a white person objects to sitting next to a Chinaman. It is simply a well-known fact that he does object, and the theater must govern itself accordingly.[5]

Frazier's decision was upheld by the Oregon Supreme Court in 1906. And, until 1953, discrimination in public accommodations was a socially acceptable and legally protected practice.

In the decades of the 1920s and 1930s, the African American community continued the fight for the right of equal seating in theaters, but success was limited to individual victories and occasions. Beatrice Cannady, assistant editor of the *Advocate* and the first African American woman to practice law in Oregon, reported her own experience at the Oriental Theater in 1928, where she was finally given the seats she wanted only after repeatedly refusing inferior seats. Speaking of herself, she wrote, "Guests see the show but can't enjoy it because of the humiliation in obtaining seats."[6]

Occasionally the intervention of a white attorney was successful. In 1929, Milo King persuaded the manager of the Pantages Theatre to give complimentary tickets to a black man and his children who had been refused tickets. The same year, W.D. Allen simply refused to be intimidated and attended a performance with his son at the Orpheum Theater, ignoring the protests of the usher and manager. When the lights went up at the end of the show, Allen noticed Chinese and Japanese patrons seated in front and in back of him.[7] These small victories were celebrated in the pages of The *Advocate*. But while African American Portlanders tried to push the agenda of equal access to public accommodations forward, they also had to work hard to prevent the grounds for legal discrimination from widening.

The fear of racial intermingling was a commonly used excuse to justify prejudice, and, in the 1920s, Portland nearly passed an ordinance banning racial association. In 1922, the cabaret license of African American entrepreneur R.D. Stuart was revoked following a police raid, which discovered white women dancing with black men. Mayor Baker declared that, while no statute prohibited racial association, the law of common decency did. Claiming to represent both white and black Portlanders, he denied that any racial prejudice was involved in the matter.

> . . . when you take our white girls and allow them to get drunk in your establishment, and allow them to consort with negro men, I want to say that it is humiliating to the white race and an insult to the decent negro people as well.[8]

Stuart argued that he had tried to keep white people out of his cabaret, but declining profits had forced him to open his place of business to everyone. He pointed out that he didn't advertise and that the white clientele had come of their own accord. City police had worked with him to evict intoxicated patrons and had assured him he was running his business according to the law. Nevertheless, the city council decision to revoke Stuart's license was unanimous. The city council also considered an ordinance aimed at barring interracial dancing. The National Association for the Advancement of Colored People (NAACP), worried that this could set a precedent, sent a formal letter of protest to the city council opposing the enactment of any discriminatory ordinance:

> . . . the language of which conveyed the impression that any colored people, regardless of their position in life, are lower than the lowest element of the white race, is not only a damaging statement to yourself and the white race, but is a direct insult to the colored people of this city.[9]

The NAACP argued that any ordinance banning interracial association might be used as a legal precedent to impose further discrimination in public transportation, public education and higher education. The city council determined that an ordinance banning interracial dancing would not be necessary, but supported Mayor Baker's decision to revoke the license of any cabaret owner who allowed this practice, in the interest of "common decency." Baker hoped he would have the support of the black community:

> We can only assure those negroes who have signed their names to resolutions that they need have no fear of any action of the city council being taken to encourage in any way any race prejudice or anything against any law-abiding person of their race. We have found that no additional legislation is necessary and will handle the situation through police vigilance.[10]

Though interracial dancing was not strictly illegal, the Mayor's point was clear. Police vigilance would be the instrument by which prejudice could legally be practiced, in the name of "common decency." Further, black Portlanders were on notice that their rights were protected only insofar as, on an individual basis and with the policemen on the beat, they were not breaking the law.

Discrimination was commonly practiced in Oregon restaurants, with or without Jim Crow signs on the premises. In fact, it was the exception rather than the rule for white-owned restaurants in Portland to serve black people, as one resident recalled:

> I can remember the signs in all the eating places: "We Reserve the Right to Serve Whom We Please." I can remember around the corner a place called "Porky Pig," a hamburger place, my son and one of the boys who grew up next door to us going around there one evening to get a hamburger and being told, "Get out of here. We don't serve 'niggers' in here!"[11]

In 1907, A.D. Griffin reported that complaints of discrimination had increased over the preceding ten years, and, characteristically, blamed the black community.[12] When the *Advocate* reported discrimination, it suggested a different strategy:

> It might be advisable for colored people who have been patronizing the Morning's store to cease it . . . from now on and until the Mannings's stores cease to draw the color line, we shall find other stores [in] which to spend our money. Colored people must learn not only not to spend their money where they cannot work but also not to spend their money where they cannot eat.[13]

On another occasion, in reporting a Jim Crow sign in Portland, the *Advocate* noted:

> The Million Dollar Club Restaurant on Fourth Street, so we are told, has hung out a sign reading: we employ white help and cater to white trade. Heretofore

this restaurant has served colored people as well as any other. However, colored folk can buy bread and doughnuts there to take home. But will they?[14]

The local branch of the NAACP was able to persuade restaurant owners to remove Jim Crow signs, but until 1953 when a statewide public accommodations law was passed, the removal of these offensive signs was strictly voluntary.

Elsewhere in Oregon, small communities of African Americans organized resistance to overt discrimination. One instance occurred in 1925 in Bend, when a group of black citizens presented the city council with their complaint concerning local Jim Crow signs. They argued that this was a deliberate public humiliation in a small town where all persons of color knew which local restaurants would not serve them. Seeking redress for hurt pride, they argued that they had no desire to eat where they were not wanted, but preferred that owners refuse black patrons privately. The city council adopted the resolution and had the signs removed.[15]

In the early decades of the twentieth century, when Oregon's African American population hovered at around .25% of the total population, most black people lived in Portland, scattered in various parts of the city. As one long-time resident recalled,

At that time black people lived wherever they chose . . . wherever they were welcomed as tenants and buyers . . . there were a few in Alberta, there were a few in Montavilla. They were scattered, they weren't in one congested district.[16]

But in the 1920s and 1930s segregated housing patterns began to form in Portland, and opposition to black people buying homes or renting apartments in white neighborhoods intensified. Sometimes, vocal neighbors tried to use the petition process to keep out unwanted people. As one black Portlander recalled,

When we bought this place [. . .] the neighbors had a petition for us not to buy the place. But we did have a black neighbor across the street and to the side of us. But they didn't want any more in here.[17]

Although it sometimes was possible to by-pass a realtor and negotiate with buyers using a sympathetic white attorney as a go-between, realtor organizations were able to effectively exclude African Americans from white neighborhoods beginning in 1919. That year the Portland Realty Board amended its code of ethics to include a provision banning its members from selling property in white neighborhoods to African Americans or Asians, arguing that such sales caused a drop in property values.[18]

In 1930, Dr. DeNorval Unthank, one of Portland's first African American physicians and a prominent leader in the community, moved into a suite in the Panama Building in downtown Portland, where Dr. E.L. Booker, a black dentist, had his offices. Because of tenant opposition, Unthank and Booker had to find offices elsewhere. Booker was able to return to the Panama Building and Unthank moved to the Commonwealth Building, although he moved his practice once more before settling into a downtown location on SW 6th Avenue, where he would remain until 1944.[19]

The Unthanks also had difficulties finding a place to live. In 1930 they bought a home in S.E. Portland in a previously all-white neighborhood. They had already been forced to move four times because of racial opposition. A petition asking them to leave was circulated and signed by seventy-five of their neighbors. The house was vandalized, windows were broken, and garbage and even a dead cat were thrown on their lawn. Determined to stay, they cleaned up the mess. A few months later, windows were broken again. The tensions escalated when Mrs. Unthank accused their neighbors, Mr. and Mrs. Fred Jones, of vandalism, and was herself charged with a threat to commit a felony. Ultimately, the charges against Mrs. Unthank were dropped and they moved from the neighborhood.

The redlining practices continued, tightly controlled by the real estate industry. As late as 1949, a realtor was kicked out of the Portland Realty Board for selling property to an African American in a so-called white district. The NAACP fought segregated housing patterns, as a report for 1939 attests:

[We are] still working on real estate boards discrimination to colored homebuyers. They take down payment, let them clean house and then say sorry they cannot let them live there. Because a neighbor complained. Investigation says neighbor is usually blocks away.[20]

The *Advocate* took pains to point out the black community's struggle for equal access to housing, which, without a law to protect African Americans, had to be fought one case at a time. In an article published in 1930, it accurately and eloquently predicted the results of segregated housing:

We all know what residential segregation means. It means poor housing, bad streets, and if the streets are paved, poorly kept, deficient lighting. It also means separate schools and their attendant shortcomings. It invites race riots, because the stronger race will feel that the weaker has no rights outside of its restricted district and any attempt on the part of the weaker to exercise its rights of liberty, at all, is met with opposition from the stronger; the trouble begins. It is segregation that is the root of all interracial troubles.[21]

In Portland, the issue of school segregation was tied to segregated housing. In the years before World War II, when Portland's black community was small and scattered around the city, black children went to neighborhood schools, wherever they lived. The NAACP report of 1939 included three school cases of prejudice: a suspension of a child that was resolved, and two teachers in separate incidents apologized after their inflammatory remarks were reported to the civil rights organization.[22]

Catholic schools in Portland were briefly segregated; in 1926 the *Advocate* printed a harsh editorial condemning this practice. The article, titled "The K.K.K. and the Katholics," pointed out that in two recent attempts to enroll black children in Catholic schools in Portland and nearby Vancouver, the children were rejected due to their race. Since African Americans and Catholics were both objects of the Klan's terrorist activities, the *Advocate* wondered aloud if it had been wise to urge African Americans to vote to support parochial schools, since here was evidence of Catholic hostility toward Blacks. The article concluded, "We admit that we are puzzled over the thing and wonder if it is true that the policy of the Catholic Church is to draw the color line."[23] In the 1930s, St. Mary's and St. Andrew's Catholic schools in Portland admitted black children.[24]

Elsewhere in the state, school segregation became an issue from time to time. In 1903 in Coos Bay, three black children tried to attend school but were refused admission by the principal. The school board directed him to provide a separate room where the black children could be taught, to hire a teacher, and insure, as the *New Age* reported, "that equal school privileges are provided for said Negro children as are now enjoyed by the white children of this district."[25] In other words, separate but "equal," a doctrine that would not be overturned until 1954 in *Brown v. Board of Education*. School segregation was practiced in the 1920s in a few small communities in situations where a number of African Americans were brought in to fill a worker shortage. In Vernonia, a small town in the Coast Range, 35 miles from Portland, African Americans emigrated from the South to work for the Oregon-American Lumber Company. The first five children of school age were forced to attend school in Portland, as the Vernonia school would not admit them. The local school district tried to set up a segregated school in a shack, but Mrs. Beatrice Cannady, a black attorney, went to Vernonia to intercede for them, and one year later, all the black children were attending public schools. One local resident, who taught in the Vernonia school in 1927, recalled that, at least in her experience, the black students were treated fairly.[26]

The situation in Maxville, a small town near La Grande in eastern Oregon, was similar. Bowman Hicks Lumber Company had recruited people from the

South, both black and white, to work in its lumber mill. In 1926, Beatrice Cannady received a letter from J.L. Stewart describing the situation. The black children were not allowed to go to school, but were taught by a black woman in her home. Cannady advised Stewart not to accept a segregated school, even if it meant teaching the children at home. Ellen Law lived in Maxville as a child, and attended a public school in the nearby town of Enterprise. Her parents had moved to Oregon from Arkansas, hoping to find better conditions, only to discover that they were the same or worse in Oregon.[27]

Economic improvement was a common motivation for migration among African Americans. But, when black people moved to Portland, they found that job discrimination was widely practiced, and in some cases conditions were actually worse in Oregon than in the South:

> There weren't any good jobs. The only jobs here in Portland at the time we came here was if you didn't [work on the] railroad, the Portland Hotel, and the women [had maid work] at Meier and Franks, and the barbershops . . . there weren't any good jobs.[28]

When the local Laundry Workers Union refused to open their membership to black women in 1902, A.D. Griffin, editor of the *New Age,* charged that this situation was worse than in the South, where black people who worked in menial jobs at least had the protection of a union. Griffin also noted that other local unions, notably the Teamsters Union and the Cooks and Waiters Union, refused to allow African American workers to join. He predicted that in the end black workers would be admitted, but in the meantime,

> . . . as long as the Unions discriminate against our people, let us show them that they cannot expect our help or sympathy. Let us call the attention of all our friends to their attitude toward us and in the end they will be compelled to grant us our rights.[29]

Griffin applauded a black truck driver who replaced a striking white driver from the Banfield, Veysey Fuel Co., and suggested that as long as unions excluded African Americans from membership, they should not hesitate to cross the picket line.

> We have repeatedly warned [the Unions] that [. . .] in case of a strike or difference between them and their employers the Negro would have no cause to feel any pangs of conscience about taking the place of the strikers.[30]

When the Civil Service and Police Commission ruled that no one who had worked as a janitor or porter in a saloon could qualify for a position on the police force, Griffin wondered if the same rule would be applied to white applicants, and concluded:

> Shut out by the Unions, who refuse to admit the black worker to membership, from securing more lucrative employment, the fact that he accepts menial labor rather than steal or starve, in the eyes of our Democratic commissioners counts against him. Verily where an excuse is wanted, it is not hard to find one.[31]

In 1924, the *Advocate* reported that white waiters were being hired in the Portland Hotel's grillroom, because the unions insisted that these jobs should not be given to black waiters.[32] The NAACP lobbied on behalf of African American employees who were discharged by Olds and King, and the women were rehired. A new position in the department store was created and filled by a black man. The NAACP was able to make small gains with other employers, but discrimination in employment continued. Jobs were limited and promotions out of the question. As one Portlander recalled, "Every job you took or were accepted for, or went after, there was no progress, no promotion. That was it. You stayed right there."[33]

Job discrimination in Oregon worsened during the Great Depression, when black men were displaced from jobs that white men had previously refused. Thus, many waiters, elevator operators and janitors found themselves out of work, and, by 1941, the overwhelming majority of African American men worked as waiters, cooks, porters, redcaps and shop laborers in the railroad industry, while African American women were almost exclusively employed as domestic servants. Often, economic survival required multiple jobs.

> I always worked two jobs. You ran on the road, you waited tables at the Portland Hotel, then in later years the racetrack opened and you worked [there] . . . . I always worked two jobs. All the men did . . . . We had to do it to make ends meet, if we expected to have a roof over our heads and provide for our children.[34]

Black people were generally barred from unions until 1949, when the Oregon Legislature passed a fair employment practices act, which nominally made discrimination in employment illegal. The unions, however, continued to resist integration, and trade unions in particular remained closed to African Americans for many decades.

Oregon's links to Southern-style racism are apparent in instances where the color line was drawn, whether it is in public accommodations, housing, school segregation or limited job opportunities. But Oregon was also a place where the Ku Klux Klan (KKK) practiced its white supremacy ideals in terrorist acts that ranged from threats of violence to cross burnings and lynchings.

The Ku Klux Klan had been reorganized nationally in 1915, six months after the release of D.W. Griffith's film, *Birth of a Nation*. This documentary-style film claimed to represent a true picture of the South during the Civil War and Reconstruction, but it was sensationally and violently anti-black. The NAACP lobbied the National Board of Censorship to have some of the film's most obnoxious scenes removed, but the attempt failed, and it became the responsibility of local governments to approve or deny permits to show the film. *Birth of a Nation* was scheduled to be shown in Portland in 1916. Leading black citizens met with the city council, and an ordinance was passed which would ban the showing of any film that would stir up race hatred.[35] Despite this ordinance, the film was at times shown in Portland during the 1920s and 1930s.

Although the Ku Klux Klan was organized in Oregon in 1921, groups of its type had existed in Oregon previously. Settlers coming from the border states and the South carried the baggage of prejudice with them: The Knights of the Golden Circle, active during the Civil War, are only one example of the appearance of southern white-supremacy organizations in Oregon. Shortly after the turn of the century, an instance of small town violence and southern style justice took place in Coos Bay, Oregon, then called Marshfield. *The Oregon Journal* reported: "Alonzo Tucker, the black fiend who assaulted the wife of Benjamin Dennis, at Marshfield yesterday, was captured and lynched by his pursuers this morning."[36] The article continued in lurid language to describe the brutal assault of a white woman, and the pursuit, capture and death of Tucker, whose body was then strung up over the south Marshfield bridge. A brief inquest was conducted during which it was concluded that Tucker's death had resulted from a single rifle shot and that no crime had been committed. An article on the same subject appearing in the *Oregonian* concluded: "The sentiment of the community is in sympathy with the lynchers, and it is extremely improbable any arrests will be made."[37]

In 1924, after the Klan had officially been reorganized, another black resident of Marshfield, Timothy Pettis, was murdered. His mutilated body was found in the bay, and the local African American community offered a reward for the capture of his murderer. The NAACP telegrammed the governor of Oregon asking that a special investigator be assigned to the case and also informed James Weldon Johnson, a national officer of the NAACP, of the local situation.

Marshfield is infested with the Ku Klux Klan, and we are of the opinion, and so are the colored people who live in Marshfield that all efforts are being made to cover up the crime. Colored people there demanded a second autopsy of the body which revealed that the testicles had been removed and it developed that it could not have been done except by [a] person or persons.[38]

The murder apparently remained unsolved. In the annual report for that year the Portland branch of the NAACP wrote, "The brutal murder of a colored man at Marshfield, Oregon was investigated by the organization . . . it gave us satisfaction in having accomplished our aim as far as physical power could act.[39]

The phenomenon of the Klan's rapid growth in Oregon in the early 1920s cannot be attributed to a large influx of their target ethnic and religious groups. Catholics, Jews, Chinese and African-Americans were few in number and therefore posed no actual threat to the white Protestant majority. The nation as a whole, however, had reverted to a new conservatism; the war had failed to eradicate communism, there were race and labor riots elsewhere in the nation, an economic recession, increased immigration and the prohibition of alcohol. It was an age of national paranoia, ripe for a movement that promised to restore law, order and 100% Americanism to the nation.

The Klan's reign in Oregon was brief, but spectacular. The organization was able to influence the election of 1922, defeating its outspoken critic, Ben Olcott, the incumbent candidate for governor. The KKK was instrumental in the passage of a law requiring compulsory public education, which would have forced the closure of all parochial schools, but this law was ruled unconstitutional by a 1925 U.S. Supreme Court decision.

In January 1922, a Klan chapter was organized in Medford. One of its first terrorist acts was against George Arthur Burr, a local bootblack. Released after serving a three-day sentence for bootlegging, he was taken into the mountains, a rope was put around his neck, and he was told to run. Another necktie party was held for a white man, J.H. Hale, who had initiated a lawsuit against a known Klan member. Again, a rope was put around his neck, he was raised off the ground, and then told to leave town or be killed. A second African American, Henry Johnson, a resident of nearby Jacksonville, was treated in the same manner and ordered to leave town. A grand jury indicted six men in Jackson County on charges of riot and assault with a dangerous weapon, but all the men were either acquitted or the charges against them were dropped.[40] The Klan threatened Charles Maxwell, a black businessman in Salem, in 1922. He received a letter which was then published in the *Capital Journal,* warning, "We have stood you as long as we intend to stand you, and you must unload, if you don't we will come to see you."[41] Although Maxwell refused to leave town and later opened a barbecue restaurant in Salem, he left following a bank foreclosure and moved to Los Angeles.

In Oregon City the following year, Perry Ellis, the only black resident of the town and owner of a car wash, was nearly lynched by men thought to be members of the Klan. He had been accused of sleeping with a white woman, although charges against him were dropped when the woman failed to appear in court. He was called out of town, allegedly to pick up a team of horses stranded on a country road with a broken-down wagon. Ellis arrived with a white friend, Ira Thrall, and found two cars parked across the road. A spotlight was turned on the pair and six men appeared wearing masks. They ordered Thrall to return to Oregon City and drove Ellis about thirty miles out into the country where he was interrogated and threatened with lynching. He denied the charges concerning the white woman and was driven to a lake where more threats followed. The men finally let him go, telling him to leave town or he would be killed. Although both Ellis and Thrall were able to identify several of the men by their voices, no charges were brought. Ellis left Oregon City and settled in Tacoma, Washington. The previous examples of Klan violence reveal a pattern—all the victims were businessmen living in small communities in Oregon.

In Portland, which contained Oregon's only sizeable black community at that time, the appearance of the Klan was also noted. In 1921, the Portland branch of the NAACP sent a telegram to the governor of Oregon.

> . . . representing more than three thousand colored people in the state of Oregon . . . [we] call your attention to the formation and rapidly spreading organization known as the Ku Klux Klan, under the pretense of promotion of law and order but aimed unquestionably at the persecution of individuals who may incur their disfavor. And to the end that all citizens may have a sense of security in their homes at night, and peaceable protection in their places of business and employment during the day, we humbly pray your honor to prevent in our State, any organization or public demonstration of the said notorious [KKK] under any pretext whatsoever.[42]

The same year, a committee of black Portlanders visited the Mayor's office to protest a KKK street parade.[43] The Klan threatened the Reverend Moses Riley, a black Portland minister, because his congregation included white people. There were other threats involving black families moving into white neighborhoods, but the black residents of Portland were, themselves, armed and prepared for the Klan, and protected individuals whose property was threatened.[44]

Between 1900 and 1940, the degree of discrimination that black Oregonians experienced varied from person to person and place to place. The most extreme examples of Klan violence occurred in small towns where the Klan was strong and African American individuals were isolated and therefore more vulnerable. Black Portlanders faced continued inequalities in employment, housing and public accommodations. An active leadership developed to protest discrimination, and they were often successful. But the power of the black community was limited and without the force of law. Further, Oregon's minority population wasn't large enough to exert economic and political pressure. Many black residents simply left Oregon. Those who remained faced a daily struggle for economic survival.

> We were just a mere handful of people here in Portland [. . .] we were so scattered. We had people living as far as Lents, St. Johns, and heck, you couldn't get them together! Then, on top of that, the majority of men were railroad men. They were out of town.[45]

With the coming of World War II, conditions for black Oregonians would change dramatically. The influx of African American war workers resulted in a backlash of increased discrimination and the promise of real political clout. Ultimately, the economic gains achieved during the wartime economy were reversed as veterans returned to the workplace and old racial lines were redrawn. But, some among the political leadership, dismayed at the evidence of wartime prejudice and aware of the contributions of African Americans and others to the war effort, were ready to enact legislation that would remove some of the barriers to progress. The Fair Employment Practices law was passed in 1949, followed by the repeal of the ban on intermarriage in 1951. That same year, the Vocational Schools Law was passed, guaranteeing the right of equal access to vocational training. Two years later, the Public Accommodations Law was passed, which finally banned discrimination in restaurants, hotels and public places of recreation and amusement.

While the post-war period saw the beginnings of civil rights legislation, the long history of discrimination continues to cast its shadow. And, although progress toward full equality in education, housing, employment and economic opportunities has been achieved, it has been hard fought and is still incomplete. The promise of equal opportunity enshrined in our laws has yet to be fulfilled, but it is hoped that a better understanding of our common history can lead us towards that unfinished task.

NOTES

1. Oregon Black History Project Oral History Collection. All citations are anonymous to protect the identity of the informants.

2. *New Age,* 8 Sept. 1902.

3. *Advocate,* 11 Aug. 1923.

4. Oregon Black History Project (OBHP).

5. *The Oregonian,* 20 May 1905.

6. *Advocate,* 8 Dec. 1928.

7. *Advocate,* 24 Aug. 1929; 5 Oct. 1929.

8. *The Oregonian,* 18 Apr. 1922.
9. *The Oregonian,* 18 Apr. 1922.
10. *The Oregonian,* 22 Apr. 1922.
11. OBHP.
12. *New Age,* 6 Apr. 1907.
13. *Advocate,* 26 July 1930.
14. *Advocate,* 26 Apr. 1923.
15. *Advocate,* 15 Aug. 1925.
16. OBHP.
17. OBHP.
18. *Oregon Journal,* 6 Mar. 1919.
19. *Cornerstones of Community,* 1997.
20. NAACP microfilm.
21. *Advocate,* 12 July 1930.
22. NAACP microfilm, OBHP.
23. *Advocate,* 11 Sept. 1926.
24. OBHP.
25. *New Age,* 17 Oct. 1903.
26. Garner, OBHP.
27. Crowell, 1973.
28. OBHP.
29. *New Age,* 31 May 1902.
30. *New Age,* 5 July 1902.
31. *New Age,* 10 Oct. 1902.
32. *Advocate,* 1 Nov. 1924.
33. OBHP.
34. OBHP.
35. *Advocate,* 14 Mar. 1931.
36. *The Oregon Journal,* 18 Sept. 1921.
37. *The Oregonian,* 18 Sept. 1921.
38. NAACP microfilm, OBHP.
39. NAACP microfilm, OBHP.
40. *Oregon Voter,* 12 Aug. 1922.
41. *Capital Journal,* 25 Oct. 1922.
42. NAACP microfilm, OBHP.
43. NAACP microfilm, OBHP.
44. OBHP.
45. OBHP.

BIBLIOGRAPHY

Cornerstones of Community: Buildings of Portland's African American History Portland, Bosco-Milligan Fnd.: 1997.

Crowell, Evelyn. "Twentieth Century Black Women in Oregon." *Northwest Journal of African and Black American Studies* 1, no. 1 (1973).
Garner, Mrs. Mss. Oregon Black History Project Oral History Collection. Oregon Historical Society.

Newspapers

Advocate
Capital Journal
New Age
Oregon Journal
Oregon Voter
The Oregonian

Oral History Projects

Oregon Black History Project Oral History Collection. Oregon Historical Library (OBHP)

Chapter Six

"We are tired of cookies and old clothes:" From Poverty Programs to Community Empowerment among Oregon's *mexicano*[1] Population, 1957–1975

Erlinda Gonzales-Berry with Dwaine Plaza

Oregon's multimillion-dollar agribusiness industry has long depended on migrant labor. In the early half of the twentieth century, much of this labor was provided by itinerant White workers, though in Eastern Oregon Mexican and Mexican American workers were regularly employed in the sugar beet and potato industries as early as the 1930s. During WWII, the shortage of workers forced Oregon growers to draw part of their labor pool from the bi-national guest worker program developed by Mexico and the United States. While this program lasted from 1943 until 1964, Oregon growers gradually weaned themselves from dependency on *braceros* (popular name for this program and the men who participated in it), and by 1950 they had begun to supplement Caucasian migrants with Mexican and Mexican American migrants from South Texas and with workers recruited directly from Mexico. *Tejano* (Mexican-origin Texan) migrants began to "settle out" in the Willamette Valley and beyond in the 1950s and '60s, and by the late '60s, towns like Woodburn and Hillsboro in Oregon had a sizable Mexican origin population.[2]

There have been some previous though not extensive studies on this population in Oregon. What is known about these pioneer migrants and the struggles they endured to make it in a hostile environment is included in research previously conducted by Slatta, Loprinzi, and Gamboa[3] or is covered in institutional reports, newspapers, and a few archival collections scattered throughout Oregon. The purpose of this chapter is to document the migration, settlement and struggles of this group to Oregon through oral life history interviews, content analysis of local newspapers, government studies, agency reports, and archival materials. A series of oral interviews conducted in Central Oregon in 2004 and 2005 will highlight what took place for both the first and second generations of Mexican-origin migrants in Oregon.[4] The testimony of key community stakeholders will highlight what life was like for these early settlers, most of whom worked in agriculture.

IN THEIR OWN WORDS

Ms. Elena Peña came to Oregon as a young child in the early '50s. In a recent interview conducted in her home in Independence she recalls the rush for mattresses, as families were unloaded at one labor camp only to find that they were crawling with bedbugs. Her parents refused to allow their children to sleep on the infested mattresses, so they spent the night in their truck. The next day, her father negotiated with his employer to allow them and another family to camp out by the Willamette River. They did so for a week, sleeping in their truck and in a tent. At the end of the week, the work at that farm was completed and the two families moved on to another crop. Ms. Peña stresses that having their own vehicle gave her family a measure of independence as well as additional money, because now they did not have to give the contractor a cut of their wages.[5] These developments also facilitated the process of settling out in a shorter period of time. In 1967, just five years after arriving in Independence, Ms. Peña's parents, Moncerrat and Antonia Vasquez, bought a small house on an acre of property. They still live in that house, and their daughter Elena and her husband Raul have constructed their home next door to the original property purchased by her parents thirty-eight years ago.

Ms. Peña's husband, Raúl—whose family also followed the migrant stream from South Texas to Oregon—provided an assessment of his life as a migrant child that is interesting when viewed in relation to David Laing's "cycle of poverty" theory, in which migrant workers are seen as victims lacking in agency with only their hard work and faith to sustain them.[6] The life of the migrant child, Mr. Peña recalls, was a life of adventure that involved the entire family. For a child that thought "going north" meant a trip to Plainview, Texas, rolling across the vast Western landscape was exciting and educational. He recalls winning a geography bee, not because he was the smartest kid in his class in Reynosa, Texas, but because in addition to knowing the names of the state capitals, he *knew* many of them because his family had passed through these sites while on their way to different job sites. The news that a Mexican kid had won the contest moved Raul's buddies to express their jubilation by carrying him on their shoulders throughout the auditorium. Mr. Peña, who recently retired from the Oregon Department of Labor where he worked as a labor compliance officer, added:

Yeah, we were poor. Actually, I didn't know we were poor but my father sure knew it. If I had stayed in Texas my life would have been very different. I would probably still be working in the fields, or I would be pushing drugs or in jail for pushing drugs, or I would be dead. Coming to Oregon increased my life chances. But what I learned as a child of migrants is to value work. My father taught me that no matter what the job was, I was being paid for it, and I was obliged to do it the very best I could. 'If your boss asks you to dig a ditch,' my father told me, 'ask how deep and how wide.'[7]

In order to fully appreciate Raul Peña's assessment of the potential outcome of a life lived in Texas, one must understand the racial politics of the state of Texas where, according to David Montejano, Jim Crow laws applied also to Mexicans:

'Jim Crow' may appear to be an odd description of the situation of Mexicans in Texas. There was no constitutionally sanctioned 'separate but equal' provision for Mexicans as there was for blacks. According to the prevailing jurisprudence, Mexicans were 'Caucasian.' But in political and sociological terms, blacks and Mexicans were basically seen as different aspects of the same race problem. In the farm areas of South and West Texas, the Caucasian schools were nearly always divided into 'Anglo schools' and 'Mexican schools,' the towns into 'white towns' and 'little Mexicos,' and even the churches and cemeteries followed this seemingly natural division of people. This was not a natural phenomenon, however, but the cumulative effect of local administrative policies. In the farm districts, the result was a separation as complete—and as 'de jure'—as any in the Jim Crow South.[8]

Under these conditions, Raul Peña reported, "people stayed on their side of town," and speaking Spanish in public was akin to committing a crime. He recalls also the time he, his father, and his uncle were refused service and asked to leave a restaurant in Texas. Regarding this painful incident, Mr. Peña is thankful that his father did not teach him to hate. Instead he told him, "It's all right. We'll just go to the other side and be with our people." Raul's wife, Elena, acknowledges that not all *tejano* settlers feel this way. "They see a different story, because they had probably already been poisoned with that attitude." She is of course referring to the resentment that frequently develops among victims of bigotry in response to the pain of rejection and discrimination. But, for *mexicanos* like the Peñas, accustomed as they were to a life of segregation and deeply entrenched racial discrimination in Texas, Oregon indeed was a welcome change.

Despite the blatant discrimination of *mexicanos* in Texas, the state seemed quite concerned with how *mexicanos* would represent Texas as they left to work elsewhere. In a letter given to migrant workers by the Texas Extension Service in 1946, émigrés were warned:

> 'The eyes of Texas are upon you, all the live long day. The eyes of Texas are upon you, you cannot get away.' No matter where you go, to the people of other states you represent Texas. All Texans are proud of their citizenship and their fellow Texans. All Texans are interested in what their citizens do when they get to other states. We want to see them make good. We also want to see that they are treated right wherever they go .... Let's stay by our contracts. Let's do a good job so that those who stay in Texas can always say that they are proud of the Texas Latin Americans.[9]

One wonders whether this attempt to embed in the conscience of *mexicano* migrants the controlling gaze of the "Eyes of Texas" was more about warning them not to air dirty (state) 'family' secrets than about making a good personal impression.

AFTER TEXAS THERE WAS OREGON

To say that migrants felt liberated from the humiliation of the Jim Crow environment that prevailed in Texas is not to say that Oregonians were beyond prejudice and discrimination. A member of the Leos family, whose arrival in Oregon was in 1954, reported the following incident: "When Raul Sr. and Anna were putting the children to bed they heard a noise outside the window. They both went out to check and what they found was a letter tacked to their door stating, 'leave wetbacks.'"[10] Discrimination could also be found among educators. Infante and Current reported that "One of the concepts expressed by some schools was that the Spanish-American child is mentally inferior. One official even went out on an unscientific limb to state, 'I have noticed that if the children are more on the Indian side, they are slower in learning than those who are more on the Spanish side.'"[11] In a 1959 report, the same authors found that in one Oregon County the practice of "price-jacking" was common, with prices of staples increasing by as much as 15 percent once migrants arrived. In another county one tavern made it a practice of refusing service to "Spanish American" migrants, though white migrants were not turned away. The law enforcement official in this same county counseled "businessmen and townspeople to handle the Mexicans with extreme caution and give them no chance to start anything. As far as he is concerned, all Mexicans are dangerous."[12] At another location, a town officer, speaking of migrant youth, affirmed: "If we see the young boys dating white girls, we tell them to go only with their own."[13] In 1962 Gilbert López reported to *The Oregon Journal* that "transient workers in the Boise Valley area of Eastern Oregon were unable to meet socially because of discrimination against them by bar and club owners." Everywhere they turn, he reported, "they are met with signs stating 'No Mexicans Allowed.'"[14] Despite these blatant displays of bigotry, the Texas migrant stream increasingly was finding Oregon a better place to be.

Like Independence, Woodburn became an attractive site for the Mexican-origin population in the early fifties. Miguel Salinas, whose father jumped off a train he was riding as a hobo in the Willamette Valley in 1947, considers his family one of the earliest pioneer families to settle in this area. In a recent interview at the Woodburn Public Library, Salinas recalls, "when I was growing up you would walk through Woodburn and see maybe one brown face. Today you don't see any white faces."[15] Salinas finished high school with the certain knowledge that he would get a job. However, he was turned away time and again "for lack of experience." Finally he offered to volunteer, that is, work for free at a gas station in order to get experience. Within two weeks, this young man had proven his mettle and was hired part time at a wage of $1.25 per hour (Interview 3-31-05). By the end of the '50s there were sufficient *mexicanos* in Woodburn to make it a profitable venture for the local theater to run Spanish movies once a week. Moreover, the Woodburn Motor Vehicle License office was the only one in the State to contract Spanish-speaking employees in order to administer the driver license test in Spanish. Current and Infante report that "Spanish-Americans" from all over the state traveled to Woodburn in the '50s to get their drivers license.[16] By the '60s the large presence of *mexicanos*, most of them from the Texas migrant stream, prompted the Chamber of Commerce to organize its first Mexican fiesta "for the purpose of recognizing 'the many Spanish-speaking peoples in the area for the harvest season,'"[17] and to create "reciprocity between these two cultures."[18] Thousands of descendents of *tejano* migrants live in Woodburn today. With the largest Latino population in the state, it is the epicenter from which much of the state's activism on behalf of *mexicanos* and Latinos—both early settlers and new immigrants—continues to emerge.

MINISTERING UNTO MIGRANTS: TOP-DOWN ASSISTANCE PROGRAMS

Conditions affecting the lives of migrant workers had become a priority item on the national agenda in 1950 when President Harry Truman, in response to pressure from labor unions, the NAACP, and numerous religious and social reform entities, formed the Commission on Migratory Labor. In its report to the President in 1951, the Commission found that migrant households in Colorado were making an average wage of $1,424 per year, and this included the work tendered by women and children of the family. The report stressed that migrant workers enjoyed none of the workplace protections such as the right to organize, unemployment insurance, or minimum wage guaranteed to other workers in the United States.[19] Moreover, they were subject to all manner of calamities, as cited by one observer: "A truckload of workers smashes up and many are killed; an ex-chicken coop catches fire and migrants living in it are burned to death; laborers of migrant families are reported to have died from malnutrition and neglect."[20] In short the commission found that the lives of migrants throughout the country were governed by "uncertainty, insecurity, poverty and filth."[21]

The new spirit of migrant labor reform that overtook the United States in the 1950s significantly affected Oregon, with its heavy dependency on migrant farm labor.[22] This is not to say that migrant workers had been completely neglected before that date. The Oregon State Council of Churches had been active in ministering to migrants as early as the 1940s. However, the Council did not specifically call attention to *mexicanos* until 1957 when it refers, in its annual report, to "Spanish Speaking" clients. In its 1959 report, reference is made to "Texas Mexican" migrants in Eastern Oregon. Activities designed specifically for these migrants included English, sewing and home nursing classes for adults, Spanish language radio programs, recreation, and summer church camps for children. In 1958, the Council was joined by the Oregon College of Education in providing summer school programs for migrant children at various camps in the Willamette Valley.[23] The following year, 1959, the legislature provided funding to continue these summer school programs for migrant children. In 1961, additional funding was allocated for permanent programming to accommodate migrant children during the regular school year. In 1962 *The Oregonian* reported that "Oregon was one of a very few states that offer special school opportunities to migrant children."[24] Gradually, the Council became a strong political voice in advocating for social change for migrant workers. Among its major accomplishments was its success in lobbing the state legislature for the establishment of an Interim Committee on Migrant Affairs and for the enactment of legislation beneficial to migrant workers.[25]

The Catholic Archdiocese also became involved in ministering unto the spiritual needs of *mexicanos* in Oregon, the majority of whom were Catholic. In 1952, in an action predating a mandate from the Vatican to have Mexican priests accompany *braceros* to the United States in an effort to avert the danger of Protestant proselytism,[26] the Oregon Diocese recruited its first Catholic priest, Father Ernesto Bravo, from Mexico. The Catholic Migrant Ministry Office of Oregon, established in 1955, however, might have been a bit reluctant to advocate for migrant workers and risk antagonizing farmers, many of whom were members of the Church and contributors to its coffers. Loprinzi suggests this possibility in her assessment of the mission of the Migrant Ministry in its early years: "In their 1955 report, the Catholic Migrant Ministry clarified its position, documenting that their members were only there to conduct research and provide religious services, not change conditions."[27] As the Church recruited additional priests from Mexico, the latter soon became involved in "providing culturally relevant masses, sacraments, and spiritual retreats to Mexican Americans in the Willamette Valley. In this way, Catholic parishes like St. Luke's in Woodburn started to emerge as the hub of the growing Mexican-American community."[28] The Church, as it became transformed by the liberal reforms of Vatican II and its clergy increasingly influenced by the new ideas of Latin American Liberation Theology,[29] was to become an important catalyst for political activism among settled out *mexicanos* and migrant farm workers in Oregon and other areas of the United States.

At this time, several government-sponsored agencies also appeared on the migrant labor reform scene in Oregon. In response to pressure from the Oregon Council of Churches and the Bureau of Labor, the Legislative Assembly created a Legislative Interim Committee on Migrant Labor in 1957. Subsequently, Governor Robert Holmes created an Interagency Committee on Migratory Labor.[30] These two groups generated three reports between 1958 and 1959, one of which was a substantive statewide survey commissioned by the Oregon State Bureau of Labor. The survey was carried out by 300 volunteers, whose services were coordinated by the Oregon Council of Churches, the Portland Archdiocese of the Roman Catholic Church, Willamette University Sociology Department, Mount Angel Seminary, and the Latin American Club. The project sampled growers, contractors and crew leaders, Anglo and "Spanish-Americans"[31] migrant workers, community members, and agency personnel. A broad range of topics, including working and living conditions, wages, education, health, life style, recruitment and contracting practices, transportation, migrant morale and morals, community attitudes toward migrants, vice, and the question of Mexican Nationals in Oregon were covered in the final report.[32] Recommendations made in these three reports resulted in the passage of four bills that covered labor contracting, worker transportation, housing standards, and an education pilot program for migrant children, the same bills around which the Migrant Ministry Council mobilized. According to the Bureau of Labor's report, this legislative action represented "the most comprehensive, balanced and studied legislative program for the welfare of migrants ever enacted by any state at one time."[33]

Migrant reform also arrived in the field of health, and rightly so, as health problems stemming from substandard working and living conditions besieged migrant workers. When it came to illness, they had few options, as indicated in the testimony of Mary Thiel, whose family moved to Eastern Oregon in the 1930s when she was a young child. Sixty years later Ms. Theil recalls:

> If you got sick, you died if it was a disease that would take your life. In fact, we lost three that way. They got sick and all you did was try to take care of them the best you could. If we did go to a doctor, the doctors would tell you if you didn't have the money, they wouldn't take you. We did take a baby to a doctor with measles, and my mother didn't know how to bring the fever down and things of that nature, and the doctor turned her away. So she brought the baby back and it died that night.[34]

In 1963, the Migrant Health Act provided federal funds to establish migrant health programs throughout the country. The mission of the Oregon Migrant Health Project was to provide diagnosis and treatment services to migrant workers and their families and also to oversee sanitation in the camps. Nurses tending to migrant workers throughout Oregon found that families suffered from skin infections, bedbug and lice infestations, and diarrhea. These conditions were exacerbated by substandard conditions in worker camps: filthy toilet and shower facilities, lack of drainage, filthy mattresses, polluted drinking water, and a lack of refrigeration. In field after field, inspectors found that only one drinking cup was provided for workers, thus contributing to the spread of infectious diseases.[35] One positive outcome of this project was that on occasion inspectors were successful in shutting down sub-standard labor camps. Loprinzi's assessment of the Migrant Health Project upon its cancellation in 1970 was that it was "the best program that had thus far existed for migrants."[36] This speaks well for the program, as Loprinzi's sense of government and especially politicians' actions is that they talked the talk, but when it came time to act, they tended to bend before the powerful farm lobbies.

THE VALLEY MIGRANT LEAGUE FACILITATES COMMUNITY EMPOWERMENT

Of the many organizations and agencies that arose to serve the needs of migrant workers, the Valley Migrant League stands out for its overall impact on *mexicano* communities and, more important, for the role it played in training and empowering cultural brokers. Article II of its Articles of Incorporation clearly lays out the intent of this organization: "[Our mission is] to assist the migrant and seasonal agricultural worker and his family to deal effectively with their own problems of poverty so that they need no further assistance."[37]

The VML's first action was to secure a $700,000 grant from the Office of Economic Opportunities. Regarding this victory, Rev. Ken Lawrence, one of VML's founding members, reported to *The Oregonian:* "[The money] will make possible a program of education and social service, unparalleled in the United States and previously impossible in Oregon."[38] Over the years, and with numerous hefty grants, the VML set up opportunity centers at Woodburn, Hillsboro, Independence, West Stayton, and Dayton; sponsored summer school programs for migrant children in 14 communities; ran a day care program and nursery facilities;[39] and oversaw a corps of Vista Volunteers. At its various centers, it offered adult education programs in English, vocational skills, citizenship, social and legal skills, health, childcare, home making, and credit management. Their Head-of-Household Program assisted migrant workers in getting a college degree at Linfield and Mount Angel Colleges in 3 years; many of today's leaders in *mexicano* communities in Oregon came through that program.[40] Another successful initiative was a self-help housing program, which helped migrant workers get low interest government loans for homes and involved them in the actual building of these homes. In addition, VML administered a migrant health program and sought to convince growers to improve their labor camps.[41]

Concomitant to the growth and impact of the VML was the emergence of a powerful socio-political movement that had taken hold in Mexican-American communities throughout California and the Southwest. Reverberations of this movement spread to the Pacific Northwest and found willing participants among VML workers. In fact, it was the VML that sent thirty to forty *concilio* members to California to a Chicano training conference in the late '60s. John Little recalls that event: "It was a great training session. What was so great was that they went down there and met with Corky Gonzales. They met with César Chávez. They met with all the great leaders at that time. They all stayed in this camp and established a good spirit. When they came back, all the area directors were now Chicanos."[42] While in California, this group of VML workers was exposed to the Movement discourse of cultural and social revolution, and they returned with a burning thirst for community organizing and self-determination. As Chicano leadership developed, more mexicanos were added to the VML staff. Tensions soon arose between "conservative, charity-oriented volunteers and ex-migrants"[43] and between growers and religious activists within the organization. John Little's words again are instructive in helping us understand the power struggles that developed within the VML:

A lot of the people in the VML were either old bureaucrats or do-gooders. So what happened was they were going to help people. We had one bureaucrat who was a social worker and he gave a training lecture in which he said, 'it's like these people are sick and we're the doctors. We're going to get them well.' We had people there, for example who were working as job counselors. They were Anglos. They didn't know the language, they couldn't talk to the workers. Like the one I inherited, was so incompetent he couldn't go around and get a job, so his assistant Sonny Montes was the one who was going around and getting the jobs and talking to the people. And the guy was doing nothing. Sonny was getting minimum wage and this guy was getting big money.

A statement made by an Assistant Director to *the Oregonian* lends credence to Little's harsh observations: "They [migrant workers] naturally mistreat facilities . . . They haven't any idea of respect for their own, much less someone else's property. . . . that's why the Valley Migrant League was created . . . We're trying to educate the migrants."[44]

Little's philosophy, influenced greatly by Paulo Freire[45] and Maryknoll missionary values, played an important role in determining the direction taken by the VML. He came to the director's job knowing full well that this was a bureaucracy and as such there were limits to what it could accomplish. Nonetheless, his stance was the following: "What I was saying was I'm here to change the institution. You can make the institution friendly to self-organization, then the people have to take charge and take responsibility for the decisions. But the institution has to permit them to make those decisions."

In fact, it was his own philosophy that forced him to step down as Executive Director to make way for a Chicano. He recalls, "When I took the job as Executive Director I said 'I will only take this job on one condition. That is, I will take the job until we can find somebody who can survive in Washington D.C. and who is from the raza [the *mexicano* people], preferably an ex-migrant worker." Frank Martínez was identified as his potential replacement and was brought in as a staff member. He was given the responsibility of organizing the Poor Peoples' March in 1969 and, as a result of the strong leadership exerted in that capacity, he was hired to replace Little as Executive Director.

With Martínez' appointment it was just a matter of time before Chicanos took control of the organization. In 1972 the VML bylaws were amended to require that 51 to 100 percent of the board members be migrant representation. Community response to this action was jubilant: "The crowd of over 150 Chicanos and supporters of VML packed inside Jason Lee Church then cheered wildly. After nearly seven years, farm workers had finally taken over complete control of the Valley Migrant League."[46] Martínez triumphantly observed, "This is probably the greatest victory for farmworkers in Oregon's history. No longer will it be possible for the Establishment to manipulate the VML. The day when the bureaucrats in Washington could tell VML what to do is over . . . This means that the man who gives slave wages and the man who runs the slave market will no longer have a say in formation of VML policy."[47] To the broader Oregon community Martínez sent a simple message, revealing that the fundamental principles of the Chicano movement—community empowerment and self-determination—had indeed found fertile ground among Oregon's *mexicano* communities: "Whenever the dominant society thought about us, it was in terms of 'Oh, these poor migrants. Let's take them some cookies and old clothes . . . Well, we are tired of cookies and old clothes."[48]

GRASS ROOTS ORGANIZING IN WASHINGTON COUNTY

The case of Washington County provides additional examples of grass roots organizing led by migrants and cultural brokers—educated, English-speaking Hispanics who mediated between migrants and mainstream agencies and individuals—some of whom were trained by the VML. Ruby Elly, who had worked for the VML in Woodburn, became the Director in Hillsboro in 1966. Growing increasingly disillusioned with the power structure of this organization, she became interested in finding ways to facilitate community leadership development, which she saw as essential for grass roots mobilization. She brought José Jaime, a seminarian from Mexico and José García, another seminarian from California, to work with her during their summer break from Mount St. Angel Seminary in Oregon. José Jaime was a program aid and José García, who in prior years had worked as a labor organizer in Chicago, eventually became the temporary executive director at the Hillsboro VML. As their education in the seminary progressed, these two young men increasingly had come to understand that spiritual service was not enough for *mexicano* communities, bereft as they were of adequate educational and social services. Finding themselves, in José Jaime's words, "converted by the people,"[49] they actively strove to interweave "faith and practice." Their exposure to Saul Alinsky's agenda for social change had given them a clear understanding of how structures of power operated as well as how to access resources for their community. Hence they clearly saw themselves as cultural brokers who could play a useful role in linking community members with activist inclinations to resources and in helping them acquire skills necessary for operating within mainstream structures and institutions, albeit from a firm grassroots position. Crucial to their advocacy work was the identification of potential community leaders who could replace them when they returned to the seminary, though they continued to work in Hillsboro on weekends during the academic session and, indeed, José Jaime ended up staying permanently. He still lives in Hillsboro and continues to be an advocate for *mexicanos'* rights.

Jaime and García found their leaders in twelve *mexicano* Hillsboro families that had already come together to "do something for the community."[50]
Under José Jaime's mentorship they formed *Los Amigos Club* in 1966, which
became an incorporated organization in 1971. The main purpose of this club
was to help community members buy homes and to assist them in time of
need, particularly with shipping the remains of deceased individuals to Mexico or Texas for burial, as was customary among *mexicano* families.

The idea of self-determination spawned in this small circle of families indeed had taken root in Washington County. VIVA (Volunteers in Vanguard
Action) was founded by Emilio Hernandez and Ruby Ely after they splintered
off from the VML. Their actions influenced the formation of El Hogar del
Campesino, a program that sought to empower migrant workers. Its director
Guadalupe Bustos did not mince words when he stated: "One of the most difficult jobs we have is trying to convince all state and private agencies that
work for betterment of migrant worker conditions that among the workers
there are people who can lead and direct if given the opportunity."[51] Staff
member, José Morales, added, "Nobody can do it for us. Only we who have
experienced it can end this so called war on poverty."[52] Bustos, under the auspices of VIVA, was also instrumental in starting up a co-operative full-service
gas station for Mexicanos in Hillsboro. Hector Hinojosa, who was an adoles-
cent when he came to Oregon with his family from Texas in the sixties and
whom we interviewed in 2004, recalled with relish, "This was unbelievable
for 1969, *el concepto de hacer una cooperativa entre Mexicanos* [the concept
of starting a co-op for Mexicanos]. Across the street was Texaco. There were
gas wars between us."[53] He recalls also working at the co-op where he learned
about bookkeeping, inventory, and purchasing at the age of 15. Bustos and
Morales, both college-educated sons of migrant workers from Texas, clearly
represented the new breed of cultural brokers engaged in helping *mexicano*
communities take control of their destinies.

The next step for this community was the founding of a cultural center.
Again Hinojosa recalls what a monumental accomplishment this was: "The
first time I heard of this concept of the centro cultural, was from my parents,
coming home from the meeting of *El Club de los Amigos* and talking. Our
need was for education, for having a resource center, a place for celebrations.
Then the fund raising started. *Vendiendo* [selling] tacos, *tamales, bailes*
[dances], in order to raise funds to first purchase the property—two properties—one house in Cornelius and an old house here. We needed a safe haven
from *la migra* [border patrol]." Hinojosa assured us that it was not just the
men leading the way: "It was both the men and the women. Couples always
working together."[54] In 1972 they opened Washington County's first *mexicano* community center. The Centro's mission, as stated in its by-laws, was

"to help provide basic emergency needs and to promote economic development, education, and cultural awareness between the diverse groups that make up our community. To provide a cultural and educational bridge, where rich and poor, young and old, educated and illiterate, could meet to discuss and find solutions to common problems."[55] As the Centro grew in strength and influence it spawned several new initiatives. The most impressive of these was the Virginia García Health Clinic.

In 1973 young Virginia García stepped on a rusty nail and her foot became infected. She was refused medical attention at the community hospital because the family had no insurance. She was then taken to St. Vincent Hospital where she was treated, given medication, and sent home. Because the family did not receive treatment instructions in Spanish, they did not administer the medicine as indicated, and young Virginia died. It became clear that medical care was a critical problem for the *mexicano* community, and the Centro, which was about to start a training program in auto mechanics, rose to the occasion. They had the space for the garage and had bought the tools. However, when the community mobilized around the death of Virginia Garcia, the board decided to use the resources for the training program to start up a health clinic. With support from Tuality and St. Vincent Hospitals, the Centro founded the Virginia García Health Center, which is still in operation today serving thousands of patients each year. The Centro was also instrumental in establishing a cultural center in Cornelius on property bought several years before by the twelve founding families of the Hillsboro center.

A COLLEGE OF OUR OWN

The formation of a university, El Colegio César Chávez, aimed primarily at educating migrant workers and other working class people, was yet another example of community empowerment led by cultural brokers. Sonny Montes, who had gained solid leadership skills working seven years with the VML, went to work for Mount Angel College in 1971. His job was to direct the Ethnic Studies program and to recruit *mexicano* students for the financially strapped but socially conscious institution. When it became apparent that the school could not meet its financial obligations, Sonny Montes proposed to the archdiocese that it give him a stab at forming a Chicano college. His idea was to create a "college without walls" that would give credit "for prior experience gained outside the classroom."[56] Hence, the only Chicano college in the nation was founded on an auspicious date, December 12, 1973,[57] with, according to Montes, an inherited "debt of almost one million dollars . . . from the former administration" as well as a hefty debt owed by the Benedictine

Sisters to HUD.[58] From the beginning, César Chávez, who was regularly visiting Oregon to promote the UFW's grape and lettuce boycott, was supportive, so much so, that the college was named in his honor. Montes fondly recalls the time when Chávez, who happened to be in Washington D.C. when
administrators from the college were attempting to negotiate with HUD,
showed up and used his masterful organizing tactics to influence the outcome
of the meeting. Within a year the *colegio* had 125 students, most of them migrants from the Mt. Angel area. *El Chavista*, the college newspaper provides
a clear sense of the strong influence of Chicano Movement discourse among
its student body:

> Colegio is a living picture of la familia, a constant reminder of the rural, urban
> and migrant barrios. It is a spirit of carnalismo [brotherhood]. It is a mirror of
> you and us and of all raza. Colegio represents our admiration, acceptance, un-
> derstanding, respect and love for our padres y madres [mothers], for our abueli-
> tos [grandparents], our principios [principles]. Who are we? We are the people
> who do not accept any less than your fullest potential in living, in learning, in
> creating. We are the people who will help the chicana/chicano to get a GED Cer-
> tificate, and to get a college degree. We do not accept that a chicana belongs in
> the kitchen. We recognize that women, too, must contribute their fullest to la
> raza. If you are not afraid to defend our people and the poor, if you really be-
> lieve that you should participate in decisions which affect our people, and if you
> truly believe that in unity there is strength, then you should come to colegio and
> learn to become a leader of our people.[59]

The passion that moved the *colegio's* student body and the administration's
success in gaining accreditation candidacy and in establishing an educational
program that was relevant and empowering for the student body notwithstanding, the college's financial burdens simply could not be overcome.[60]
Consequently, this inspiring experiment came to an end in 1983. Montes en-
thusiastically recalls those years:

> *Teníamos muchas ganas de hacer cosas*, (we had the desire to accomplish
> things) and considering that we had paid our quotas it was a perfect fit for those
> days, because one thing that we didn't lack was energy and knowing people here
> and there. I remember when they said the only way you're going to be able to
> have financial aid is if you guys get some institutional self-studies. I didn't even
> know what the hell that was. So you know you do common sense stuff. We
> asked Father Waldschmidt at the University of Portland if he could come over
> and talk to us about institutional self-studies, what they look like and all these
> kinds of things. And he did. So we put together a plan including 20–25 people.
> We started writing (laughs). A lot of people involved in this. We submitted the
> report, with a request to the Northwest Accreditation Association for candidacy

status. We went to a hearing in Idaho and we were on the news every day because we were kind of ridiculous. We didn't have any money, we didn't have accreditation. After the site visit and so on we made a presentation before the association and, lo and behold, they gave us candidacy status. It turned out to be a brand new ballgame after that, because they had to release some federal monies. So it worked out. It worked out. But again it was the effort of a whole bunch of people. A lot of struggles. It was hard. It was hard because—I'm not exaggerating or anything—but right after HUD started coming after us, we went about 6, no maybe 7, 8 or 9 months without any pay. How we were surviving was that any time I would go out and speak at different places, and I would say, we need to get paid. And then we had an agreement that anybody who generated monies would bring it back into a pot and we distributed among everybody else. But you know what . . . fantastic experience. I don't think I'll ever go through that again. We never fought with each other. We were too busy trying to make the Colegio become a reality.⁶¹

We cite Mr. Montes at length because his words bear testimony to the stuff that early m*exicano* activists and settlers were made of; they bear witness to the fact that through sheer will and hard work they were able to extricate themselves from paternalistic poverty programs and to take control of their communities. We must point out, however, that not all *mexicanos* view the accomplishments of the *"Movimiento"* with equal candor. Manual Salinas, a retired educator whose family settled in the Willamette Valley more than almost sixty years ago, offered the following assessment of the activities described above: "What we lacked was how to separate reality from fantasy and too many people were focusing on the fantasy and not the reality. You got the *centro cultural* that used to be over here a mile away [in Woodburn]. What happened to that? Well when you don't have the business savvy, when you don't have the fundamentals to engage in some kind of business partnership, sometimes it's a lot of heart and not enough of the other. I think there has to be a balance. It's a shame to have a lot of this *movimiento* and not to have today, in the year 2005, not to have any tangibles."⁶² In our minds, however, there is no doubt that the pioneers and activists discussed above, and others whose stories are not told here, laid a strong foundation for future generations. This foundation provides new migrants from Mexico⁶³ a foothold upon which to anchor their very vulnerable lives as they arrive daily in Oregon to continue picking our crops, washing dishes in our restaurants, making beds in our hotels, mowing our lawns, building our houses and, equally important, enriching our cultural landscape.

The descendants of the early *tejano* settlers are scattered throughout Oregon, though they are primarily concentrated in Ontario, Nyssa, Woodburn and surrounding areas, Independence, Washington County, and Medford. Their children and grandchildren are integrated into Oregon's mainstream society, but in general their acculturation has been selective. Portes and Rumbaut characterize selective acculturation as a paced learning of the host culture accompanied by retention of significant elements and key values of the culture of origin.[64] The continual flow of migration from Mexico has contributed to the selective acculturation of *tejano* pioneer culture, and in this regard, Oregon is beginning to resemble Southwestern states that have a long-standing *mexicano* presence, which forms the bedrock upon which newer immigrants struggle to build their communities and construct their new identities as Americans and Oregonians.

NOTES

1. The use of identity labels is a very complex issue (see note 31 below). *Mexicano,* when speaking in Spanish, is the one term that is universally accepted by people of Mexican-origin in Oregon. Hence, we have chosen to use this term throughout this paper. We deliberately wish to call attention to the original language in which it is used; hence we designate this language switch through the use of italics and the use of the lower case, which is standard practice in Spanish writing.

2. The Latino population in Oregon in 2000 was 275,314; in 2003 it is estimated at 326,361. See table 1 and chart 1 in the appendices for a more precise breakdown of the Hispanic population in Oregon by county and year from 1980–2003.

3. Richard W. Slatta, "Chicanos in the Pacific Northwest: An Historical Overview of Oregon's Chicanos," *Aztlan* 6:3 (1975); Colleen Marie Loprinzi, Hispanic Migrant Labor in Oregon, 1940–1990. M.A. Thesis: Portland State University, 1991; Erasmo Gamboa, "El Movimiento: Oregon's Mexican-American Civil Rights Movement," in *Nosotros: the Hispanic People of Oregon,* ed. Erasmo Gamboa and Carolyn Baun (Portland: The Oregon Council for the Humanities, 1995), 47–60.

4. Twelve individuals, 6 women and 6 men, were interviewed between April 2004 and March 2005 for this project. They were selected because of their long-standing presence in the community and because they are recognized for their involvement as community leaders and activists. The open-ended interviews were recorded on an audiocassette and transcribed by the authors. Subsequently the data were analyzed using a constant comparative method and examined for emerging themes. Additional interviews and print materials found in two archival sources (The Independence Heritage Museum and the Oregon Historical Society Library) were also used in this study.

5. Loprinzi notes that families who operated independently of contractors faced challenges that did not affect contract workers, such as arriving without funds and not being able to find work or not being able to buy items on credit (Hispanic Migrant Labor in Oregon, 1940–1990. M.A. Thesis: Portland State University, 1991). Despite these drawbacks, one report indicates that in 1957, of the total 111,760 Spanish-speaking workers running the migrant circuit to Oregon, 2,945 (not counting children)

came independently of contractors (Oregon Bureau of Labor, *Vámonos p'al Norte 1958* (Salem, OR: Bureau of Labor, 1959), 9–10.

6. David Laing was a student at the University of Oregon who conducted a survey on the conditions affecting the lives of migrant workers in the Willamette Valley. Findings of this survey were reported in a series of articles published in *The Independence Enterprise* in the summer of 1964.

7. Interview, Raul Peña, 15 Apr. 2004.

8. David Montejano, *Anglos and Mexicans in the Making of Texas, 1836–1986* (Austin: University of Texas Press, 1987), 262.

9. Latino Oral History Project Independence Historical Museum Archives, Independence, Oregon (not indexed).

10. Latino Oral History Project, IHMA.

11. Mark Martinez Infante and Tom Current," *We Talked to the Migrants . . ." Preliminary Report* (Salem, OR: Bureau of Labor, 1958), supplement, 7.

12. Tom Current and Mark Martinez Infante, . . . *and Migrant Problems Demand Attention. Bureau of Labor Migrant Labor Division Final Report of the 1958–59* (Salem, OR: Bureau of Labor, 1959), 116.

13. Current and Infante, . . . *And Migrant Problems Demand Attention*, 123.

14. *The Oregonian,* 19 July 1962.

15. Interview, Raul Salinas, 15 Apr. 2004.

16. Current and Infante, . . . *And Migrant Problems Demand Attention.*

17. Robert Dash, "Mexican Labor and Oregon Agriculture: The Changing Terrain of Conflict," *Agriculture and Human Values* 13, no. 4 (Fall 1996): 92–93.

18. Elizabeth Flores, "*Festejando* Community: Celebrating Fiesta Mexicana in Woodburn, Oregon," in *Chicanas and Chicanos in Contemporary Society*, 2nd ed., ed. Roberto M. De Anda (Lanham, Md.: Rowman & Littlefield Publishers, 2004), 148.

19. Cited in Fuller, Varden. *No Work Today!* Public Affairs Pamphlet No. 190, (New York: Public Affairs Committee, 1953).

20. Fuller, *No Work Today!* 11.

21. Fuller, *No Work Today!* 11.

22. A report issued by the Oregon Legislative Assembly Interim Committee in 1958 found that in 1957, Oregon ranked sixth in the nation as users of migratory labor.

23. *Independence Enterprise,* 3 July 1958.

24. *The Oregonian,* 23 July 1962.

25. Oregon Council of Churches. Annual Report (n.p., 1960). Regarding the limitations of mainstream religious organizations in achieving radical social change, the following case is instructive. The State Council's sister organization in Portland, The Greater Portland Council of Churches, turned its attention to social action in matters related to the civil rights of urban African Americans living in Portland in the sixties. Eventually, it turned its attention to farm worker issues by joining the UFW grape strike, thereby trying to influence social action on behalf of Oregon's *mexicano* community. Members of the business community resisted strongly because as Nelson reports, "numerous local lay members of churches which belonged to the GPCC had

large invested interests in the supermarket being picketed and were hurt by the boy-cott, because the pragmatic intensity of the issue *directly* affected their economic well-being, many of its own members vigorously questioned the GPCC's stand" (Nelson 1974, 136).

26. Richard B. Craig. *The Bracero Program: Interest Groups and Foreign Policy* (Austin: University of Texas Press, 1971).

27. Loprinzi, Hispanic Migrant Labor in Oregon, 104.

28. Gamboa, "El Movimiento," 48.

29. The Second Vatican Council created an atmosphere that encouraged new ways of conceptualizing the world. In Latin America, theologians began to question the social problems affecting their countries. They also began to think about the relation between faith and poverty and to understand that the principals of Christianity, as espoused in the Bible, provided a blueprint for social justice. They encouraged the merging of theology with social praxis and this, in turn, prompted priests and nuns to engage actively in social movements.

30. This Committee was made up of representatives from the Departments of Agriculture, Education, Labor, Public Welfare, Industrial Accidents, Motor Vehicles, Health, and Employment Services. Their job was to "develop a cooperative program to assist in solving the many problems facing the agricultural employer and worker" and to "cooperate with the Legislative Interim Committee on Migratory Labor . . . in studying the problems of the migrant agricultural worker" (Current and Infante, . . . *and Migrant Problems Demand Attention,* 5).

31. A note of clarification on ethnic labeling is in order here. Throughout this period in all government reports, as well as in the media, the Mexican-American population—be it migrant or settled out individuals—is referred to as "Spanish-American." This usage was common in New Mexico and to a lesser extent in Texas, where the preferred label was "Latin American." The racialized white/color binary prevalent in the United States rendered the label Spanish American a designator of white status, while the term Mexican connoted non-white status. This is complicated by the fact that individuals of Mexican origin, with the exception of 1930 when the term Mexican appeared as a race designator, historically have been counted as whites in the U.S. census. In order to distance themselves from the conditions affecting African Americans in this country, many Mexican-American politicians and community leaders deployed strategies that ensured this group was being categorized as white (See Foley, "Becoming Hispanic"). It is plausible that the strong voice of Dennis Chavez, a "Spanish American" New Mexican with seniority in the U.S. Senate, may have influenced the language used at the federal level, which then trickled down to the states. In the reports issued by Infante and Current, the term Mexican is occasionally used but always in quotes, as if to signal that this is not appropriate usage. Given that Infante was himself from Mexico, it is likely that he reserved the term Mexican for Mexican nationals but found it inappropriate for designating United States citizens of Mexican origin, who could not lay legitimate claim to Mexican national identity. These labels were to give way to "Chicano" in the sixties and early seventies. Today the preferred albeit contested labels are "Hispanic" and "Latino."

32. Our reading of the reports mentioned above, even those that reveal a marked empathy for migrant workers, suggests that a preponderance of the blame for substandard labor and living conditions is laid at the feet of contractors, thereby tending to mitigate grower responsibility.

33. Current and Infante . . . *and Migrant Problems Demand Attention*, 162–63.

34. Cited in Gamboa and Braun, *Nosotros*. 135.

35. Oregon State Board of Health. Oregon Migrant Health Project. Annual Reports 1964–1965, 1968, 1961,1970, 1971 (n.p., 1965).

36. Loprinzi, Hispanic Migrant Labor, 74.

37. *El Relámpago* April 1971, 4.

38. *The Oregonian,* 20 Mar. 1965.

39. This interesting note regarding childcare appears in *El Relámpago* (Apr. 1971, 1): "Many problems face establishment of child care centers in the different areas served by the VML. Local citizens are frequently ignorant of the problems of migrant families. Farmers feel childcare is somehow subversive. Some school and church boards whose facilities are badly needed feel the political pressures against child care and are reluctant to co-operate with the program. Many people simply do not understand the relevance of day care in solving the problems of migrant families."

40. Interview with John Little, 31 Sept. 2004.

41. *The Oregonian,* 11August 1965; Gamboa, "El Movimiento"; interview, Little, 31 Sept. 2004).

42. Interview, Little, 31 Sept. 2004.

43. Loprinzi, Hispanic Migrant Labor, 110.

44. *The Oregonian,* 11 Aug. 1965.

45. Paulo Freire, renowned Brazilian educator, espoused a philosophy which sought to empower disenfranchised and marginalized populations by encouraging dialog as a step to recognizing their own social positioning and consequently defining their own needs and political agendas.

46. *El Relámpago*, 13 Feb. 1972.

47. *El Relámpago*, 13 Feb. 1972.

48. *The Oregonian*, 24 Jan. 1971.

49. Interview, Jose Jaime, 6 June 2004.

50. Interview, Jaime, 6 June 2004.

51. *The Oregonian,* 19 Aug. 1968.

52. *The Oregonian,* 19 Aug. 1968.

53. Interview, Hector Hinojosa, 6 June 2004.

54. Interview, Hinojosa, 6 June 2004.

55. Hinojosa family papers, loaned to author by Hector Hinojosa.

56. Interview, Sonny Montes, 1 Oct. 2004.

57. Dec. 12 commemorates the apparition of the Virgin of Guadalupe to the indigenous youth, Juan Diego. This date is celebrated yearly in Mexico and also in *mexicano* communities throughout the United States. In fact, a mass in honor of the Virgin of Guadalupe was the first event slated for the opening celebration of El Colegio.

58. *Rural Tribune*, 6 Apr. 1974.

59. *Chavista* Mar. 1979.

60. Interview, José Romero, 9 Sept. 2004.
61. Interview, Sonny Montes, 1 Oct. 2004.
62. Interview, Miguel Salinas, 31 Mar. 2005.
63. We consider 'new immigrants' those individuals who began arriving in Oregon after the passage of IRCA (Immigration Reform and Control Act) in 1986. Immediately after passage of this act, thousands of workers were given amnesty in Oregon, and shortly thereafter, the statistics related to "Latinos" in Oregon—the majority of them *mexicanos*—began to soar.
64. Miguel Portes and Rubén Rumbaut, *Legacies: The Story of the Immigrant Second Generation* (New York: Russel Sage Foundation; London, Berkeley and Los Angeles: University of California Press, 2001).

BIBLIOGRAPHY

Dash, Robert. 1996. "Mexican Labor and Oregon Agriculture: The Changing Terrain of Conflict." *Agriculture and Human Values*: 13:4 (Fall 1996):10–20.

Craig, Richard B. 1971. *The Bracero Program: Interest Groups and Foreign Policy*. Austin: University of Texas Press.

Current, Tom and Mark Martinez Infante. 1959. . . . *and Migrant Problems Demand Attention*. Bureau of Labor Migrant Labor Division Final Report of the 1958–59 Migrant Farm Labor Studies in Oregon.

Flores, Elizabeth. "*Festejando* Community: Celebrating Fiesta Mexicana in Woodburn, Oregon."Roberto M. De Anda, ed., *Chicanas and Chicanos in Contemporary Society*. 2nd ed. New York: Rowman & Littlefield Publishers, Inc. 2004.

Foley, Neil. 1997. "Becoming Hispanic: Mexican Americans and the Faustian Pact with Whiteness." Neil Foley, issue ed. *Reflexiones: New Directions in Mexican American Studies*. Austin: Center for Mexican American Studies, pp. 53–70.

Fuller, Varden. 1953. *No Work Today!* Public Affairs Pamphlet No. 190. New York: Public Affairs Committee, Inc.

Gamboa, Erasmo. 1995. "El Movimiento: Oregon's Mexican-American Civil Rights Movement." Erasmo Gamboa and Carolyn Baun eds. *Nosotros: the Hispanic People of Oregon*. Portland: The Oregon Council for the Humanities.

Gamboa, Erasmo and Carolyn Buan, eds. 1995 *Nosotros: The Hispanic People of Oregon: Essays and \Recollections*. Portland: Oregon Council on the Humanities.

Infante, Mark Martinez and Tom Current. 1958. *"We Talked to the Migrants . . ." Preliminary Report*. Salem, OR: Bureau of Labor.

Loprinzi, Colleen Marie. 1991. Hispanic Migrant Labor in Oregon, 1940–1990. M.A. Thesis: Portland State University.

Montejano, David. 1987. *Anglos and Mexicans in the Making of Texas, 1836–1986*. Austin: University of Austin Press.

Nelson, Leonard S. 1974. Social Action as Social Change Through a Process of Insulation. Unp. MA Thesis, Portland State University.

Oregon Council of Churches. 1960. Annual Report.

Oregon State Board of Health. 1965. *Oregon Migrant Health Project.* Annual Reports 1964–1965, 1968, 1961,1970, 1971.

Newspapers

El Relámpago
Farm Labor News Notes
The Independence Enterprise
The Oregon Journal
The Oregonian
The Rural Tribune

Oral History and Archival Projects

Latino Oral History Project Independence Historical Museum Archives, Independence, Oregon
Latinos in Oregon Oral History Project, Oregon Historical Society Library, Portland, Oregon

Interviews

John Little (10-01-04)
Celedonio "Sonny" Montes (10-1-04)
José Romero, (9-0-04)
Elena Peña (4-15-04)
Raúl Peña (4-15-04)
Miguel Salinas (3-31-05)

Part IV

RACE AND LABOR

Chapter Seven

Lumber, Railroads, Factories and Silicon: Asian and Pacific Islander Americans and Work in Oregon

Patti Sakurai

While often thought of as newcomers, Asian and Pacific Islander Americans actually have a long history of work in Oregon, one that reveals much about ways in which economic competition, gender norms, racism, and anti-immigrant sentiment have been intertwined in our state's history. Further, this early history marks both a stark contrast to and certain continuity with today's perceptions of Asian and Pacific Islander Americans, as the dominant workforce stereotype has shifted to the well-paid, high tech employee, and yet racialized anti-immigrant resentment remains. This chapter, then, will look at some of the labor history of Asian and Pacific Islander Americans in Oregon and what concerns and issues might surround employment issues and concerns for these groups today.

During the 1830s and '40s, the Hudson Bay Company listed over a dozen workers of Hawaiian and Tahitian origin among its employees at Fort Umpqua, Oregon.[1] Referring to nearby Fort Vancouver, Washington, the Oregon Historical Society notes that "Hawaiian Islanders were among the earliest Asian Pacific groups to migrate to the Pacific Northwest. Hawaiians came to the West Coast on British trading ships in the late 18th and early 19th centuries to work for fur-trading companies such as the Hudson's Bay Company at Fort Vancouver."[2] Their numbers there were substantial, and "[b]y the 1840s, forty percent of the laborers at Fort Vancouver were of Hawaiian decent [sic]. They worked as cooks, gardeners, servants, millers, and sailors and lived in an area outside the fort named Kanaka Village."[3] Native Hawaiian and Pacific Islanders' early presence in the region makes them an integral part of the area's history and is particularly worth noting given how relatively invisible this history has been to most of Oregonians.[4]

In the mid 1800s, Chinese began to immigrate in substantial numbers to Hawaii and the U.S. mainland. Many of them were initially drawn to the

mainland by the California gold rush and driven by harsh economic and political conditions at home. In Oregon, most of these early Chinese immigrants
were men working in mining or on the railroads.[5] As related in an Oregon
Employment Department report, "In 1880, as many as 78 percent of the Chinese in eastern Oregon were employed in the mining industry. The other 22
percent were employed in other occupations such as railroad workers, cooks,
laundrymen, laborers, and merchants."[6] As railroad and mining jobs de-
creased, many Chinese immigrants "moved to coastal cities and worked as laborers and factory workers, while others migrated to Portland and worked in
the salmon canning industry. By the mid-1870s, the Chinese had become the
largest ethnic group in Portland and by 1880 there were 9,510 Chinese living
in Oregon."[7] Some also worked in agriculture, while others were able to open
small businesses, such as the well known Kam Wah Chung Company store in
John Day, Oregon, run by Ing (Doc) Hay and Lung On in the late 1800s and
well into the 1900s (the building is now a museum run by the Oregon Parks
and Recreation Department and their story is discussed by Jun Xing and
Sarah Griffith in this anthology). Not everyone welcomed the immigrants,
however, and many Chinese moved to areas such as Portland and Astoria to
escape the rising anti-Chinese violence in the 1880s.[8] With the hostility came
anti-Chinese legislation, including the 1882 Chinese Exclusion Act aimed at
halting Chinese immigration, particularly laborers.

Japanese immigrants began arriving in substantial numbers soon after, as
Japan lifted its ban on emigration in 1885 and labor recruiters worked to fill
gaps left by the now excluded Chinese.[9] Many of these early Japanese immigrants worked on the railroads and in mining and lumber industries in Oregon. Forty percent of Oregon's railroad workers were Japanese during the period 1905–1907.[10] They also played a big role here in agriculture: "In 1920,
60 percent of Oregon's Japanese population was employed in the agricultural
industry."[11] While many worked as migrant farm workers, some were eventually able to start their own farms as sharecroppers, lessees, or even farm
owners, and "[b]y 1940, Japanese farms produced 75 percent of the vegeta-
bles sold in Portland."[12] Among the most successful of the Japanese farmers
in the early 1900s was Masuo Yasui of Hood River, Oregon. While well respected by many Oregonians, his success was also met with hostility as evi-
denced by the establishment of the Hood River Anti-Asiatic Association in
1919.[13] Referred to by critics as the "emperor," Yasui was supposedly leading
a Japanese takeover even though Japanese owned only two percent of the
farmland in Hood River Valley at the time, 1920.[14] Yasui tried to counter the
rising anti-Asian hostility but to no avail. Oregon followed California's suit
and passed its own Alien Land Law in 1923, barring Asian immigrants from
owning land.[15] While Yasui was able to work around the law at the time by

putting his land in the names of his U.S.-born citizen children, he lost most of it during World War II when he was wrongly arrested by the FBI and his family was forced to leave Hood River and placed in internment camps along with 120,000 other Japanese Americans—a blow from which he would never fully recover.[16]

Though smaller in numbers, Koreans and Asian Indians also came to Oregon in the early 1900s, working in agriculture, on the railroads, in lumber mills, mining, and other occupations.[17] Some early Korean immigrants also opened small businesses.[18] Korean immigration to Hawaii and the U.S. mainland in the early 1900s was rather short-lived—just two and half years—due to concerns over their mistreatment abroad and political circumstances in their homeland—namely Japan's occupation and colonization which was both reason for leaving and why many could not leave, as Japan stopped allowing emigration in 1905.[19] Immigration patterns from Korea were also influenced by Christian missionaries and labor recruiters.[20] Only about a thousand immigrated to the U.S. mainland in the early 1900s[21] *Sun Gu Ja: A Century of Korean Pioneers*, an Oregon documentary released in 2004, chronicles some of the early experiences of Korean immigrants to Oregon, including the story of Kyung Soo Park, one of the first Koreans to arrive and settle in the state.

Most Asian Indians immigrated during the period 1907–10, and like most of their other Asian immigrant counterparts, they came due to the political and economic situations they faced at home and the possibilities they saw for work here, particularly as presented by labor recruiters.[22] The story of a family of early Asian Indian immigrants in Oregon is told in Erika Surat Andersen's short narrative film, *Turbans,* set in Astoria around 1918. The film is based on the experiences of Andersen's grandmother and reflects the predominantly male presence of Asian Indian immigrants who worked in the lumber mills in Astoria. The family in the film is Sikh and faces a number of challenges, including how to handle the discrimination they encounter and issues of assimilation, particularly when it comes to their children.[23]

The 1924 Immigration Act virtually ended immigration from all Asian countries until the passage of the Immigration Act of 1965. An exception to this legislation was the Philippines, as it was by then a U.S. territory undergoing rapid change and harsh socioeconomic conditions under American colonization. Predictably, then, Filipino immigration to the U.S. mainland rose substantially in the 1920s, coinciding with anti-Asian immigration legislation that cut off labor recruitment from other Asian countries. The vast majority were single men, working a wide variety of jobs on farms, in canneries, restaurants and private homes as domestic workers, to name a few. While some Filipino immigrants were able to open their own businesses or find better-paying skilled jobs, the timing of their immigration was hardly ideal. Faced with a well-developed set of anti-Asian discriminatory laws and practices on the one hand, and the even fiercer labor competition with the coming of the Great Depression on the other, many Filipino workers were held to low-paying, largely migratory work, that is, when they could get work.[24] As recounted by historian Chris Friday, one Filipino immigrant, Ramon Tancioco, did manage to find a winter job one year during the depression at a farm in Gresham, Oregon. Willing to accept the low pay of fifteen cents an hour given the scarcity of jobs, Tancioco's luck proved questionable when he ended up being paid in stove wood rather than cash.[25] Without the cash wages to buy food to cook, the wood became a bitter ironic symbol indeed. Friday's research also points to the interconnections between work and formal education. Many of the early Filipino immigrants' hopes for a better life included attending school, and best estimates put the number of Filipinos attending school on the U.S. mainland between 1920–25 at around two thousand—about fifteen percent of their mainland population. By 1939, though their overall numbers had gone up, the number of Filipino immigrants able to attend school was down to around three hundred.[26] As one Filipino immigrant, Ponce Torres, put it, "[W]hen there was no job we could not go to school, there was no money."[27] While formal education is most often associated with better jobs and pay, this historical example makes clear the reciprocal relationship between work and being able to afford school in the first place. One Filipino man, Felix Zamora, described their treatment in those early decades, recalling a visit to the Broadway theater: "I was in Portland. . . . They segregate the Filipinos, Japanese, Chinese, Colored people on the balcony. The white on the first floor . . ."[28]

The animosity encountered by Asian immigrants of all ethnicities in the late 1800s and early 1900s was very much tied to their role as workers. Other laborers often viewed them as economic competition and cheap labor that drove down wages since Asian immigrants were usually paid less than their white counterparts for the same work. While not all Oregonians shared the prevalent anti-Asian views of the period, the call for their expulsion was quite clear. Drawing on the popular slogan, "the Chinese must go," the Reverend E. Trumbull Lee was compelled to write in the *Portland Daily News* in 1886 that the Chinese were "unclean and immoral" and "live on these shores at the expense of white laborers."[29] He refers to the Chinese Six Companies, a Chinese immigrant community and business organization, as "a slave holding corporation indeed" which could ". . . furnish any white manufacturer, firm, or corporation, with coolies who will labor for a fraction of what the white laborer is able to live upon."[30] He goes on to argue, "We have come to a situation in social and political matters when we must listen to the reasonable demands of honest labor. And labor says: 'I cannot compete with yonder yellow slaves. Send them back to their land, and for God's sake, do not degrade me any longer.'"[31] Oregon's labor commissioner echoed the sentiment over two decades later, stating in a 1909 report, "Every honest means should be used to stop Oriental immigration to our country. It is a menace to all our institutions."[32] Numerous laws and policies were passed over time at the federal, state, and local level regulating and restricting the lives of Asian immigrants in the U.S.—everything from immigration legislation like that mentioned above to school segregation, anti-miscegenation laws, and special taxes that targeted particular Asian immigrant populations. As to the "dishonest" means of stopping immigration implied in the labor commissioner's statement, one can guess his probable meaning as anti-Asian violence often backed up anti-immigrant sentiments.

In 1887, a group of white men killed and mutilated the bodies of thirty-one Chinese miners on Oregon's side of the Snake River in Hell's Canyon. Three of the men went to trial, but no one was ever convicted for the killings.[33] The violence carried over into the 1900s as it did in Toledo, Oregon. In July, 1925, twenty-two Japanese, four Filipinos, and one Korean who had been contracted to work at the Spruce Mill were threatened with violence, forced out of their homes, put in cars and driven to Corvallis by a mob of white townspeople.[34] The foreman, Ichiro Kawamoto, was beaten in front of his wife and three children during the incident. The list of violent anti-Asian incidents in Oregon and other parts of the U.S. is unfortunately a long one—too long to catalog fully here.[35] No Asian immigrant group escaped notice in this regard.[36]

While the majority of the Asian immigrants were male laborers, there were a number of women among them. Like Kawamoto's wife mentioned above in the Toledo incident, a number of them cooked for the work crews.[37] Others took in laundry, helped run family businesses or farms, and/or worked as manual laborers, often alongside their husbands. But in the early decades of Asian immigration, prostitution was also among the listed occupations for Asian immigrant women. For example, sixty-one percent of the Chinese women in neighboring California were listed as prostitutes in the 1870 census.[38] Their presence in Oregon has occasionally been noted in various materials as well. Friday mentions a significant number of Chinese prostitutes among the few Chinese women in Astoria in the 1870s and 1880s, particularly as noted in local and Portland newspapers.[39] And given the gender imbalance at the time in other Asian immigrant groups (and the West in general), the occupation was by no means limited to Chinese women. In Portland, a Japanese Consulate official reported nineteen Japanese immigrant women working as prostitutes in 1891.[40] Unfortunately, many of the Asian women who worked as prostitutes were lured or outright purchased by other Asians, bought from desperately poor families—sometimes under false pretenses of a legitimate job—or taken under the promise of a marriage that never happened.[41] Few of these women were self-employed, and many were kept in a state of "debt peonage" supposedly to pay back the expenses incurred when brought to the U.S.[42] Held in urban brothels or taken from work camp to work camp, most received no wages and "worked in conditions far inferior to those of white prostitutes."[43] In some cases, their exploitation was twofold: "[I]n the daytime they [Chinese prostitutes] were forced to do sewing work subcontracted out to their employers."[44] The trend did wane, however, and by 1880, the percentage of Chinese immigrant women listed as prostitutes in California had already fallen dramatically, to twenty-four percent.[45] Friday notes a similar decline in prostitution among Chinese women in Astoria by the turn of the century.[46] Of course, anti-Asian immigration laws certainly played a part in the decrease. The Page Law of 1875, for example, explicitly barred the entry of Asian women for the purpose of prostitution. The law also barred Asian male contract laborers and felons, though, and certainly was not passed with these women's welfare primarily in mind. In fact, the law heavily reduced the number of Chinese immigrant women regardless of actual intended occupation or circumstance, as would-be immigrant wives became intimidated and deterred by the assumptions of and rigorous interrogations by U.S. government officials.[47]

As a consequence, Chinese immigrant women comprised less than fifteen percent of the Chinese American population in the U.S. in 1920. While the wives of the handful of wealthy Chinese merchants did not have to work within the home or outside of it, most Chinese immigrant women did have to work and took on a wide variety of jobs—from farm work and family businesses to "housekeepers, servants, laundresses, seamstresses, shoemakers, cooks, miners, and fisherwomen."[48] In contrast to the Chinese immigrant community's situation, a substantial number of Japanese immigrant men were able to bring over wives because of the 1907 Gentlemen's Agreement, many of them "picture brides"—a term that refers to the photos often exchanged across the Pacific in setting up arranged marriages. Between 1910 and 1920, the number of Japanese women in Oregon rose from 294 to 1,394.[49] Korean, Asian Indian, and Filipina women entered the country in the early 1900s as well, though in smaller numbers and/or proportion to the overall population of their respective ethnic groups. Like their Chinese counterparts, all of these women worked a variety of jobs. And like most women, they were also responsible for household chores and childcare, making their workdays especially long. One Hood River woman, Hatsumi Nishimoto, recounted: "Women's work never ended. During the week, I labored in the fields. I drove the Ford tractor when we sprayed. . . . Same as the men, I worked until 6:00

P.M. But when I came home, I had to cook, too. After dinner during harvest, we boxed the fruit. Then when everyone went to bed, I cleaned the house. . . . Even on Sundays, I had laundry and housecleaning chores."[50]

As Julie Matthaei and Teresa Amott point out, the unpaid work of Japanese immigrant women and their children on small family farms is often what made the success of many of these farms even possible in the first place.[51] The same can be said for other Asian immigrant women (and all women, for that matter) and their children who have likewise worked wage-free in family businesses and on family farms. As noted by Fred Cordova, a number of Filipinas "became entrepreneurs. They owned with their husbands and managed for them restaurants, pool halls and stores."[52] There were also some Filipinas who worked as teachers and other professionals during the period.[53] But Cordova argues that Filipinas differed from most other Asian immigrant women in one regard. Having been raised within significantly different gender dynamics than other Asians and often more educated than their husbands, they held more explicitly recognized power within their families and in their communities than most other Asian immigrant women during the period.[54] Still, like other Asian immigrant women, most worked long and hard hours: "Pinays were shouldered with limited financial resources while trying to rear growing families with their mates. So, these women joined their men in agricultural work by working alongside them in the fields or cooking for work crews. . . . They prepared and sold Philippine finger-foods in the streets. They took in washing, sewing, baby-sitting and other domestic chores."[55]

While most Asian immigrant men held some privilege based on their gender within their communities, broader American gender norms were conspicuous in their employment histories as well and the phenomenon is worth noting alongside the histories of Asian immigrant women as another example of the ways in which race, gender, and class have and continue to interact in U.S. culture and society. Anti-Chinese sentiment in Oregon, for example, reflected gender roles in the dominant culture as "a number of white working women also took up the anti-Chinese cause. Women laborers often competed directly against Chinese men for jobs in domestic service, tailoring, laundries, and mills . . . With the decline of mining and the completion of railroad construction, the Chinese increasingly took jobs that had been regarded as within the 'sphere' of women."[56] Matthew Klingle goes on to note how Chinese were blamed for "driving white women out of respectable jobs and into careers of 'depravity,' i.e., prostitution."[57] In the Pacific canning industry, Friday also notes the ways in which gender notions affected employment rationales, as Chinese men were seen as being able to perform the "fine, fast, and repetitious" work often viewed as women's work but with the strength employers attributed to men.[58] As Friday puts it: "Nimble, strong hands can be found

among both sexes and all races, but the combination of characteristics can-
ners attributed to Chinese further legitimized their employment and demonstrates how tightly race and sexual prejudices were intertwined."[59]

Often underpaid and overworked, Asian and Pacific Islander immigrants of
the late 1800s and early 1900s were hardly passive in their approach to work
here. Many became active in unions and fought for equal pay and improved
work conditions. They participated in lumber mill strikes in the Columbia
River region in the early 1900s, organized as farm workers, and overcame
ethnic divisions as the multiethnic Cannery Workers and Farm Laborers
Union—including a Portland chapter—joined the CIO in the late 1930s.[60]
With World War II came more changes as broader employment trends created
through the war industries and military service affected Asian and Pacific Islander Americans as well, including Asian and Pacific Islander American
women who were able to secure jobs previously not available to them.[61] As
Valerie Matsumoto has pointed out, even Japanese American women experienced some shift in gender expectations and limitations during the war, albeit
within the context of the harsh and unjust conditions of the internment
camps.[62] After the war, while African American veterans were generally denied their rightful benefits, many Asian Pacific American veterans were able
to take advantage of GI support for school and hence shift vocations.[63] This
is not to suggest that job discrimination disappeared, however, and it is important to note that the Filipino soldiers who were called up to serve in the
U.S. military from the Philippines, then still a U.S. territory, did not receive
the benefits promised them (a bill that would restore full benefits and equal
veteran status sits before Congress at the time of this writing—2005).

Also dramatically affecting the vocational makeup of Asian and Pacific Islander Americans were changes in immigration legislation. In 1965, Congress
passed a new Immigration Act that once again allowed immigration from
Asia in substantial numbers. With renewed immigration came different demographics and trends in terms of countries of origin, gender, and varying socioeconomic backgrounds. Larger proportions of immigrants from India and
Korea came to the U.S. after 1965 than earlier in the century and newer populations from Southeast Asia, initially pushed here by war, also began to arrive. Shifts in Oregon demographics reflect this growing diversity as well,
and recent census figures show that the state has one of the most ethnically
diverse Asian and Pacific Islander American populations in the country.

Today, the dominant image of Asian and Pacific Islander Americans has
shifted from manual laborer or farmer to that of the successful high-tech professional. While somewhat reflective of actual vocational trends, the image
masks not only past work histories of Asian and Pacific Islander Americans,
but current labor issues faced by them as well.[64] While many immigrants

come to the U.S. with education, training, and economic resources, other, less visible and lower income immigrants end up in ethnic enclaves and/or "underground" economies where they are easily exploited and unprotected by U.S. labor laws. Matthaei and Amott describe the situation as a bifurcated "Uptown" and "Downtown" demographic trend among post-1965 Asian immigrants.[65] Further, as sociologist Timothy Fong points out, the idea that Asian and Pacific Islander Americans somehow constitute a socioeconomically successful "model minority" relies on a number of distortions and overgeneralizations, particularly when it comes to work and income.[66] For example, when comparing different racial groups in the US, mainstream media will often cite the average Asian American household or family income to assert the "stunning" success of the group as a whole. Asian Americans do have a higher average household income ($51,908 in 1999) than any other racial group, including White Americans ($44,687 in 1999).[67] But what is overlooked in such statistics is the dramatic diversity when different ethnic groups are specified. For example, Asian Indians in the U.S. had an average 1999 household income of $63,669, while Cambodian Americans' average 1999 household income was $36,155 and Native Hawaiian/Pacific Islander Americans" was $42,717. Moreover, Fong argues, when per capita income is cited rather than household income, the picture looks quite different.[68] According to the 2000 U.S. census, the 1999 per capita income was $21,823 for Asian Americans, $15,054 for Native Hawaiian/Pacific Islander Americans, and $23,918 for White Americans. While a number of variables contribute to per capita figures, the difference raises questions nonetheless, especially given the dramatic contrast with average household income figures.

As Fong notes, comparisons of income levels are further skewed by ignoring the fact that a dramatically higher percentage of Asian Americans than White Americans live in urban areas where costs of living and average wages/salaries tend to be higher.[69] This seems to hold true for Oregon as well, where just under 70 percent of Asian Oregonians lived in the Portland metro area in 2000 and another 19 percent lived in the Willamette Valley which includes more populated areas such as the Eugene-Springfield area and Corvallis-Albany.[70] While in 1999 the per capita income for the state was $20,940, the per capita income for Multnomah County was $22,606, Washington County $24,969, and Clackamas County $25,973. To further add to the distortion, Fong notes that Asian American households also tend to include more wage earners than others.[71]

Ironically, the other aspect of the model minority image—educational attainment—actually makes unqualified assertions of success even more suspect. Precisely because the average level of educational attainment for Asian Americans is significantly higher than the average for Americans in general, and because educational level is generally tied to occupation and income, their lower median earnings for full-time, year-round workers creates a much more complicated picture than the "model minority" image would at first indicate. In the case of Oregon, while Asian Americans over 25 are significantly more likely to hold a bachelor's degree or higher, their average educational attainment does not seem to be reflected in their median earnings levels when compared to White Oregonians as seen in the figures in Table 7.1. Native Hawaiian/Pacific Islander American figures also prove telling in the comparison and mark a disparity that often gets overlooked when statistics for Asian and Pacific Islander Americans are lumped together.

A number of questions arise when looking at this data: To what extent are Asian Americans in Oregon getting an equal and fair return on their investment in education when it comes to jobs and income? What might census data reveal about the number of Asian and Pacific Islander Americans in Oregon at the lower end of the income scale? And finally, what of Native Hawaiian/ Pacific Islander Americans and other specific groups who get lumped into the category of "Asian and Pacific Islander American" and how might their issues and concerns get lost in model minority" assumptions? While there is currently little Oregon-specific research available in these areas, hopefully future research will delve more into these questions.

On the national scale, the idea that Asian and Pacific Islander Americans face discrimination in the workplace is not without its controversies and debates, particularly when it comes to wages and notions of a "glass ceiling." As outlined in economist Marlene Kim's article, "Do Asian Men Face Wage Discrimination in the United States?," scholars clearly disagree on the answer to her title's question. While there does seem to be some consensus on the earnings disparities faced by foreign-born Asian American men when compared to similarly qualified White American men, opinions are much more

Table 7.1.   Education and Earnings in Oregon (2000 U.S. Census Figures)

	White Oregonians	Asian Oregonians	Native Hawaiian/Pacific Islander Oregonians
Percentage over 25 with bachelor's degree or higher	25.7	38.7	14.3
Percentage over 25 with graduate or professional degree	8.9	14.4	3.4
Median 1999 earnings for full-time, year-round workers	$32,740	$31,786	$25,875

varied when it comes to U.S.-born Asian Americans. Kim's own conclusion is that U.S.-born Asian American men do indeed experience wage discrimination, particularly given factors of educational attainment and work experience.[72] The debate is not a simple one, and that given, my own relation to the statistics offered here warrants some qualification. As someone trained in literary studies, I am hardly an expert statistician and hence am more than a bit wary of trying to assert any major conclusions in the same quantitative terms as Kim or other so qualified scholars. Moreover, my own educational training highlights for me the subjective aspects of statistical information and the narratives built around them, despite common assumptions about statistics' objective qualities. Obviously, how groups are aggregated, which statistics are juxtaposed with each other, what specific language is used to present them—all have an impact on what conclusions we draw from numbers, my own words in this paper being no exception. Further, census data, especially when it comes to communities of color, is not an infallible source of accurate information since underreporting and other issues of data collection can skew figures. Therefore, while I cite a number of census figures and do make some observations, my primary aim here is not to assert an objective "truth" about Asian and Pacific Islander Americans and work in Oregon but rather to offer an alternative context for some of the demographic information available and to raise some questions about the "truths" that are already often assumed when looking at this topic.

For example, the Oregon Employment Department's June 2000 report, "American Indians, Blacks, and Asians in Oregon's Work Force," asserts, "Because Asians have historically constituted a very small percentage of the U.S. population and because *every quantifiable indicator* suggests that Asians are doing as well as or better than any other of America's racial minority populations, there has been no concerted effort to compile labor force statistics"(emphasis mine).[73] Comparing Asian Americans to other groups of color, the report's assumption that all is well for Asian Americans seems quite reasonable given the glaring disparities experienced by Latinos, African Americans, and Native Americans in Oregon.[74] However, while the report is useful in many ways (I cite it several times in this essay myself), the report's particular statistical comparisons risk overlooking labor issues Asian and Pacific Islander Americans may actually have in the state—issues that may become more apparent when their figures are compared to those of White Oregonians and/or broken down into specific Asian and Pacific Islander American ethnic groups. Comparing Asian and Pacific Islander Americans to other communities of color or to general state statistics seems problematic in this light, as it renders any disparities relative to White Oregonians largely invisible and risks perpetuating "model minority" generalizations.

The report does, however, highlight the increased immigration of highly skilled and educated workers from Asia to work in Oregon's high-tech industries. Half of Asian American Oregonians are foreign-born and according to the report, often "came here specifically for education and/or were recruited for a job that requires a high level of education."[75] The report goes on to note that "an increasingly large percentage are coming as guest workers in response to employment opportunities in the high-tech industry."[76] The census figures for Asian Indian Americans in Oregon in particular seem to bear this out. Of the Asian Indian Oregonians over 25 years of age, 75.7 percent hold a bachelor's degree or higher and 42.8 percent hold a graduate or professional degree—an incredibly high percentage when compared to the general figures in Table 7.1. 75.8 percent were born outside of the U.S. and the average 1999 earnings for full-time, year-round Asian Indian Oregonian workers was $70,408—not surprising given their high educational levels (see Table 7.2 for per capita figures). And while their high average earnings seem to indicate a positive picture for Asian Indian Oregonians, consensus around findings of wage discrimination for foreign-born Asians and some specific U.S.-born groups does not bode well for this group of workers as implied in Kim's work: "[T]he most consistent finding is that foreign-born Asian men face earnings discrimination, and . . . only U.S.-born Asians of certain ancestries, such as of Filipino and Asian Indian descent, appear to suffer earnings discrimination."[77] She goes on to posit the existence of a glass ceiling for all Asian male workers regardless of nativity, however, and points to findings that "at higher levels of schooling, Asian men earn less than similar white men."[78] While Kim limits her observations to Asian males, Oregon earnings statistics certainly raise questions about such trends and white collar employment practices and rationales for both genders. The fact that these high-tech workers are well-paid relative to most other Oregonians makes concern for their fair treatment a hard sell, but questions arise nonetheless about pay equity, racialized resentment from co-workers and surrounding communities, and job instability—particularly as employment affects their immigration status.

On the "Downtown" side of this picture, to return to Matthaei and Amott's term, questions arise around the fact that while close to the same percentage of Asian Oregonian civilians (61.2 percent) and White Oregonian civilians (60.9 percent) over age 16 worked in 2000, and an even higher percentage of Native Hawaiian/Pacific Islander Oregonian civilians over 16 worked that same year (67.6 percent), Asian and Pacific Islander Oregonians were more likely to live below the poverty line than White Oregonians—12.5 percent for Asian Oregonians, 18.2 percent for Native Hawaiian/Pacific Islander Oregonians, and 10.2 for White Oregonians. The disparities in income and poverty status for some get even more pronounced when broken down into different ethnic groups as shown in Table 7.2. I have included figures for African American Oregonians,

Table 7.2. Population, Education, Income, Poverty, and Unemployment Rates for Selected Groups in Oregon (2000 U.S. Census Figures)[80]

Group	Population	% Age 25+ with Bachelor's Degree or Higher	1999 Per Capita Income	1999 Median Earnings for Full-Time Year-Round Workers	1999 % Individuals Below Provety Line	% Civilians Over 16 Employed
White	2,961,623	25.7	$22,118	$32,740	10.2	60.9
Asian	101,350	38.7	$19,790	$31,786	12.5	61.2
Asian Indian	9,575	75.7	$30,723	$60,182	7.5	66.2
Cambodian	2,569	8.9	$12,079	$27,520	18.9	56.8
Chinese	20,930	45.7	$20,858	$36,208	12.9	61.7
Filipino	10,627	37.7	$17,697	$28,811	6.8	67.4
Hmong	2,101	8.5	$8,802	$22,373	3.0	62.9
Indonesian	788	52.5	$13,912	$31,719	42.7	56.0
Japanese	12,131	45.9	$26,217	$41,224	19.1	52.0
Korean	12,387	37.4	$16,657	$27,397	15.2	57.5
Laotian	4,391	8.8	$13,299	$25,219	10.9	67.4
Pakistani	362	68.7	$26,386	$71,471	15.4	67.5
Thai	1,441	40.3	$15,819	$30,739	33.5	55.8
Vietnamese	18,890	16.6	$16,132	$27,199	10.2	62.1
Native Hawaiian/ Pacific Islander	7,976	14.3	$15,516	$25,875	18.2	67.6
African American	55,662	17.8	$14,875	$29,860	24.1	55.2
American Indian/ Alaska Native	45,211	12.2	$13,443	$26,880	22.2	59.2
Hispanic/Latino	275,314	9.6	$10,116	$21,159	24.9	62.5
Mexican	214,662	7.2	$9,428	$20,304	25.6	63.0

Hispanic/Latino Oregonians and Mexican Oregonians (the largest Latino group in the state) to offer some further context for the figures.

Table 7.2 certainly suggests a much more complicated picture for Asian and Pacific Islander Oregonians than a first glimpse at the broader data might suggest. From Hmong Americans' $8,802 per capita income to Pakistani Americans' $71,471 median earnings, from an incredibly wide range of educational attainment rates to equally wide-ranging poverty rates, the dramatic socioeconomic diversity of Asian and Pacific Islander Oregonians is clear.[79] And the data for a number of the groups also seems to suggest that conversations about the working poor need to include Asian and Pacific Islander Americans. Further, while Asian Oregonians are more likely to work in management, professional, and related occupations than White Oregonians (40.2% of those over age 16 versus 34.2% respectively in 2000), they are also more likely to work in service occupations (16.3% versus 14.5%) and manufacturing (26.6% versus 13.7%). In comparison, Native Hawaiian/ Pacific Islanders in Oregon are less likely than White or Asian Oregonians to work in management, professional and related occupations (20.3%), while more likely to work in service occupations (22.7%) and manufacturing (17.5%).[1]

Niche industries have emerged, such as the mushroom and other harvesting that occur in Oregon forests each year, predominantly the work of Southeast Asian, Mexican, and other Latino immigrants. The murder of two Asian mushroom harvesters in the early 1990s brought attention to the multimillion-dollar industry, but since then, the industry has remained largely invisible to most Oregonians. Even less discussed are the cases of human trafficking that still occur. In September 2002, as covered by newspaper journalist Maxine Bernstein, federal authorities arrested a Portland Vietnamese man in connection with a trafficking ring that allegedly lured Southeast Asian women to the U.S. under false pretenses and then forced them to work as prostitutes to pay off their "debt." Southeast Asian women had been shuttled between brothels in Southeast Portland, Seattle and Los Angeles on a regular basis for at least two years prior to the arrest.[81] The example marks just one case of the tens of thousands—most of them women and children—who are brought to the U.S. by traffickers each year for the express purpose of exploitation in prostitution, domestic work, and other industries. The treatment faced by many involuntary Asian prostitutes in the early decades of immigration discussed earlier in this paper is unfortunately still happening today and remains largely unaddressed by the mainstream as a human rights issue.

Asian and Pacific Islander Americans in Oregon today hold a wide variety of jobs, from small businesses to factory work, from social work to computer engineering. Theirs is a long and rich labor history of which I have just scratched the surface here. While demographics have changed dramatically and the early days of overt legalized discrimination have passed, one could argue that issues of wage parity, labor exploitation, and tensions wrought by ethnically-defined labor pools and economic competition are still with us. As the "model minority," today's Asian and Pacific Islander American communities are assumed to be problem-free. But as I hope has become apparent, such assumptions prove too broad a generalization indeed.

NOTES

1. See Stephen Williamson, "Asian Employees of the Hudson Bay Company." 2003. <http://members. efn.org/%7Eopal/fortumpqua.htm>. Retrieved 2 July 2005.

2. Oregon Historical Society. "Asian Pacific History in Oregon." 2005, 1. <http://www.ohs.org/ education/ focus_on_oregon_history/Asian-Pacific-History-Home.cfm>. Retrieved 9 Sept. 2005.

3. Oregon Historical Society, 1.

4. I have come across little about Pacific Islanders' early presence and experiences here in Oregon; I realize that their limited representation in this paper only compounds the problem and hope to further research the area in the future.

5. See Ronald Takaki, *Strangers from a Different Shore* (Boston: Little, Brown and Company, 1989); also, Sucheng Chan, *Asian Americans: An Interpretive History* (Boston: Twayne Publishers, 1991).

6. See Ted L. Helvoigt, "American Indians, Blacks, and Asians in Oregon's Workforce." Salem, OR: Oregon Employment Department, 2000, 13.

7. Chinese comprised 12% of Portland's population in 1880. William Toll, "The Mature Distribution Center: The Chinese Community." The Oregon History Project. The Oregon Historical Society. 2003. <http://www.ohs.org/ education/oregonhistory/ narratives/subtopic.cfm?subtopic_ID=198>. Retrieved 15 Aug. 2005. See also Helvoigt, "American Indians, Blacks, and Asians," 13.

8. See Toll, "The Mature Distribution Center"; also Chris Friday, *Organizing Asian American Labor: The Pacific Coast Canned-Salmon Industry 1870–1942* (Philadelphia: Temple University Press, 1994).

9. Chan, *Asian Americans: An Interpretive History.* 1991.

10. See Eiichiro Azuma, Historical essay. *In This Great Land of Freedom: The Japanese Pioneers of Oregon* (Los Angeles, Calif.: The Japanese American National Museum, 1993), 8.

11. Helvoigt, "American Indians, Blacks, and Asians," 13.

12. Helvoigt, "American Indians, Blacks, and Asians," 13.

13. See Lauren Kessler, *Stubborn Twig: Three Generations in the Life of a Japanese American Family* (New York: Plume, 1993), 72.

14. The Report of the Commission on Wartime Relocation and Internment of Civilians cites Robert Wilson and Bill Hosokawa's *East to America*, noting that in 1920, 4,151 Japanese lived in Oregon and owned only 2,185 acres total (Commission 1997, 35). See also Kessler, *Stubborn Twig*, 74–5.

15. The alien land laws drew on the fact that Asian immigrants were not allowed to become naturalized citizens. Some immigrant farmers were able to sidestep alien land laws by finding a white American citizen willing to purchase land for them, or, like Yasui, purchasing land in the names of their U.S-born citizen children. Use of this loophole became more common among Japanese Americans whose numbers and gender ratio made them more likely to have children in the U.S. than other Asian immigrant groups. By 1935 over half of Japanese Americans in Oregon were U.S. born (Tamura and Katagiri 1994, 4).

16. Kessler, *Stubborn Twig,* 7–27.

17. Helvoigt, "American Indians, Blacks, and Asians"; see also Stephen Williamson, "Sikhs and Hindus from India." 2003. <http://www.efn.org/%7Eopal/indiamen.htm>. Retrieved 2 July 2005.

18. Takaki, *Strangers.*

19. Chan, *Asian Americans: An Interpretive History.*

20. Chan, *Asian Americans: An Interpretive History.*

21. Chan, *Asian Americans: An Interpretive History.*

22. Chan, *Asian Americans: An Interpretive History.*

23. Two-thirds of the Asian Indian immigrants in the early 1900s were Sikh, most of the other third being Muslim and a small percentage being Hindu (Takaki 1989, 295)

24. Some of the experiences of these early migrant workers and the hostility they faced are chronicled in Carlos Bulosan's *America Is in the Heart.* Bulosan's experiences take him through Oregon a number of times, including a stay in Portland when he is working as a labor organizer (Bulosan, 1973, 297–9); see also Chan, *Asian Americans: An Interpretive History*; Fred Cordova, *Filipinos: Forgotten Asian Americans* (Iowa: Kendall/Hunt Publishing Company, 1983); and Takaki, *Strangers.*

25. Friday, *Organizing Asian American Labor*, 135.

26. Friday, *Organizing Asian American Labor*, 135.

27. Cited in Friday, *Organizing Asian American Labor*, 135.

28. Cited in Cordova, *Filipinos: Forgotten Asian Americans,* 191.

29. *Portland Daily News*, 13 Feb. 1886.

30. *Portland Daily News*, 13 Feb. 1886.

31. *Portland Daily News*, 13 Feb. 1886.

32. Kessler, *Stubborn Twig,* 66.

33. See Matthew W. Klingle, "Industrialization, Class and Race: Chinese and Anti-Chinese Movement in the Late 19th Century Northwest," in *A History Bursting with Telling: Asian Americans in Washington State—A Curriculum Project for the History of the People of the Pacific Northwest in Washington State Schools.* Center for the Study of the Pacific Northwest. University of Washington. 1997. <http://www.washington.edu/uwired/outreach/cspn/hstaa432/lesson_15/hstaa432_15.html>, 7. Retrieved 15 Aug. 2005.

34. See Ted Cox, *The Toledo Incident of 1925* (Corvallis, Oreg.: Old World Publications, 2005).

35. Chan, *Asian Americans: An Interpretive History.*

36. Other notable incidents include the forcing of 700 Asian Indian immigrants out of Bellingham, Washington to Canada in 1907 and the forced expulsion of Korean workers from Hemet, California in 1913 (Takaki 1989, 297; Chan, 1991, 52).

37. Cox, *The Toledo Incident.*

38. Takaki, *Strangers,* 121.

39. Friday, *Organizing Asian American Labor,* 60–1.

40. Azuma, *In This Great Land,* 13.

41. See Julie Matthaei and Teresa Amott, "Race, Gender, Work: The History of Asian and Asian-American Women." In *Rethinking the Color Line: Readings in Race and Ethnicity.* 2nd Ed. Ed. Charles A. Gallagher (New York: McGraw-Hill, 2004), 277, 281; also Takaki, *Strangers, 41–2, 51.*

42. Matthaei and Amott, "Race, Gender, Work," 277, 281; Takaki, *Strangers,* 121–2.

43. Matthaei and Amott, "Race, Gender, Work," 277.

44. Matthaei and Amott, "Race, Gender, Work," 277.

45. Takaki, *Strangers,* 123.

46. Friday, *Organizing Asian American Labor,* 61.

47. Takaki, *Strangers.*

48. Matthaei and Amott, "Race, Gender, and Work"; Takaki, *Strangers,* 121.

49. Azuma, *In This Great Land,* 20.

50. Cited in Linda Tamura, *The Hood River Issei: An Oral History of Japanese Settlers in Oregon's Hood River Valley* (Urbana: University of Illinois Press, 1993), 100.

51. Matthaei and Amott, "Race, Gender, and Work, 283.

52. Cordova, *Filipinos: Forgotten Asian Americans*, 149.

53. Cordova, *Filipinos: Forgotten Asian Americans*, 150.

54. Cordova, *Filipinos: Forgotten Asian Americans*, 147–8.

55. Cordova, *Filipinos: Forgotten Asian Americans*, 149.

56. Klingle, "Industrialization, Class and Race," 7.

57. Klingle, "Industrialization, Class and Race," 7.

58. Friday, *Organizing Asian American Labor*, 34.

59. Friday, *Organizing Asian American Labor,* 34.

60. Friday, *Organizing Asian American Labor,* 148–71. Granted, as Friday makes clear, the interethnic alliance was fragile and short-lived for both internal and external reasons (172).

61. Matthaei and Amott, Race, Gender, and Work, 279, 285.

62. See Valerie Matsumoto, "Japanese American Women During World War II." *Frontiers* 8.1 (1984): 6–14.

63. Chan, *Asian Americans: An Interpretive History*; see also Karen Brodkin Sacks, "How Jews Became White," in *The Social Construction of Difference and Inequality: Race, Class, Gender, and Sexuality,* ed. Tracy E. Ore. (Mountain View, CA: Mayfield Publishing Group, 2000).

64. Further, it is worth noting that the high tech image is more often associated with Asians as separate from Native Hawaiian/Pacific Islanders. While a discussion of the complexities and debates surrounding the lumping together of Asians and Native Hawaiian/Pacific Islanders in the first place is beyond the scope of this paper, I do feel the need to acknowledge the difficulties surrounding such categories of identity in their ongoing construction, and I negotiate them here as best I can. I also want to acknowledge the politicized use of the term "Pacific Islander" in reference to Filipinos, though I include Filipino Americans under the 'Asian American" umbrella here, in no small part due to the difficulties involved in reconfiguring census data if included as "Pacific Islander" instead (the census data sets from which I draw keep the two groups distinct).

65. Matthaei and Amott, "Race, Gender, and Work," 280, 286–7.

66. See Timothy P. Fong, *The Contemporary Asian American Experience* (Upper Saddle River, New Jersey: Pearson Education, 2002).

67. Contemporary figures are drawn from the 2000 U.S. Census unless otherwise noted and were the most recent available for all groups for the purpose of comparison.

68. Fong, *The Contemporary Asian American Experience*, 70–72.

69. Fong, *The Contemporary Asian American Experience*, 70–72.

70. Helvoigt, "American Indians, Blacks, and Asians," 3, 17.

71. Fong, *The Contemporary Asian American Experience*, 70–72.

72. Kim herself takes issue with Arthur Sakamoto and Satomi Furuichi's findings that U.S.-born Asian Americans do not face wage discrimination in the U.S. (Kim 2003; Sakamoto and Furuichi 2000). She points, for one, to Sakamoto and Furuichi's particular means of calculating work experience to determine job qualifications and argues that due to a number of factors including average age, years of education, and average age at graduation, Asian Americans' years of work experience are actually higher on average than Sakamoto and Furuichi's methodology indicates. See Marlene Kim, "Do Asian Men Face Race Discrimination in the United States?" Occasional Paper (University of Massachusetts Boston: Institute for Asian American Studies, 2003).

73. Helvoight, "American Indians, Blacks, and Asians," 41.

74. The report generally refers to Asian Americans alone, though on some occasions Native Hawaiian/Pacific Islander Americans are included with Asian Americans and the two are treated as a single category.

75. Helvoigt, "American Indians, Blacks, and Asians," 26.

76. Helvoigt, "American Indians, Blacks, and Asians," 34–5.

77. Kim, "Do Asian Men Face Race Discrimination," 1.

78. Kim, "Do Asian Men Face Race Discrimination," 2.

79. The U.S. census site's threshold for generating statistics for specific Asian ethnic groups in Oregon was 100 and a number of groups including Bangladeshis and Sri Lankans were below this population threshold. The category "Other Asian" was too small to provide data as well.

80. Figures for poverty rates for some groups differ substantially from national percentages. For example, the percentage for Hmong Oregonians is extremely low

(and actually quite puzzling) considering the national poverty rate for Hmong Americans was 37.8%. Indonesian, Japanese, and Thai poverty rate were higher on the other hand, their national rates being 20.9%, 9.7%, and 14.4%, respectively.

81. Granted, in the 2000 census figures, manufacturing is listed as an industry rather than occupation, making it difficult to determine the specific types of jobs and their distribution among individuals within that industry.

82. *The Oregonian*, 19 Sept. 2002.

Chapter Eight

Mixtec Farmworkers in Oregon: Linking Labor and Ethnicity through Farmworker Unions, Hometown Associations and Pan-Indigenous Organizing

Lynn Stephen

Beginning in the early 1980s, the Mexican immigrant farmworker population in Oregon began to reflect the emergent pattern in California: its composition was increasingly indigenous. By the mid-1980s, Mixtec (one of the indigenous peoples of Mexico) farmworkers were a significant presence in the state and were among those who received legal residency in the U.S. through the Special Agricultural Workers (SAW) program of the 1986 Immigration Reform and Control Act (IRCA). Since that time, family members of amnestied workers, and others, have joined the population of indigenous immigrants in the state. By 2002, indigenous immigrants accounted for probably 40 percent of the temporary and permanent farmworker population and have moved into other sectors as well, including canneries, nurseries, construction, home care and childcare, and other service and food-related industries. A non-random sample (snowball) survey done of Marion county labor camps in the summer of 2003 by the Oregon Law Center counted 231 out of 387 people, or 59 percent, as indigenous. A majority of those indigenous workers surveyed were Mixteco (145). And, the indigenous languages recorded in the labor camp surveys included several varieties of Zapotec, Yucatec Maya, Chinanteco, and Mixe. In a separate survey, 200 Triqui-speaking workers were found in one camp and 80 in another.[1]

As their numbers grew in Oregon, Mixtec workers became a significant constituency for Oregon's farmworker union, Pineros y Campesinos Unidos (PCUN). The union was able to attract Mixtec members initially through its Immigration Service Center and through organizing campaigns in the growing season that targeted farms with significant numbers of Mixtec workers. The multiple legal statuses (undocumented, legal resident, citizen) occupied by Mixtec workers and their family members, as well as their position as low-wage agricultural workers, were all significant facets of the Mixtec experience that the union supported. This support among many Mixtec workers remains strong.

For many Mixtec farmworkers, the ethnic dimensions of their identity and experience in Oregon came to be realized through family networks and through participation in hometown associations such as the Comité Pro Obras de San Agustín Atenango (Public Works Committee of San Agustín Atenango), which has committees in Chicago, Las Vegas, Madera, Oxnard, Santa María, Vista and Santa Elena, California; Portland and Salem, Oregon; and in the Grand Canyon area of Arizona. The Salem branch began in October of 2001. Such associations provide a social framework for men and women to come together and work towards a common goal in relation to their communities of origin. They also help maintain the rights and obligations that members of a particular community have, to institutionalize political practices that allow community members to engage in collective projects that benefit their home town and to engage in information exchange and practices that stretch across national boundaries, reworking the concept of community in a transnational space.[2] The cultural and even physical sense of "place" or community of origin is accommodated to the realities of individuals and families who live their lives in several locations simultaneously and have for quite some time.[3] In the process of participating in hometown associations, the pan-Mixtec and local (community of origin) dimensions of their ethnic identity are often reinforced.

This chapter takes an ethnographic approach to understanding the multiple ways that Mixtec farmworker men and women have organized collectively in the state of Oregon and how their participation in multiple organizations works to validate the different dimensions of their experience of living and working in Oregon. I will focus in particular on Mixtec participation in PCUN, in one hometown association branch in Salem, and in the Organización de Comunidades Indígenas Migrantes Oaxaqueños (OCIMO, Organization of Indigenous Oaxacan Migrants), a new pan-indigenous statewide organization formed in 2004. Because of their unique position as indigenous people within the Mexican immigrant population and the institutionalized racism against indigenous peoples, both in Mexico and in the U.S., combined with their status as low-wage workers (often, undocumented low-wage workers), the Mixtec populations in Oregon and elsewhere have developed survival strategies that defend, maintain and strengthen their ethnicity, as well as their status as workers. In a state where indigenous politics refers to the original native peoples of Oregon (Coquille, Grand Ronde, Siletz, and others), being Mixtec is not part of the "native peoples map." On the other hand, when diversity is discussed in terms of the state's population, the categories of "Latino" or "Mexican," are often used to identify Mixtec immigrants, thus erasing their ethnic identity through Mexican nationalism or a pan-Latino identity. As discussed by Kearney,[4] hometown associations can act as visible forms of Mixtec self-differentiation (distinguishing them from U.S. Native Americans and Latinos). Thus, they serve as a focal point for ethnicity, and what we might call a public self-consciousness about ethnicity. As discussed here, participation in such ethnically-identified and constituted organizations can occur simultaneously with people's participation in class-based forms of organization such as labor unions. The recent emergence of OCIMO with the support of PCUN and CAUSA[5] (Oregon's statewide immigration rights coalition) suggests ways that ethnic and class-based organizing can work together.

PCUN AND MIXTEC FARMWORKERS

Oregon's farmworker union, Pineros y Campesinos Unidos del Nordoeste (PCUN, translated as the Northwest Treeplanters and Farmworkers United), has its origins in the 1970s. At that time, several organizers, inspired by the work of César Chávez, began to plan how they could build a social movement of Mexican immigrants and farmworkers in the state of Oregon. Their initial organizing strategies were influenced by the climate of harassment and fear faced by Mexican immigrant farmworkers in the Willamette Valley. In May 1977, the Willamette Valley Immigration Project (WVIP) opened its doors to provide legal representation for undocumented workers. While the WVIP started in Portland in 1978, it later moved permanently to Woodburn. The staff and organizers of WVIP went on to facilitate the creation of PCUN in 1985. The initial goal of the PCUN was to change working conditions for treeplanters and farmworkers. The eight-year track record of the WVIP was key to building trust in the farmworker/treeplanter community so that open discussion of a farmworker union could begin. During the 1990s, the union engaged in a series of actions aimed at opening up political and cultural space for immigrant Mexican farmworkers and raising farmworker wages. It achieved its first contracts with small organic growers and by the summer of 2002, the union was finalizing negotiations with Norpac Foods Inc.—a large cooperative of 240 Oregon growers that had been a focus of a ten-year boycott by PCUN.[6]

SECURING AMNESTY FOR OREGON FARMWORKERS

Most Mixtec farm workers and tree planters first came into contact with the Union in the mid-1980s. Some of them were living in labor camps targeted by PCUN for organizing. The vast majority, however, came to know the Union through help they received in processing their amnesty cases in 1986 and 1987. Within days of Immigration Reform and Control Act's (IRCA) enactment in November of 1986, PCUN held a number of large forums attended by more than 800 people in Woodburn, Salem, Independence and other locations in Oregon.

The first meetings focused on informing people about the different ways that undocumented people could apply for U.S. residency under the 1986 law. PCUN staff also warned people about potential discrimination against Latino workers because of the employer sanctions included in the IRCA legislation. During 1987, PCUN and the Centro de Servicios Para Campesinos (CSC or Service Center for Farmworkers) staff devoted most of their time to working with those seeking amnesty through the IRCA and SAW programs. By the summer of 1987, PCUN and the CSC had a combined staff of ten. With this small staff, they managed to process 1300 legalization cases from June 1987 to June 1988 (this represented, at that point, more than 10 percent of the total cases in the state). Their work in this area also significantly increased their membership. In the period from October of 1986 to June of 1988, PCUN signed up nearly 2000 new members. Probably up to a third of these new members were Mixtec men and a few women.[7] Later, when these men brought their wives and children to live with them, some of them returned to the Service Center for Farmworkers to receive assistance in petitioning for their residency. Since 1986, the immigration services offered by the Union are a key reason why Mixtec workers have continued to relate to PCUN in an ongoing way. Mixtec workers became deeply involved in negotiating the first contracts PCUN won more than a decade later, were recruited as labor organizers and came to occupy key spots on the union's governing board and in a spin-off women's organization.

IMPROVING CONDITIONS FOR
MIXTEC FARMWORKERS AND OTHERS

For Mixtec workers who had been laboring in Oregon for up to six years without documentation, the assistance PCUN offered them in securing legal residence was, and is, greatly appreciated. After PCUN's membership grew dramatically in 1987, the Union began to concentrate on the struggle to achieve collective bargaining. They organized the first union organized strike in the history of Oregon farm labor in 1991, and, in 1992 widened the pressure on key growers by beginning a boycott of NORPAK, a grower cooperative that included some of the growers that workers had most complained about. In 1995, PCUN began a massive organizing campaign to honor their tenth anniversary and to raise strawberry wages.

During the campaign, PCUN used trilingual radio spots in Spanish, Mixtec, and Triqui. PCUN also sent organizers to Madera, California to alert workers headed to Oregon about the campaign. Madera has been a stopping point for many Mixtec and some Zapotec migrants who come seasonally to Oregon to work. In this campaign, the union self-consciously acknowledged the indigenous ethnicity of a significant number of the workers they sought to represent and defend. In 1995, and, to this day, there are Mixtec and Triqui workers who speak little or no Spanish who are completely under the thumb of labor contractors. In order to communicate with them, the Union has used multilingual organizers and radio broadcasts and announcements to reach workers who are not literate.

Lorenzo Alvarez Meza, a Mixtec immigrant worker, began working with the Union as an organizer during 1997 and continued until April of 2002. He was an important example of the union's efforts to reach out to and organize Mixtec workers. During the winters of 2000, 2001 and 2002, he spent several months in Mexico working for the Union and visiting workers in their home communities in Oaxaca, Guerrero and Veracruz. During these visits he warned potential workers about the kinds of "come-ons" contractors used and tried to tell them about the real working conditions and about the Union. For two years he was able to track some workers from labor camps in Oregon back to their home communities. Visiting workers in these three states was an important part of the union's strategy in building confidence and support on one farm in particular, where some of the same workers returned several years in a row.

The late 1990s brought PCUN a historic victory through the signing of Oregon's first farmworker collective bargaining agreement. It was with Nature's Fountains Farms. Later, three others were signed. The agreements provided for more than a dozen rights and protections for farmworkers not afforded by law, including seniority, grievance procedures, overtime, paid breaks and union recognition. María de la Luz Contreras, a Mixtec immigrant worker, was the leader of one of the negotiating teams that worked on the first PCUN contracts. For her, the contracts were an important step in better treatment and working conditions. We discussed what the contracts meant to her in her living room in the fall of 2000.

Lynn: *What were the working conditions like when you had the contract? Were they no different than before?*

Luz: *No, of course they were not the same [with the contract]. We had clean bathrooms, we had fresh water to drink, we each had a glass with our own name on it for water. We got our break and we got to eat lunch. Before, we never got this. In the other places the bathrooms were filthy, they gave us warm water to drink, and we never even drank water, took breaks or ate lunch because we had to keep pick-*

ing in competition with others, or we wouldn't have enough work. In other places I worked, if you didn't get to the fields early and keep working in a big hurry, you wouldn't even earn enough money to pay for your food. Under our contract, they paid us the minimum and guaranteed us eight hours of work per day.

For Mixtec immigrant workers like Luz and Lorenzo, PCUN offered legal assistance at a crucial time (in 1987 following the IRCA and SAW legislation). By demonstrating that they had the resources and skills to help people like Lorenzo and Luz gain legal residency in the United States, staff from PCUN won their confidence and began to talk to them about the conditions they labored under as low-wage workers in the fields. Lorenzo and Luz became active in Union activities and eventually came to be key parts of the organization and important links to its growing Mixtec membership. As the 1990s progressed, some of the Mixtec membership of PCUN settled permanently in Oregon and began to move into other sectors of work, particularly nurseries, canneries and food processing. In helping workers like Luz and Lorenzo meet two of their primary needs (legal residency, and improved working conditions), PCUN was able to engage with them about their experience of marginality in the United States.

STAYING CONNECTED AS A MIXTEC: THE TRANSBORDER COMITÉ PRO OBRAS DE SAN AGUSTÍN ATENAGO IN SALEM, OREGON

Apart from the Union, participation in a home-town association is a different form of organizing for Mixtec immigrant workers. It allows them to focus more centrally on their links to Oaxaca, linguistic and cultural identity and transnational status.

It's really nice having this language Mixtec. But there is going to come a time when this language is going to be lost, when it will be forgotten. Our children do not want to speak it. I tell them that it would be good for them to learn a little bit of Mixtec. But they don't listen to me. I tell them that it is important to have this Mixtec language and that they shouldn't forget it. For my generation, speaking Mixtec makes me think about my youth and the kids I knew growing up. We used to speak Mixtec in school. There, we had a teacher who told us that we shouldn't speak Mixtec, that we should speak Spanish among ourselves. That is what he said. But we didn't know how to speak Spanish. Our parents spoke pure Mixtec. My mother and father didn't know how to speak Spanish. That is why I couldn't speak Spanish growing up. Now speaking Mixtec reminds me of where I am from. When I get together with other men here and talk in Mixtec, I feel different (Victor Léon Gómez, age 55).

Victor first came to Oregon from Ensenada in 1979 where he worked a circuit picking berries. He later returned in 1981 and again in 1988. From 1981 until 1986 he served his community as *comisariado de bienes comunales*, or, communal land commissioner, a position of local leadership that later pushed him to the forefront of a transborder public works committee. He became a member of PCUN and, today, sometimes goes to their events. His passion in 2002 was the transborder public works committee and his involvement with other migrants from his hometown of San Agustín Atenango.

The Oaxacan town of San Agustín Atenango straddles a paved road that runs between Huahuapán de León and Santiago Juxtlahuaca in the Mixteca Baja region of Oaxaca. On the way into town you can see two-story houses in various states of completion. Some are occupied with satellite dishes perched on top and people inside. More than half are empty, being watched by neighbors or relatives in the absence of their owners who are invariably somewhere in "El Norte," with the largest clusters of paisanos residing in Santa María, Madera, Los Angeles and Vista California; Flagstaff and Grand Canyon, Arizona; Las Vegas, Nevada; Salem, Keizer and Portland, Oregon; and Chicago, Illinois. San Agustín is a transborder community and its border-crossing members are transborder migrants.

The reason I use the term "transborder" migrants rather than "transnational" is that I want to suggest that we have to look beyond "the national" in order to understand the complex nature of what people are moving or "transing" between. In many communities such as San Agustín, where migration to and from other places has become a norm that spans three, four and now five generations, the borders people cross are ethnic, cultural, colonial and state borders within Mexico, as well as the U.S.-Mexico border. When Mixtecos come into the United States, they are crossing a new set of regional borders that are often different than those in Mexico, but may also overlap with those of Mexico (for example the racial/ethnic hierarchy of Mexico which lives on in Mexican communities in the U.S). For these reasons, it makes more sense to speak of "transborder" migration in the case I am describing here, rather than simply "transnational."

People from San Agustín have a history of labor migration in the 20th century going back to the 1920s and 1930s when they went to Veracruz and Pinotepa Nacional in Oaxaca to work in coffee and sugar cane. Some participated in the Bracero program in the U.S. from the 1940s through 1964, and, at the same time, they began to go to other parts of Mexico, such as Sinaloa, to work in commercial agriculture. By the 1970s, Mixtec migration was well established and significant not only in Northwest Mexico, but also into the United States.[8]

By the late 1980s and early 1990s, there was a significant population of Mixtecos in Baja, California—up to 20,000.[9] Yet, their numbers fluctuated because many who were residing in Baja, California (in places like San Quintín) were further recruited by agents of farm labor contractors who operated in the U.S.[10] Men from San Agustín came to work in the agricultural areas of Del Mar, Oceanside, Vista and Oxnard in the late 1970s. Later in the 1980s they came up to Oregon and Washington as well.

Mixtec immigration to the West Coast of the United States appears to have increased very significantly from 1995 to 2005. One recent estimate put the number of Mixtecos in California at 100,000.[11] One of the premier destinations for workers from San Agustín is Santa María, California, in the county of Santa Barbara. There were an estimated 200 people from San Agustín living there in 2004. There is a local San Agustín Atenango Mixtec community group in Santa María that is affiliated with the Oaxacan Indigenous Binational Front (FIOB), which changed its name to the Indigenous Front of Binational Organizations in March of 2005.

In the fall of 2001, the *presidente municipal* (mayor) of San Agustín sent out an official letter to the townspeople living in Salem. Victor describes this event:

> On October 19th, we received an official letter from our town authority, telling us that there was a piece of land for sale. The piece of land was called Inocencia. The letter said that this person was willing to sell this land to the community for our cemetery. After we got the letter, we called up all of the people from our town living here. We had a big meeting in a large park near here to see who was interested. Whole families came to the meeting. We asked if they wanted to help out in purchasing the land. They said yes, they agreed. So they named some of us to a committee. It had a president, secretary, treasurer and 2 vocales. Everyone nominated us. And they voted.

While we were talking, Victor asked another friend (also in the leadership of the committee) to bring out the list of names. His friend Lorenzo (introduced previously) returned with a computerized list of names in very tiny type. He and Lorenzo counted the names and announced that there were 80 people total, including children. There were even single mothers on the list. Victor looked up and continued describing the committee:

> The work we do is really important. Because it is about the needs of the town we really worked hard on this. Every person gave $200 and we raised $7,899 right here in Salem. We were in touch with all of the other committees and we had a big meeting in Santa Maria. We rented a hall and we had a meal. Then we began to report on our money.

Lorenzo becomes animated as Victor is talking and begins chiming in with details about the get-together in Santa Maria, the phone calls to other committees and their ideas for new projects. By the fall of 2002, more than $60,000 had been raised from all branches of the San Agustín Atenango Public Works Committee. The ten federated committees came together to meet in Santa María, California. After that, delegates from the federated committee took the money to San Agustín. When the original parcel of land became unavailable, a different one was purchased. From 2002 to the present, those who were living in the community were contributing volunteer labor or *tequio* to build a wall around the new cemetery and to cut a new road that runs between the community and the land. I visited the cemetery project in August 2004 and saw that it was well on its way. People are already being buried there. This is a very concrete example of a new form of political organizing that has harnessed economic remittances from agricultural workers and others in the U.S. directly to a collective development project in rural Mexico. The federated public works committees are now looking for a new project to carry out.

For Victor, Lorenzo and others who have participated in the Comité Pro Obras de San Agustín, the experience has been rejuvenating, and they have found it exciting to have ongoing contact with other committees from their community. Another male member described the committee as "like a community." Men involved in the committee have clearly found it to be an important cultural and social space. While they reported that most meetings are run in Spanish because the young people don't speak dialecto (Mixtec), when the leadership of the committee gets together to plan for larger meetings they will often break into Mixtec. This, they stated, reminded them of how community assemblies were run at home in Oaxaca. "There we have to speak in Spanish and Mixtec," reported Victor. "There are old people there who don't speak Spanish and now young people who don't speak much Mixtec. So we really need both languages."

While women attend meetings and vote, none were named to the leadership positions on the committee initially. This mirrors the dynamics of community assemblies in San Agustín, where women can now attend meetings, but still have not been named to important positions. While community leaders used to be chosen in the assemblies by those present, since 1987, the most powerful civil authorities such as the mayor and the city counselmen, are elected as part of a party platform. An elders council, police commanders and a wide range of committee heads and members continue to be appointed through the traditional community assembly. While the presence of political parties is in part responsible for the inclusion of women in local meetings in San Agustín, it has not resulted in their election to leadership positions there (although some have been nominated). In Salem, Oregon, in the context of the transborder public works committee, women are present but not particularly vocal or central to its activities beyond paying their quotas and discussing projects. The San Agustín transborder public works committee does not appear to be a mechanism for expanding women's political participation, and may sometimes serve to preserve and strengthen male-dominated political culture in the U.S.[12]

For the men from San Agustín (particularly for those ages 30–60), many of whom also belong to PCUN, the transborder public works committee seems to have opened up an important cultural space where they can reconnect with the Mixtec language, with the governance structure of their community and with their childhood memories and experiences. The emergence of the San Agustín Atenango Transnational Public Works Committee has also further connected them with other clusters of paisanos from home and increased their feeling of connectedness to them in the U.S.[13] Community is thus reconstituted not only in specific locales, but also through networks in the U.S. and in Mexico.[14] For Mixtecos in Salem, Oregon, the San Agustín Transnational Public Works Committee has provided an ethnically-based mode of organization.

PAN-INDIGENOUS ORGANIZING
OF OAXACAN MIGRANTS IN OREGON

In 2004, the basis for ethnically-based organizing of indigenous Mexican migrants in Oregon was broadened with the formation of Organización de Comunidades Indígenas Migrantes Oaxaqueños (OCIMO, Organization of Oaxacan Indigenous Migrant Communities). OCIMO identifies itself as a coalition of organizations and individuals from the state of Oaxaca that focuses on the problems encountered by indigenous migrants in the state of Oregon. In June of 2004 the group of people that came to make up OCIMO invited a candidate for the governorship of Oaxaca to visit Woodburn, Oregon. In September of 2004, OCIMO participated in a hunger strike with PCUN, UNETE (Unite with Us, a Medford-based volunteer organization dedicated to helping Latinos, many of them new immigrants), and other Oregon immigrant rights organizations in support of the Dream Act. The Dream Act is a bipartisan piece of legislation that was still pending in Congress as of September 1, 2005 to clear up the immigration status issues and address barriers to education and work confronted by U.S.-raised children of undocumented immigrants.[15] In September of 2004, OCIMO opened up an office in Salem in a ceremony attended by more than 150 people from a wide range of organizations. PCUN has been supportive of OCIMO and maintains a close relationship with its Board of Directors. The leadership of OCIMO includes two Mixtec women, one of whom works with PCUN. As of the spring of 2005, OCIMO's program was focused primarily on indigenous rights and promoting indigenous women's participation at cultural events. Its active volunteer base included thirty to forty men and women from primarily Mixtec communities such as Santa María Tindú, San Juan Cahuayaxi, Tlaxiaco, Santa Rosa and San Juan Mixtepec.

When Mixtecos and other indigenous peoples from Oaxaca go elsewhere in Mexico, as soon as they identify themselves as from Oaxaca they are immediately classified as "chaparitos" (short ones), "Oaxaquitos" (little people from Oaxaca), "Inditos sucios" (dirty little Indians), and sometimes told that they can't "speak" because of use of their native language.[16] These derogatory terms not only follow them through Mexico, but are frequently employed in the U.S., by the Mexican-origin population there as well. Whether it is in the public schools, in local businesses or the surrounding labor camps, the belittling of indigenous peoples that occurs in Mexico is often repeated in Oregon. Because of this discrimination, OCIMO has made the promotion of indigenous cultural events and activities a priority. OCIMO Secretary Valentín Sánchez explained, "We promote indigenous cultural events in order to decrease the discrimination toward indigenous people among Hispanics. We think that one of the reasons why discrimination exists is that many Hispanics don't know about the cultural wealth of the indigenous people of Oaxaca." OCIMO is functioning not only as a cultural space for indigenous migrants in Oregon, but also hopes to make a difference in lowering the levels of discrimination against indigenous migrant workers.

While the public works committee I researched in Salem, Oregon includes women in its membership and meetings, its organizational structure is dominated by men, and the national and international networking aspects of the committee appear to be carried out primarily by men.[17] In 1997, PCUN formed a spin-off women's organization called Mujeres Luchadoras Progresistas (Women Fighting for Progress). It became independent in 2002. Many of the participants are Mixtec women and they have often participated in the leadership of the organization as well. The women's group has been the source of many up-and-coming leaders in PCUN and in the Woodburn area. OCIMO has made a conscious effort to promote women in its leadership and activities. Mujeres Luchadoras Progresistas, and the more active inclusion of women in the leadership of OCIMO, points to the importance of venues outside of hometown associations that are tied to traditional political cultures in order for women to develop their political participation and their leadership skills.

CONCLUSIONS: LINKING LABOR
RELATIONS AND ETHNICITY

The patterns of organizational participation I have documented here suggest that the concerns of transborder Mixtec migrants remain focused on a range of issues including the relations of production, the politics of immigration and immigrant rights, culturally-based issues such as language and local cultural expression and maintenance, combating racism and discrimination in both Latino and non-Latino communities, collective memory and connection to communities of origin, and the creation of community across borders and through networks. This list of concerns certainly suggests that Mixtec migrants are not assimilating into "mainstream" U.S. culture and continue to cultivate ethnic distinctiveness in relation to both people of Mexican descent in the U.S. and Native Americans. They have created transborder communities that operate in multiple sites and social fields.[18] In the coming years, as global competition for cheap rural labor heightens, indigenous workers leaving rural Mexico are likely to continue as an important source of labor in Oregon. Our state is an important site for transborder indigenous communities and their issues need to be paid attention to in a wide range of arenas, including in education, in the legal system, in the health care system and in many workplaces.

NOTES

1. Julie Samples, 2003.
2. Gaspar Rivera-Salgado, 1998 Radiografía de Oaxacalifornia. *Masiosare*, domingo 9 de Agosto, 1998. <http:/www.jornada.unam.mx/1998/ago98/980809/mas-rivera.html>
3. See Roger Rouse, 1992; Michael Kearney, 1998.
4. Michael Kearney, "Transnationalism in California at End of Empire," in *Border Identities: Nation and State at International Frontiers*, ed. Thomas Wilson and Hasting Donnan (Cambridge: Cambridge University Press, 1998).
5. CAUSA member organizations include Centro Cultural, Cornelius, Oregon; Eugene-Springfield Solidarity Network, Eugene, Oregon; Farmworker Housing Development Corporation (FHDC), Woodburn, Oregon; Jobs with Justice, Portland, Oregon; Latinos Unidos Siempre (LUS), Salem, Oregon; Mano a Mano Family Center, Salem, Oregon; Movimiento Estudiantil Chicano de Aztlán, Eugene, Oregon; Oregon Farmworker Ministry, Portland, Oregon; Organización de Communidades Indígenas Oaxaqueñas (OCIMO), Salem, Oregon; Pineros y Campesinos Unidos del Nordoeste (PCUN), Woodburn, Oregon; Rainbow Coalition, Portland, Oregon; Rural Organizing

Project (ROP), Scappoose, Oregon; Salem/Keizer Coalition for Equality, Salem, Oregon; UNETE, Medford, Oregon; Voz Hispana Causa Chavista, Woodburn, Oregon; VOZ, Portland, Oregon.

6. See Lynn Stephen, 2001b, for a general history of PCUN.

7. PCUN archive.

8. Felipe López and David Runsten, "Mixtecs and Zapotecs Working in California: Rural and Urban Experiences.," in *Indigenous Mexican Migrants in the United States*, ed. Jonathan Fox and Gaspar Rivera-Salgado (La Jolla: Center for U.S.-Mexican Studies, Center for Comparative Immigration Studies. University of California, San Diego, 2004), 255.

9. Carol Zabin, Michael Kearney, Anna Garcia, David Runsten, Carole Nagengast, *Mixtec Migrants in California Agriculture: A New Cycle of Poverty* (Davis: California Institute for Rural Studies, 1993).

10 López and Runsten, *Mixtecs and Zapotecs,* 255.

11. Eduardo Stanley, "Se Fortalece Organización Indígena," Pacific News Service. <eduardostanley @comcast.net> (17 Mar. 2005).

12. See Goldring for a discussion of male domination in hometown associations.

13. As pointed out by Felipe López, Luis Escala-Rabadan and Raúl Hinojosa-Ojeda (2001), hometown associations can also provide collective remittances that are used to build shared community infrastructure and collectively engage migrants in efforts to develop their communities.

14. As written about by Kearney and others (1992), 232.

15. The Dream Act would grant a six-year grace period for illegal aliens who grew up in the United States and graduated from a U.S. high school. During that time, they would be exempt from deportation. If they finished two years of college or served two years in the military, they could earn permanent legal residence in the United States (DeBose 2005).

16. See Jonathan Fox and Gaspar Rivera-Salgado. "Building Civil Society among Indigenous Migrants," In *Indigenous Mexican Migrants in the United States*, ed. Jonathan Fox and Gaspar Rivera-Salgado (La Jolla: Center for U.S.-Mexican Studies, Center for Comparative Immigration Studies. University of California, San Diego, 2004), 12.

17. See Goldring, *Creating the Countryside,* 303–329.

18. See Goldring 1999; Kearney 1996, 1998; Rivera Salgado 1998, 1999; Smith 1999.

BIBLIOGRAPHY

DeBose, Brian. "Alien Still Hopes for Dream Act." *The Washington Times*, 5 July 2005. <http://www.washingtontimes.com/national/20050705-122611-6540r.htm>. Retrieved 31 Aug. 2005.

Fox, Jonathon and Gaspar Rivera-Salgado. "Building Civil Society among Indigenous Migrants." Pp. 1–68 in *Indigenous Mexican Migrants in the United States*, edited by Jonathan Fox and Gaspar Rivera-Salgado. La Jolla: Center for U.S.-Mexican Studies, Center for Comparative Immigration Studies. University of California, San Diego, 2004.

Goldring, Luin. "Gendered Memory: Reconstructions of Rurality Among Mexican Transnational Migrants." In *Creating the Countryside: The Politics of Rural and Environmental Discourse*, edited by Melanie DuPuis and Peter Vandergest, 303–329. Philadelphia: Temple University Press, 1996.

———. "The Power of Status in Transnational Social Fields." In *Transnationalism From Below*, edited by Michael Peter Smith and Luis Eduardo Guarnizo, 165–195. New Brunswick: Transaction Publishers, 1999.

Kearney, Michael. "The Effects of Transnational Culture, Economy, and Migration on Mixtec Identity in Oaxacalifornia." Pp. 337–353 in *The Bubbling Cauldron: Race, Ethnicity, and the Urban Crisis*, edited by Michael Peter Smith and Joe R. Feagin. Minneapolis: University of Minneapolis Press, 1995.

———. "Transnationalism in California at End of Empire." In *Border Identities: Nation and State at International Frontiers*, edited by Thomas Wilson and Hasting Donnan. Cambridge: Cambridge University Press, 1998.

López, Felipe H., Luis Escala-Rabadan, and Raúl Hinojosa-Ojeda. "Migrant Association, Remittances, and Regional Development Between Los Angeles and Oaxaca, Mexico." Research Report Series No. 10. Los Angeles: North American Integration and Development Center, School of Public Policy and Social Research, UCLA, 2001. <http://naid.sppsr.ucla.edu>

López, Felipe and David Runsten. "Mixtecs and Zapotecs Working in California: Rural and Urban Experiences." Pp. 249–278 in *Indigenous Mexican Migrants in the United States*, edited by Jonathan Fox and Gaspar Rivera-Salgado. La Jolla: Center for U.S.-Mexican Studies, Center for Comparative Immigration Studies. University of California, San Diego, 2004.

PCUN Archive. Organizational Archive located in PCUN office in Woodburn, Oregon.

Rivera-Salgado, Gaspar. "Radiografía de Oaxacalifornia." *Masiosare,* domingo 9 de Agosto, 1998. <http://www.jornada.unam.mx/1998/ago98/980809/mas-rivera.html>. 1999, Welcome to Oaxacalifornia: Transnational Political Strategies Among Mexican Indigenous Migrants. Ph.D. Thesis, Department of Sociology, University of California, Santa Cruz, 1998.

Rouse, Roger. "Making Sense of Settlement: Class Transformation, Cultural Struggle, and Transnationalism among Mexican Migrants in the United States." *Annals of the New York Academy of Sciences* 645 (July 1992): 25–52.

Runsten, David and Michael Kearney. *A Survey of Oaxacan Village Networks in California Agriculture.* Davis, CA: California Institute for Rural Studies, 1994.

Samples, Julie. "Personal communication regarding indigenous migrant workers counted in labor camps." Oregon Law Center, Woodburn, Oregon. 18 Sept. 2003.

Smith, Robert C. "Transnational Localities: Community, Technology and the Politics of Membership within the Context of Mexico and U.S. Migration." Pp. 196–238 in *Transnationalism from Below*, edited by Michael Peter Smith and Luis Eduardo Guarnizo. New Brunswick: Transaction Publishers, 1999.

Stanley, Eduardo. "Se Fortalece Organización Indígena." *Pacific News Service*. 17 Mar. 2005. <eduardostanley @comcast.net>.

Stephen, Lynn. "Globalization, the State, and the Creation of Flexible Indigenous Workers: Mixtec Farmworkers in Oregon." *Urban Anthropology and Studies of Cultural Systems and World Economic Development* 30, no. 2 (2001): 189–214.

———. "The Story of PCUN and the Farmworker Movement in Oregon." Department of Anthropology, University of Oregon Publication, 2001.

Zabin, Carol, Michael Kearney, Anna Garcia, David Runsten, and Carole Nagengast. *Mixtec Migrants in California Agriculture: A New Cycle of Poverty*. Davis: California Institute for Rural Studies, 1993.

Zabin, Carol and Sallie Hughes. "Economic Integration and Labor Flows: Stage Migration in Farm Labor Markets in Mexico and the United States." *International Migration Review* 29, no. 2 (1995): 395–422.

Part V

HISTORY AND MEMORY

Chapter Nine

Oral Narratives of the Klamath Termination: Using Video to Record Memory

Linc Kesler

THE KLAMATH TERMINATION IN INDIGENOUS HISTORY

For many Americans, the idea of the end to traditional ways of life in American Indian culture is associated with a long history of representations of the Plains Indian wars of the later part of the nineteenth century and the subsequent formation of reservations. These narratives glorify the formation of the U.S. nation-state and encourage the conscious association of American Indians only with the past. Though recent independent films such as *Smoke Signals* have brought to many a greater consciousness of the present circumstances of Indian life, blockbusters such as *Dances With Wolves* (1990) have continued to more firmly entrench the long term pattern by focusing on that most iconic symbol of historical transition, the extermination of the buffalo herds, that made traditional ways of life impossible for tribes that followed the herds for sustenance.[1] Those who have thought about it in more detail recognize that such iconic moments were only part of a much larger process beginning with contact and proceeding through many different periods and forms of dispossession, dislocation and change. Fewer people recognize the extent to which that process extended throughout the twentieth century and continues today, not only in North America, perhaps especially in the far north, but in other Indigenous communities throughout the world as the result of economic changes and the incursions of industrialized society, and, often, as the result of complicit government policy.

For the tribes of what was then the Klamath Reservation in southern Oregon, the most critical period in the loss of traditional ways of life did not occur until the mid-20th century when, through a federal policy generally known as "termination," federal recognition of the Klamath and dozens of other tribes was officially withdrawn. This policy, though established in principle in the 1934 Wheeler-Howard Indian Reorganization Act as movement towards self-sufficiency, was more actively pursued during the 1950s, and then with an explicitly assimilationist intent. For the Klamath tribes, termination came in 1954 with an act of congress, and its effects, fully realized over a space of several years, were massive economic and social changes—a devastation keenly felt within the community, but generally unrecognized outside of it.[2]

The Klamath Reservation had been established by treaty in 1864, though its land base diminished, as did many others, through a series of later government actions. Three major cultural groups were eventually located within the reservation: the Klamath, indigenous to the area surrounding Klamath marsh and lake; the Modocs, relocated during the Modoc wars from their original territory that extended southward into northern California; and, the Yahooskin band of Paiutes, whose original nomadic range had stretched farther to the east into Nevada. Even after the various reductions, by mid-twentieth century, the reservation still included some 860,000 acres, rich in timber, wildlife, and other natural resources. In addition to tribally operated commercial enterprises, the reservation lands still supported many traditional hunting and gathering practices, and the cultural and religious practices that accompanied them.

With the termination, the tribes lost control of this land base, the ability to sustain the practices that had supported them for centuries, and the core of their social and cultural life. A whole set of consequences followed, including a general diaspora of reservation families to other areas, a loss of cultural cohesion, and a range of ancillary effects that adversely affected the health and well-being of tribal members. Since the withdrawal of federal recognition also meant the loss of federal services including those for health care and education, tribal members who had lost their traditional livelihoods now also found themselves thrown on the social service networks of surrounding communities that were poorly equipped to receive them. A period of deteriorating inter-ethnic relations followed. Conditions for many were extremely difficult, and the tribes suffered significant attrition through alcoholism and suicide.

After more than three decades of struggle, tribal status was restored to the Klamath tribes in 1986, though restoration did not, of course, include the return of the land base. Today, the Klamath tribes, like other restored tribes, are working, through gaming and other initiatives, to expand a viable economic base, rebuild their land holdings and cohesion in their communities, and preserve and restore cultural traditions. The generation that lived through the termination period has reached their seniority and many have passed away, and the history of earlier reservation life and this period of catastrophic change, not widely known outside of the community, is now passing within it.

It was with this present circumstance in mind that Klamath elder Morrie Jimenez and I began *Oral Narratives of the Klamath Termination*, an oral history project to record, in digital video, the recollections of tribal members who had survived this critical period in tribal and Oregon history. In initiating this project, described in more detail below, we were addressing a pedagogical as well as historical need. Through the many presentations that Morrie and others had given in classes throughout the state, we had become aware of how little awareness most students had of Indian history in Oregon, and how poorly Indian history, especially recent Indian history, was reflected in their curriculum. Time and time again when Morrie and other elders spoke in our classrooms, students, many of whom had grown up within a few miles of Klamath or one of the other communities affected by termination, expressed outrage that they had lived their entire lives in Oregon and been educated in Oregon schools, and yet knew nothing of this history. And at the end of the 1990s, as the water wars in southern Oregon began to take shape, virtually none of them knew the integral relation between Oregon environmental history and this pivotal Indian history—the process through which the rapid degradation of this once pristine landscape had been so catastrophically effected.

The invisibility of such transforming and often catastrophic events in Indigenous communities to surrounding societies is one of their most consistent features, and points to the complicity that educational systems and other institutions of public information have often had in the expropriation of Indigenous lands. In addition to its other purposes, it is this condition of invisibility that this project and others like it are designed to address. The original set of interviews forming *Oral Narratives of the Klamath Termination* is now available as a set of DVDs, and may also be accessed on line in a fully searchable video and text format that supports citation for scholars and transparent browsing for all users. It will soon be accompanied by a teacher's guide and other materials supporting its inclusion in curriculum. We have also included information on the methods and techniques of this project for others who would like to develop similar projects of their own.[3]

This project has recorded a very particular type of information, and we have been concerned for many reasons that what it is, and what it is not, be clearly understood. This project records recollections of personal experiences and personal observations on historical events and processes. It is not an attempt to provide a complete or final account of the Klamath termination, nor does it constitute, at least at this point, an account that has any official status with the Klamath tribes or any other organization. Rather, it is a record of how those events were perceived, understood, and remembered in different ways by individuals who were affected by them. While some may view that dedication to personal recollection as a limitation, it is, in our perception, a significant strength, since what it documents is the complexity of lived experience. At a recent meeting in which the results of the initial project were returned to the participants and community officials, one participant observed that, in contrast to other projects that have presented themselves as more complete accounts, this project has recorded many perspectives and left room for the inclusion of others. We hope that, over time, other perspectives will be added that will make this record, if not more complete, even more informative and satisfying.

While the events surrounding termination are the focal point for the interviews included in this project, the project reflects more broadly on a whole set of themes that are common to many Indigenous communities that have experienced rapid periods of loss and cultural change, and have survived and adapted to changing circumstances. There is much here to understand about such processes and their effects, about the challenges faced by communities that experience them, and about the resiliency of individuals and communities in responding to them. There is also much to understand about the ways in which surrounding societies have viewed or failed to recognize such changes. The urgency we felt in undertaking this project was the realization that people's accumulated experience and knowledge was as vulnerable as it was valuable: without a record, their ability to share their experiences might soon be lost. Below, we will be describing some of the observations that were made during our interviews and identifying as best we can what seemed to us to be their most significant features. However, we urge you to view the interviews themselves and hear these observations in more detail from their source.

OBSERVATIONS ON TRADITIONAL CULTURE

One of the most noticeable features of Morrie Jimenez's many presentations at universities was the profound effect his narration about his childhood memory of the traditional harvesting cycles and their accompanying social and religious practices had on students. Students were often drawn into the particular calm of these narratives, from which Morrie's later description of the effects of termination came as a rude awakening. Their passage from comfort to unsettling awareness replicated, in some small ways, the experience of the historical circumstance they were hearing described. The parts of these narrations describing the traditional rhythms of life on the reservation prior to termination, though unfolding in a calm and measured manner, were dense with information, as are the corresponding narratives that form parts of this project. In a general sense, they relate as a group the very specific kind of functionality that the reservation economy and social structure was sustaining through the 1930s, '40s and early'50s.

Perhaps the clearest example comes in Morrie's description of the chuam (ling. /c'waam/) harvests of his youth. In his interview of 27 August 2002, he describes the arrival of the yearly fish runs in the Williamson River and the gathering of various family groups to join in the harvest. The harvest, as he describes it, was highly organized, with a highly-developed organization of labor that was mapped out geographically up the river bank. There were men at the waterline spearing and hooking the fish and tossing them on the bank. Then boys were hauling the fish up the bank to the younger women, who would then clean and fillet the fish, and pass them to the older women for staking and drying. The process would last for days and was also the site for community gathering and communication and the renewal of family ties. It was also an important moment for ceremonial and religious instruction. In specific, Morrie recounts the moment in which his aunt, who was a spiritual leader within his family, would take the children at dawn to view the sun rising over the river and reflecting off the backs of the fish, which were thick on the surface of the water, to remind them of the wonder and significance of that abundance and the need to appreciate and respect it.

> And we set up camp there and I can remember my grandmother and my aunts and my mothers, and my mother, during that first day of the chuam season, you know, looking down river and seeing as the sun came up behind us, and flashing down on the river glancing off the top of the river surface, my grandmother, I can remember grandma saying, "look down the river, what do you see?" And we can see the fins of the, of those big sucker fish because they were so deep in the water and they were coming up so profusely that you could see the backs, their backs glimmering in the sun and those fins glimmering in the sun as far down river as you could see.

These cultural values, in turn, reinforced the community attitudes that would support this fishery as a sustainable and self-sufficient resource. This description gives a way to understand the close relationship between natural resources and their temporal cycles, with social organization forming recurrently around a specific economic purpose. In addition, ceremonial and spiritual life and instruction occurred within the frame of this economic and social activity thereby reinforcing the values that sustain the system. As community members migrated among different locales in the yearly cycle of

harvests, they also migrated among different economic and social roles defined by the different kinds of work that needed to be done. As people aged
in the recurrent pattern of such yearly harvests, they also migrated among different age-defined roles, the young boys carrying fish up the banks becoming
the men who take the fish from the river, and the young women who clean the
fish becoming the older women who dry it. In all these respects, the society
worked to order activity in an integrated, defined, and flexible system that
prepared people for different roles and followed the rhythms of the resources
and the passage of time.

The experience of the chuam harvest reverberates at other points throughout these interviews. In his recounting of his childhood on 19 October 2002,
Ramon (Porky) Jimenez recounts going into a storage shed to retrieve some
of the dried fish hanging there, and putting it inside his shirt to eat later in the
day when traveling far from home on horseback. While the harvesting was a
single, temporally distinct event in the yearly cycle, its effects were experienced throughout the year as a constant reminder of the activities and
processes that linked the community and its systems together in an interre-
lated web.

A second set of traditional economic practices that receive considerable attention in this project center around the geography of Klamath marsh and the
resources available there. One of the most significant was the harvesting of the
wocus (ling: /wok?sam/), or water lily, the nutritionally rich seeds of which provided a major food source for the tribes. Both Morrie Jimenez (16 September
2002) and Ivan Jackson (22 September 2003) describe the traditional harvesting and processing of this resource. It was quite complicated and involved the
harvesting of the seeds by dugout canoe and the processing of the seeds through
several stages of drying, winnowing, rotting, and milling. Ivan Jackson recounts the sophisticated and difficult process of constructing the dugout canoes
used in this process. And, both Ivan and Morrie recount the storage of canoes
in the water as markers of families, much in the way that fishing hooks left on
trees marked family harvesting locations along the river during the off-months
of the year. In earlier times, the marsh was also the source of tule reeds used in
making mats, baskets, and clothing as well, though such uses were no longer as
common during the lifetimes of the participants in this project. Lynn Schonchin
(19 October 2002) also recalls the kinds of social interaction that took place
during his childhood in yearly camps near the marsh. Again, the camps combined the work of the yearly harvest with continual instruction, providing both
social interaction and entertainment:

> Those guys also taught us a whole lot on their own: how to take care of deer,
> what . . . you know you didn't waste anything. You didn't kill to just kill a deer;

you kill for meat and subsistence only, and never wasted anything. It's all of those kinds of lessons were taught with that freedom of running around as a kid, camping and everything. So I think those kinds of things, when I look back now, probably didn't think about it then, but when I look back now, are pretty important teachings and learnings that I got from those guys and my grandparents and my great-grandma, 'cause I got to spend time around her. So that was kind of like growing up.

While the narration of many of these recollections points to the survival and continued operation of traditional practices in the mid-twentieth century life of the Klamath reservation communities, many other observations throughout these interviews show the ways in which reservation life had also come to embody other, newer rhythms, while still preserving a strong sense of community. Much centered on the newer economies of commercial timber harvesting, and, on the growth of settlements, such as the Klamath agency and Chiloquin settlements, as hubs of economic and social activity. These are described in detail by Morrie Jimenez (12 November 2002), Lynn Schonchin (19 October 2002), and Delphine Jackson (13 December 2002). They point to ways in which reservation life had also begun to incorporate other cultural influences. Two particularly interesting examples will be discussed here.

The first is the development of a thriving community at Algoma, between Chiloquin and Klamath Falls, along the railroad line that follows the shore of Klamath Lake. Algoma was developed as a company town organized around a milling operation. Morrie Jimenez in particular remembers it, however, for its unique cultural aspects (20 August 2002). It included members of the tribal community, but also Mexican railroad workers, European and Japanese Americans, and recent immigrants, primarily from northern Europe, who had come to work in the timber industry. In Morrie's recollection, the community was remarkable in its inter-cultural harmony, with frequent celebrations originating in one cultural group including all the others.

A number of small communities that developed on the lakeshore there and every one of them had, were really diverse little communities and so when they got together, we always got together as a diverse, as a diverse group, and growing up in that little community, I think helped me, great deal in learning acceptance of other people's belief systems, in other people's way of life, because we shared. They were such a sharing community. We shared, food, on a regular basis, we shared celebrations on a regular basis, we shared ideas, beliefs, thoughts.

This is a particularly striking circumstance in the segregationist America of the 1930s and 40s, and, especially, in rural Oregon, which, as other parts of these accounts remind us, has not always been renowned for its climate of racial tolerance. The special circumstances of the close-knit multiculturalism of Algoma made the sudden disappearance of the Japanese families in the community at the start of WWII a very vivid recollection in Morrie's memory.

The second example of an unusually strong community experience that nearly all of the participants noted in some fashion was the institution of the Indian Shaker church, which had a large following during the pre-termination era. The Indian Shaker church dates from the late nineteenth century and has had a strong presence in many northwest Indian communities. Large meetings were held in Chiloquin. While Morrie Jimenez notes that the church at Chiloquin had some Christian elements and employed some Christian iconography that may have helped deflect government censure, both Morrie (27 August 2002, 12 November 2002) and Modesto Jimenez (19 October 2002) remember its long services and continual use of bells in healing ceremonies. Most especially, they recall the strong sense of community that marked its services and the integration of people of all ages into the communal work supporting the services and accompanying meals. They cite that sense of community as one of the most positive memories of their childhoods and something they would like to see supported again. Morrie notes that:

> It was just an extension of everyday lessons that were taught to us, but they had a great deal more meaning; and for me individually, I know other people as well, most of us who participated in that old traditional belief system remembered that, and how, what an influence it had, what an impact it had on us, in terms of what a close experience that was, in terms of communal, communal experience that was . . . . And the fact that you were together, you were practicing a religion together, you were visiting, you were talking, you were sharing stories. And, at the same time, you were learning lessons, at the same time. And very important lessons, because we all had practice, we all practice responsibility to each other. And there was a . . . It was all done in a respectful manner, but the responsibility, of the responsibility, aspects of teaching responsibility, began at a very early age. Everybody had a role to play and that. And of course, since then I've learned that's, that has been one of the keys to Native American survival over the years, is they all, they were all relying on each other, they all share. They all had accepted the responsibility for themselves and for their family and for their community.

Morrie further explains that his memories of the egalitarian spirit of the Indian Shaker religion drew him back to Indian religions after his deep involvement with Christian churches that, he came to feel, were too hierarchical in their organizational structure.

The importance of the sense of community is perhaps the single most clearly noted memory of participants in recalling their experience of pre-termination life, and is well illustrated by a story told by Lynn Schonchin (19 October 2002). On his birthday as a child he was being chased by other boys who wanted to give him a celebratory spanking. When he ran around a corner in town he collided with the legs of an older man who had a reputation for his strength and toughness. Lynn recalls being somewhat intimidated in this encounter, but explaining to the man why he was running.

> I run smack into him and kind of boom went backwards, you know, and he looked down and said, "what's going on," you know and helping me get back up and I told him, "those guys are going to spank me," and he thought, you know it was a serious, for real thing, and I said, "no it's my birthday." "Oh ok, well come on," and we went kind of in front of, there was a golden rule store, Norvel's Golden Rule: he sold dried goods. Horrie took me in there and bought me a shirt for my birthday. I'm not a member of his family or, but that's the way those folks were with us kids. And they spoiled us. But yet they taught us and so like I said, I was in the right place at the right time and those folks really had an impact on my life.

Many other recollections in this collection focus on the relationships between adults and children and the concern and informal, but persistent, transfer of values that accompanied daily exchanges.

TERMINATION

In his interview of 22 October 2002, Morrie Jimenez explains at length the processes of termination and its effects on the reservation communities, as well as detailing some of the subsequent processes through which tribal members worked to mitigate some of these effects. Morrie details the effects of the loss of the tribal land holdings and supporting services, the subsequent Diaspora of tribal members to other predominantly white communities, and the subsequent impact on cultural integrity and the personal well-being of former members. These recollections are echoed by others, and many of the factual details may be found on the Klamath web site and in other published accounts of termination. The Public Broadcasting System also did a short documentary on the effects of termination that, while not fully satisfying to all tribal members, did give an account of some of the social effects of the policy.[4] At the end of this interview, Morrie returns to the question of control of natural resources. He analyzes the reasons for termination within the long process of the dispossession of Indigenous communities that have had the dubious fortune to be located in resource-rich areas, echoing the sentiments of Lynn Schonchin (19 October 2002).

These interviews, however, are not so much about the general or statistical understanding of termination as they are about the experiences of people who lived through this process, how they understood it at the time and how they have come to think of it over the intervening years. In this respect, the recollection of two participants are particularly powerful in their different vantage points. Both Morrie Jimenez and Delphine Jackson left the Klamath area at different points during termination process only to return later to a transformed physical and social landscape. Morrie, who left to pursue his education and career, first in Klamath Falls, and later at Southern Oregon College (now Southern Oregon University), had been working in teaching jobs around the state for several years before deciding to return to Chiloquin, in part to ensure that his growing children had contact with their tribal roots. Upon his return to work in the Chiloquin school, he recounts the sadness he experienced in taking his children out for a day trip to see the important sites of his youth. What he encountered was a landscape transformed by privatization, widespread clear cutting, and other extractive economic practices.

> And I was so anxious to get them to share in that. The first time I took them out on the, onto the reservation, in the station wagon, and I took them way up on the Klamath Marsh area and the Yamsay Mountain Region, it turned out to be not a very pleasant experience, because all of that pristine wilderness area, that natural beauty, had pretty been, had pretty well been changed, by the timber that had been cut, the roads that had been built through the area, the barbed wire fences that had been erected, the gates that we had to go through, and so forth. And, and it actually turned out turned out to be, for me, a very depressing experience. And so I had, I brought my children back to the house. And like you do at that particular time, at that point on, from that point on was just to try to explain to them what it used to be like, the rivers that we swam in, the water that we drank out of the natural streams, the deer and the elk and the hunting experiences that we had, the fishing experiences (20 August 2002).

Delphine Jackson recalls similar experiences (13 December 2002). Having left the reservation for schooling as a young girl, she returned at various points to watch aspects of termination process play out. She recalls, in specific stories, the knowledge people of her grandfather's generation had of the landscape, but the feeling of total disorientation she and others had at later points as fences were built and access restructured (Ramon "Porky" Jimenez also recalled the earlier prediction of a white farmer, admired in the community, that the land would some day be completely restructured by fencing, 19 October 2002). Her sense of disorientation and displacement, so immediately tied to landscape, resonates in every aspect of the life she feels transformed.

The first time I went back after the termination, and the Forest Service took over, this was after all the land was sold and the Forest Service then took over the land, I was amazed how new roads were put in. The old roads that I used to know were not, they were no longer there. And I actually got lost; I'd never gotten lost before, in the dark you know? It was really upsetting because it, it was something that I knew almost like the back of my hand. And then they go in, and then wonder where I was. And I, I think perhaps, this is how the termination effected our people. One time we knew where we were: we had a land, we had a lifestyle, we had families and, and once the termination came, it, it was different. And I feel that a lot of people, lot of our people got lost. And I think their children are lost right now, because they didn't have what we had.

Her recollection points back to Morrie Jimenez's accounts of the chuam harvest and its integration of location, the natural world, social organization and spiritual values that give us a way to understand just how disruptive the loss and transformation of the landscape was on all these other levels. After another absence, in which she worked and studied overseas, Delphine recalls her return to Chiloquin, a community that she finds is only a remnant of its former self. She expresses particular sadness that the young children she meets there had no idea, and, at that time, seemingly no way of forming an idea, of what the former society of the reservation had been.

So, it's, it's completely different, completely different. There's a few signs of what used to be there, but very few and only if you're my age, you might be able to recognize them. Again, the younger generations have no idea, no idea what it was like. And even trying to explain to them I don't think makes sense to them. They only know what's there and what has been there since they've been born. And, and that, that's changed, it changed at termination time; and many of whom who were born during or after termination. There was very few, there was very little visibility as to the fact that a tribe at one time lived there.

It seemed to her that the reservation itself had been erased, not only from the landscape, but also from the cultural memory of the community, a sentiment that Morrie Jimenez also echoes (20 August 2002).

Other memories, sometimes in oblique ways, point forward towards the effects of termination in the present. Though the Klamath tribes were restored to status in 1984 and are now rebuilding their tribal and community structure, they have not recovered their land base and the natural resources on which the former tribal economy and social system were built are now severely compromised. Ramon "Porky" Jimenez was also away at the Chemawa Indian school during termination, but has since returned to live in the Chiloquin community. Having concentrated on work and the daily processes of his life, Porky did not immediately recall the specific effects of termination. But, he did note several specific practices, such as the mass harvesting of chuam by non-Indians for sport or for use as fertilizer that, in conjunction with irrigation practices and chemical fertilizer, run off back into the water system, and would result in the eventual listing of the chuam under the Endangered Species Act and the transformation of the tribe's yearly activity around the chuam to purely ceremonial acts (19 October 2002). These recollections allow us to understand the ways in which the loss of land and other effects of termination were experienced and understood differently by different people, and the ways in which, in various ways, they came to affect, and in many ways, to restructure their lives.

RESILIENCY AND RESPONSE

While termination was the explicit focus of this project, much of what has emerged from the interviews are the narratives of these individual lives, and, as a group, they demonstrate the ways in which the kind of rapid cultural change that has affected so many Indigenous communities has played out in the trajectories of individuals who have responded to its challenges. Two of the participants, Lynn Schonchin and Morrie Jimenez, pursued careers in education, and, for both, their early experiences with traditional teaching practices were highly influential. Both returned, at different points, to teach in the Chiloquin school. Morrie, returning at an earlier point after termination, found it a difficult and disheartening experience due to the school's incorporation into an uncooperative and culturally insensitive school system (8 October 2002). Lynn, returning later to a better institutional circumstance, has continued to live within the Chiloquin community and completed his teaching career there. His aim was to be someone that students could rely on, in this way replicating, in this very different social setting, the kind of relationships he had experienced in his youth (19 October 2002).

In part because the project began with the attempt to record some of the materials that Morrie Jimenez had shared with classes at OSU, Morrie's contribution to the project is by far the most extensive, and his recollections detail the trajectory of his own response to the cultural changes that affected his community and his family. Morrie returns many times in his interviews to underscore the importance of the solid platform that his family and indeed the whole community gave him to work with throughout his life. And, he acknowledges not only the profound influence of his mother, his aunt, and other Klamath elders, but that of his Mexican father, who was accepted into the community, and brought his own traditions (a high regard for the importance of family and a dedication to hard work) and influenced all of the children (10

September 2002, 8 October 2002). Morrie also notes, however, that his family recognized that, even in the circumstances of his youth, in which many traditional practices were vibrant, their society was, in some respects, a "remnant" society, affected by the distortions of the reservation system and its systems of cultural and political control. His family, and especially the strong women figures in it, recognized the changing circumstances that were surrounding them and set for him, very early on, the task of acquiring an education in the terms defined by the mainstream society that surrounded them, and their support was essential to his overcoming adversity:

> I'd have this tremendous need to go back and have her reinforce for me the reason for my being and how important it was that I be able to deal with the negative experiences in my life, and, which came in different forms, in one fashion or another, in some cases, nothing more than a need to go back, because, to be with your people, you know, to be amongst, amongst your people, and the way, and what they believed in and the way they practiced life on a regular basis. And so invariably I'd wind, I have a tremendous need to go back and do nothing more, to visit with my Aunt Helen so she could reinforce for me again, the reasons for being and why I needed, why I needed to sustain the effort. The way she put it, you know, "you're, there's a need for you to do what you've been asked to do." You know, and "because eventually it's going to be very helpful to your people and hopefully to other Indian people at the same time. And even though, and even non-Native people, you know, because they need to be exposed to Indian people out there at the same time." (10 October 2002)

Both Morrie (8 October 2002) and his brother Modesto (19 October 2002) recount their experiences of moving from the closely knit reservation communities of Modoc Point and Algoma to the predominantly white schools in Klamath Falls, a city in which they, and other members of their family and community, had frequently felt at risk (27 August 2002). Both succeeded in forging places for themselves in school through what has often served as route for minority students, athletics. Morrie notes that through his involvement in athletics he was able to secure not only a greater level of social acceptance, but also a greater degree of scholastic attention. Athletics also provided a route to postsecondary education at Southern Oregon College. Morrie also notes the importance of the individual teachers who chose to work with him, challenge him, and help him reach his full potential. While at Southern Oregon, Morrie began his academic investigation of other world cultures and religious traditions, and became interested in the study of cultural survival. The study of other cultures led him back to the study of other American Indian cultures and to American Indian history and the history of relations between Indian communities and the U.S. government and broader society. That study, which has continued throughout his life and later led him towards civil rights work, has also provided a context for better understanding termination policy and its effects.

Morrie recalls that at many points, negotiating the challenges of his education off the reservation and his later work as a teacher proved to be very difficult. But, that the foundation of his early training, as well as the constant encouragement of his family and other tribal members, and, the support of his wife Lois, allowed him to continue. He recounts in particular the very positive experiences he had in one early posting, where he worked with poor white migrants from Louisiana. The migrants proved to have a similar regard for family, community and work, but a much more difficult circumstance working in this small Oregon community in which racial prejudice was a constant, insurmountable obstacle in daily life (8 October 2002). He also recounts the periods in which his work, even within his original community, was very difficult due to particular circumstances, but other times in which significant progress was possible. In his interview of 20 November 2002, he also discusses at length the challenges facing people with advanced education and outside expertise who are returning to their communities. These observations are valuable in alerting viewers not only to the difficulties of working in cross-cultural settings, but the need to assess the possibilities for effecting change at different points in different environments.

In later parts of his career, Morrie worked with the civil rights office of the Oregon Department of Education and was able to participate in national civil rights projects. The interview conducted on 31 October 2002 includes one very interesting story. It recounts the filming of a PBS documentary in a Pueblo community in the southwest and Morrie's role as a mediator between the community and a non-Native producer who did not adequately understand the importance of working with community processes. This interview will be of particular interest to people working with communities when they are "outside experts," whether they themselves are Indian or not, since Morrie shares the ways in which an awareness and respect for community processes can determine the success of a project. Following his retirement from the Salem school system, Morrie has worked as a consultant to tribes, as a founding member of the Oregon Indian Coalition for Post-Secondary Education, as Klamath Tribal Council Chair, and as a guest lecturer on many campuses (31 October 2002).

The life stories of all of the participants demonstrate the resilience that allowed people to survive the changes resulting from termination. Morrie's story charts a particular trajectory across the cultural boundaries of the pre-civil rights era and the cultural divide of termination, to a position in mainstream education and government from which he has been able to use the skills and experience he has gained to contribute to the survival of his and other Indian communities in a changing world.

RESTORATION AND THE NEW CONTEXT FOR ACTION

Though federal status was restored to the Klamath tribes in 1986, the challenges facing tribal members in rebuilding the community remain significant. Morrie recounts aspects of the Restoration process in his 22 October 2002 interview, and Morrie, Modesto, and Lynn have all taken active roles in tribal government during this restoration period. Due to the loss of tribal lands and the degradation of the Klamath basin environment since termination, it is clear that no comprehensive return to prior conditions will be possible. The economic base of the tribes has shifted from a subsistence and resource base towards other kinds of development, such as the Kla-mo-ya casino. Cultural restoration is also proceeding along other lines, since, as the interviews in this project clearly indicate, traditional culture had deep involvement and integration into the landscape and the traditional economies of subsistence. Where even Morrie described the culture of his youth as a "remnant" culture (in some respects), the culture of the Restoration era might be thought of as a "recovery" culture, with efforts being undertaken to stabilize, and, where possible, to recover older cultural practices. Some of these efforts, such as those aimed at language recovery, have involved outside experts, while others have been focused more tightly within the community.

Ivan Jackson is one of the people who has dedicated much of his life to the preservation and recovery of traditional knowledge, as his two interviews with this project attest. Both of these interviews were conducted at a site near the tribal administration buildings, where Ivan was developing a restoration area centered on the construction of traditional pit houses. The first interview, conducted on 19 October 2002, took place during an early phase of construction, as the beam framing of the first house was nearing completion. The second interview, conducted some ten months later on 22 September 2003, took place inside a second house, which was nearly complete. Both interviews describe construction methods, their purpose, and their relation to traditional use patterns, as well as Ivan's motivation for undertaking the work of cultural preservation. The second longer interview also includes Ivan's memories and acquired knowledge surrounding many traditional practices, including house construction, the construction and use of tule mats and clothing, basket and hat weaving, the construction of dugout canoes, the construction of bows and arrows, and the preparation of traditional foods.

Ivan's accounts are particularly interesting for the ways in which even small details relate particular practices to a range of larger functions, or indicate the sophistication of traditional practices in addressing technical problems. The processing of wocus is one clear example of a highly developed and sophisticated system of realizing the nutritional potential of a valuable resource that would otherwise be of little use. The use of sinew laminates in the construction of bows to increase their strength under tension is another. A final example is his explanation of the use of deer antler in obsidian flaking. The capacity of the slightly resilient antler (as compared to a harder material such as stone) to adhere to the obsidian face (in effect, its "tooth") is the key to finer and more successful control. This critical technical refinement would, no doubt, be lost on the casual observer, who might well assume this choice of tool was related to convenience or shape, rather than material properties.

Ivan's recollection of his lifetime of gathering information is equally interesting. He acknowledges the fortunate circumstances of his youth, in which he moved with his family through the pattern of the yearly harvests and other activities, acquiring knowledge in the traditional way of taking a designated part in each form of activity, observing the actions of others engaged in other aspects, and learning more as his role transitioned when he grew older. But, he also describes his active efforts, at later points, to gain knowledge of specific skills and activities that were no longer practiced:

> I'll back up: about twenty three years ago I really, really started wanting to know everything I could about our old ways. Even that I was told and taught a lot of it, there was a lot of gaps in between, like a putting a big puzzle together. In 1990, by 1994 there was ten elders that participated in the culture camp, and once they seen that I was doing this right and everything was accurate, then they started coming forward and filling in those gaps, ok? But there was still a lot missing, so way before I even got hired by the Klamath tribes, I would travel to other tribes, that I knew we'd gambled with, or that we were participating in pow wows, or rodeos, or whatnot, and I'd talk to their elders. And I'd also had books, ethnic background of all the different tribes around here, and I'd find out that they were doing the same type of twining we were. The only difference was the material. So then I came back and started researching the material, and all I had to was find the right material and then put them into the twining and the rest is history.

This process of restoring knowledge, by reconstructing it from local and neighboring resources, has been key to other restoration processes (e.g., that of David Gladstone in restoring Heiltsuk culture on the coast of British Columbia), but has only been significant in those instances where dedicated individuals have taken an active role. Ivan's interviews, his vision of linking the knowledge of elders to the curiosity of youth through summer camps and other activities, and his way of describing his own role will be of interest to others wishing to initiate or better understand this form of cultural restoration.

The first interview with Ivan on 19 October 2002 arose somewhat by chance. Modesto Jimenez was speaking on camera near a partially restored Shaker church site when some men in a pick-up truck stopped to see what we were doing and suggested that we visit Ivan's pit house site. When we arrived there, Ivan was standing with a group of men by a flat-bed truck. As we were explaining to Ivan what we were doing, he signaled to the men and they left in the truck. Later, as we were driving from Chiloquin to Klamath Falls, Modesto began talking about the tribe's establishment of a community-based restorative justice program in cooperation with the Klamath County court system. The program had been so successful, he noted, that Klamath County had begun to extend the system to non-tribal members. In fact, he related, the men we had seen standing by the truck were non-tribal members who were helping with the construction of the pit house as part of their community service. During the previous winter they had driven through Chiloquin discharging firearms in anger over what they took to be tribal opposition to farmers in the previous year's water rights disputes. Modesto observed that he thought that their experience of the community and the good treatment they received during their restitution was allowing them to better understand tribal perspectives and the possibilities of more cooperative interactions. The cultural restoration program, in other words, was functioning, somewhat surprisingly, not only to preserve and restore knowledge within the community, but also to forge new links to a surrounding community that has traditionally chosen to remain ignorant of tribal culture and perspectives.

REFLECTIONS ON TECHNOLOGY
AND HYBRID CULTURAL PRACTICES

Thinking through some of the issues involved in these narratives, especially those surrounding the Restoration process, returns us to a consideration not only of the status of such efforts in their relation to tradition and cultural survival, but to the function of projects such as this one, which are, in various ways, combinations of traditional and decidedly non-traditional methods. The Kla-mo-ya casino, for instance, is within a couple of miles of both Ivan's restored pit house site and the mouth of the Williamson river, where the traditional chuam harvest took place. And, it is the casino monies that are the likely source of funding for the Klamath culture and heritage center as it is built. This is a circumstance replicated in different permutations in many Indigenous communities across North America, and indicates the many varying ways in which communities work to maintain continuity with a cultural and ancestral past while adjusting to a history of suppression and a changing present circumstance. Each combination, preservation, adaptation, and new development reconfigures identity and in some way either erodes or contributes to cultural survival while inevitably changing its terms. The examples of all the lives recounted in this project emphasize the need for adaptability, while demonstrating the strong need for preserving the most positive aspects of the past. Morrie, in particular, emphasizes time and time again the critical function of the support and perspective he was fortunate to receive from the previous generation that helped him to face the challenges of his adaptation in a contentious, and, at times, very hostile majority culture. Yet, it is through that adaptation that he gained the skills that would later be of such significant benefit to his community and others. The stories and evaluations of those processes of adaptation are as valuable as the recollections of traditional culture in understanding the critical tasks facing Indigenous communities today.

Ivan's efforts also remind us that the recovery and representation of culture is also its re-creation. While the houses he has built and the knowledge that he shares with others within them is no longer embedded in the same way in the daily economic processes of survival, its reenactment is critical, in other ways, to the cultural survival and well-being of the community. Technology, too, plays a role. First, in the obvious ways in which modern construction techniques and telecommunications support daily life and economics, and in the ways technology may sometimes operate to support traditional practices that have fallen under the stress of changing circumstances. All of our participants recall the life of the community before termination as one in which a close-knit community transmitted information from the old to the young through routine daily interactions, as well as through more identified yearly circumstances tied to the cycle of economic and social life. Termination, the resulting diaspora of tribal members, and the correspondent shift towards a more nuclear family structure severely compromised that system—with the effect Delphine Jackson noted of erasing young people's awareness of the reservation, even as it had existed only a few years before. Similarly, the critical relationships between extended family members were broken as young parents moved out of the community to survive economically. Morrie's experience in returning for his children's benefit demonstrates just how difficult that situation had become.

In his final interview in this series, Morrie recalls the ways in which the intensity of his involvement in many of the activities that not only secured his family's livelihood, but contributed to the more general survival of Indian communities, took him away from more extended contact with his children, who grew up in circumstances in which extended family members were not available to fill some of those gaps. He expresses the hope that the record of the interviews, which they and their children may at some point watch on a TV or computer screen, may provide a way of understanding those circumstances and serve as a form of contact (13 October 2003):

> And I finally reached a point a number of years back, several years back, where I became aware of the fact that a lot of what I want to share with people on these tapes, and these interviews was something that I should've been sharing all along with my own children. And they only, I was only able to give them bits and pieces over the years. But I never took the time to really sit down and share with them what I've shared with you on these tapes over the years. And so, I wanted, I felt a critical need to share with them those experiences as a means of, of hopefully them understanding the impacts of, of my former reservation experiences; and what's happened since then. That might give them a better explanation of why things went along the way they did over the years. That might give them some understanding of, of what their mother and I have gone through over the years. And, and the various experiences that impacted – that may or may not have impacted their personal experiences within, as a family, as a family unit too. I felt this need primarily of, eventually because of the fact I realized that over the years, I've never taken the time to do that.

While no one would claim that a video resource in any way duplicates the circumstances, relationships or effects of traditional oral transmission (and there is always the potential danger that viewers might assume that it does), a video resource does serve as a way in which some kinds of information may be preserved and transmitted within a culture and be made available as a resource for greater understanding to others outside it. Because the participants in this project have chosen to act now, their perspectives *will* be available to others and other generations.

In this way, this final interview returns, from the specific issues of Klamath history, to some of the critical and methodological discussions that occurred as this project began. Technology has the potential to erode and displace traditional culture, but in situations such as the one described here, in which many other factors had already accelerated that erosion and displacement, and perhaps in many other circumstances in which the engagement with technology is either inevitable or desirable for other reasons, it may also provide an avenue for cultural stabilization, recovery, and growth, and other important forms of interaction. It is up to producers, participants and communities to explore, evaluate, and decide.

NOTES

1. *Smoke Signals,* screenplay by Sherman Alexie, dir. Chris Eyre, Miramax, 1999; *Dances with Wolves,* dir. Kevin Costner, Orion, 1990.

2. For information on the Indian Reorganization Act, see Vine Deloria, Jr., ed., *The Indian Reorganization Act: Congresses and Bills* (Norman: U Oklahoma P, 2002); Graham D. Taylor, *The New Deal and American Indian Tribalism: the Administration of the Indian Reorganization Act, 1934–1945* (Lincoln: U Nebraska P, 1980); Elmer R. Rusco, *A Fateful Time: the Background and Legislative History of the Indian Reorganization Act* (Reno: U Nevada P, 2000). For a history of the termination era, including a specific and detailed treatment of the Klamath situation, see Donald L. Fixico, "Termination of the Klamath and Timberlands in the Pacific Northwest," *The Invasion Of Indian Country In The Twentieth Century: American Capitalism And Tribal Natural Resources* (Niwot: UP Colorado, 1998): 79–102. See also Theodore Stern, *The Klamath Tribe: A People and their Reservation* (Seattle: U. Washington P, 1966); Susan Hood, "Termination of the Klamath Indian Tribe of Oregon," *Ethnohistory* 19.4 (Fall 1972): 397–392. For more concise overviews that include accounts of the restoration era and current prospects, see Native American Rights Fund, "The Economic Viability of the Klamath Tribes," *NARF Justice Newsletter* Summer 1997, 26 Oct. 2005 <http://www.narf.org/pubs/justice/1997summer.html>; see also *Klamath Tribes Website*, 26 Oct. 2005 <http://www.klamathtribes.org>.

3. *Oral Narratives of the Klamath Termination: Individual Elders Reflect on Time and Cultural Change,* recorded, edited and produced by Linc Kesler, 8 DVDs (Vancouver, BC : First Nations Studies Program, U British Columbia, 2005);

4. *Your Land, My Land: the Klamath Tribe,* videorecording, Oregon Public Broadcasting Documentary Unit, 1991; Oral Narratives of the Klamath Termination Website <http://faculty.arts.ubc.ca/lkesler/klamathtermination>.

Chapter Ten

Celilo Falls: Parallel Lives Along N'Che Wana

Lani Roberts and Ed Edmo

The Oregon we know today has been shaped by innumerable forces, on her peoples and on her land; often these dynamics have profoundly impacted both. Careful examination of relationships resulting from the cohabitation of indigenous peoples, European immigrants and their descendants yields valuable lessons basic to understanding our contemporary Oregon experience, especially as it pertains to modifications of the natural world and the lived realities of her peoples.

The European Americans who sailed up the River or who moved west in the 1800s settled on land which "belonged" to everyone and to no one person in particular until that time. The parceling of this land through grants of homesteads resulted in the phenomenon of private ownership of pieces of the earth by specific individual people. This process involved conflict, cooperation and profound consequences for people and nature. The effects continue today as the descendants of Native peoples and immigrants struggle to live together in a depleted natural environment.

We grew up in the mid-Columbia River area, near The Dalles, on the border between Oregon and Washington.[1] Ed is Shoshone Bannock, Nez Perce, Yakama and Siletz and lived at the fishing village at Celilo Falls until its destruction in March 1957. Lani grew up just outside The Dalles, a descendant of an early settler family. Although we grew up in the same area and are the same age, our lives were lived in parallel fashion because of the differences in our ethnic heritage. Ed is Native American; Lani is European-American. Ed is a well-known storyteller, poet and author. Lani teaches philosophy at Oregon State University. Our worlds intersected some 10 years ago when Ed was an invited speaker for a conference on Environmental Justice sponsored by the Philosophy Department and then, again, when Ed's daughter, Se-ah-dom, became one of Lani's students. This provided an opportunity for us to

173

talk and to share stories of our childhoods growing up near The Dalles. It soon became painfully clear that our lives were divergent and at odds in ways explainable only by the racism and sexism the dominant culture imposes on Native peoples. We believe the alternative perceptions and experiences of our lives inform the tangible and actual harms done to some by the sheer blindness, ignorance and arrogance of others.

We have very different memories of growing up, living near the River, the destruction of Celilo Falls, the local city-owned swimming pool, the Granada Theater and The Dalles High School mascot. We grew up in the same geographical space but lived in radically different worlds. Ed, his family and other Native people have suffered profound effects of racism that Lani, her family and most of the white people did not comprehend.

WE LIVE TOGETHER YET APART. WE ARE ESTRANGED.

I grew up in a house built by my great-great grandfather in 1868. The land upon which the house and cherry orchard were located was deeded as a homestead. This acreage, like much of the North American continent, was considered empty and unused by the immigrating Europeans. I grew up with just this conception but learned later that the local Native peoples had ceded millions of acres in the mid-Columbia area in an 1851 treaty. In addition to the cherry orchard, the Roberts family had also homesteaded a wheat and cattle ranch running alongside the Deschutes River, lost to the family in the Great Depression. My great-grandfather served in the Oregon Legislature in the 1920s and the room at the back of the Congregational Church sanctuary, opened for overflow crowds on Christmas and Easter, is dedicated to him as well. I was the fourth generation of my father's family to graduate from The Dalles High School. My roots are deep in the mid-Columbia region.

I was born on the Duck Valley Indian Reservation in Owyhee, Nevada in 1946. My grandparents lived at Celilo, a fishing village located at the falls for about 15,000 years. Celilo was a central seasonal gathering site for tribal people throughout the northwest, walking in from what is now southeastern Idaho, the Spokane area, Burns and the Washington and Oregon Coasts to fish, trade and socialize. We traded dentillium shells, buffalo products, Wocas (roots) and stories. My Grandma was Nez Perce; my Grandpa was Yakama. I guess that Mom wrote Grandma and they made a plan that we'd all visit. It's been a long visit! We moved to the River when I was six months old.

My home is the river. The river was a welcome playmate which never had to be called in for supper. The sound of the river is soothing to my ears, like a lullaby. The river was always a friend. We have been on the River for a long, long, long time, fishing, root digging, hunting and trading along "N'Che Wana," "The Big River," as we called the Columbia River. There were legends about white people coming.

In my youth at Celilo, my family would talk and talk around our dinner table with a warm wood-stove fire. When we ran out of food, we went to the missionary's house to eat! I remember that we always had a warm welcome fire at our house.

Our house was built out of discarded railroad ties my father had salvaged from the Union Pacific Railroad where he worked on the section gang. I remember being the three year old boy "straw boss," as my half-brother, "Frenchie," called me. I believe that I used my "straw boss" authority and fired my brother "Frenchie" a few times.

I learned to read by coal oil lamp before I started the first grade in The Dalles, Oregon. My mom would get me the classic comic books. I broke my reading teeth on the classics!

The Destruction of Celilo Falls
Celilo Fisherman
You tested your knots, seeing that they held
Little did you know what was to hold you
After the sound of water falling
Over what used to be.

Without doubt, the single most tragic and traumatic wrong done to the mid-Columbia River and to the peoples who live there was the flooding of Celilo Falls. Although both of us still grieve this tragic loss, the direct impact and experiences were radically different, then and still today.

When the government man came, he seemed to be constipated all the time. He never smiled. It seems like that there weren't any children to greet him at the end of the day with a glad, "Daddy! Daddy." He sure was a sour puss. It was the attitude of the government man, the many government men who came, the same attitude the townsfolk of The Dalles, as they "threw rocks at us with their eyes," that attitude of racism I don't like. My dad, Edward M. Edmo, Sr., saw the plans of The Dalles Dam at the Chamber of Commerce and tried to warn the Indians at Celilo. The Indians just scoffed at him and called him "Old Chinaman" because my father had short hair and didn't wear his hair in traditional braids like most of the men of Celilo Village. But when the workers began leveling the land for the right of way of the Union Pacific Railroad, they saw my dad was right. "We'll stand on our treaty rights," the Indian said. But many elders remembered when the

Bonneville Dam was built in 1938, the Herman Creek Indians were forced to move and were not given anything for their fisheries or houses. My father organized the Celilo Community Club to get monies and houses for our fisheries and homes.

I remember one of the meetings which were held in people's houses. Henry Thompson, Chief Tommy Thompson's son, told the government man, "You should give us fifty dollars for every board in our drying sheds, because this is our way of life." The government man got angry and shouted, "You Indians will take the government's fair offer. If you don't take the fair offer, I'm going to Judge Webber and condemn your land and you won't see a red cent." This white man who lived at Moody, owned the store and gas station. He held out for a higher price. It was announced that the bulldozers would come and take down his house and business. I remember that the white man was standing there, crying into a red bandana. The government made him an example, so we had to accept the "fair" offer.

It was a time when there were no hearings as to the environmental impact, cultural impact or anything like that. It was the "Red Scare" and the U.S. Government needed electricity to make aluminum to build ICBM missiles to point at the Russians. It was done in the name of "progress" and no one stuck up for us Indians except the Democratic Society of Wasco County, the local chapter of the Daughters of the American Revolution. We told the government man that we wanted to settle together by The Dalles Dam, to show people what the government did to us. The government man said we couldn't do that. We didn't know that the land was being looked at for development for hotels and gas stations. One of the agreements was that when the park was built, we were to have a curio shop there to sell beadwork, coffee and food to tourists. What happened?

When I was a girl, about 10 years old, my mom and dad took me to see Celilo Falls. I remember it well, mostly because the mood was serious and somber, almost spiritual, very much like it feels at a funeral. My parents explicitly told me that they wanted me to see Celilo Falls because it would never exist again. That impressed me. How could something as huge and powerful and magnificent as Celilo Falls cease to exist? The water roared, the falls were taller than any building I'd ever seen and the Indian fishermen dangled dangerously over the water, dip-netting salmon from the river. My dad explained that The Dalles Dam was near completion and when it stopped the flow of the mighty Columbia River, the backwater would flood the falls out of existence. This became an actuality in March of 1957.

I have mourned the loss of Celilo Falls my whole life. When I understood what had happened, I used to scare my parents by wishing that someone would blow up The Dalles Dam; I doubt I am the only person who imagined such a thing. I also doubt that The Dalles Dam could be built today in the same location since an environmental impact statement would be required and I hope the utter destruction of such a magnificent natural wonder and an ancient fishing village would be unthinkable. The cost has been incalculable, both to the natural environment and the lives of the original peoples who lived there. Not only was a 15,000-year-old fishing village destroyed, but the salmon and steelhead runs have greatly diminished, to the extent that the federal government has proposed counting hatchery salmon in species populations. The dynamic flow of a living river has ceased and in its place is a series of manmade lakes behind the several hydroelectric dams constructed to provide cheap electricity.

It seems completely wrong, a mistake, to call the Columbia a river anymore.

It was a springtime day as Dad took me out of Wishram Elementary to go watch the flooding of Celilo Falls It was a bad dream that something so big, so wonderful was flooded. I had watched my Grandpa, uncles and father fish, and I too believed that when I grew up that I'd become a fisherman. But my role model was taken by the flooding of the falls.

Nowadays, I tell legends from the river, tell stories about Celilo Falls and go fishing for an envelope with a check in it, to take to Fred Meyer's and get groceries. I'm a fisherman in a different way.

THE NATATORIUM—COOL, CLEAR WATER ON A HOT DAY

It is really hot in The Dalles in the summertime. The hottest I can remember was 116 degrees and there are nights when it does not cool down below the 80s. Relief was available, though. Kids (some kids) could go swimming at the Natatorium, more commonly called the Nat. It is a city-owned and operated swimming pool just west of the downtown area. It is a concrete pool surrounded with a chain link fence which must be eight feet tall, to prevent access when the Nat is closed. There is a concrete building in which the changing rooms and showers are located. There is a little bit of lawn out front and around a wading pool, maybe 10 feet on a side, designed for parents with toddlers. Like lots of kids, my siblings and I walked to the Nat nearly every day in summer. As a child, I did not notice that the Indian kids weren't swimming with us, even on the hottest days. As is all too often the case, people of ethnic minorities are invisible to the dominant culture and my childhood was no exception. With shame as an adult, I recall that it simply did not occur to me to even notice that "kids" meant "white kids" and no adult in my life pointed out this fact. I sometimes think I can remember Indian kids pressed up against the chain link fence surrounding the pool, looking in at us splashing around for hours in the cool water. I don't know whether this is actually a memory or the result of the guilt I feel.

For some reasons a five-year-old can't understand, us Indians were not allowed into the big swimming pool, with its deep greenish-blue water and the high diving boards. If we wanted to get wet at the pool, we had to go to the toddlers' wading pool – even grown men and women. I guess the white people believed a little of their white would rub off and we would experience some, but not all, of their privilege.

One time, the Boys and Girl's Club had a "Swim Day." My brother was a member, and we were to go to the swimming pool on Saturday morning. On that Friday night, the tension in the kitchen oozed out like the dull light of the coal oil lamp. Mom and Dad talked in hushed voices, and I could see the seriousness on Mom's face. She was straining to get her words out. Dad gestured with his forefinger extended like he hammered nails, and I saw him hammer nails a lot.

When we arrived at the swimming pool, we joined a long line of kids who were members of the club. Behind the counter, a young teenage white boy was red-faced mad. Mr. Warren, the flamboyant leader of the club, had a receipt in his hand and was waving it in the air like a flag over the top hat he wore on special occasions.

Finally, he phoned the new manager of the pool. Looking back at my brother and me, Mr. Warren said that the Boy's and Girl's Club membership was open to needy children. Well, I had Mom and Dad, and my grandma lived on the hill above me, we had a warm, welcomed wood stove. I didn't think that I was "needy." Sometimes we ran out of food, and then we just went to the missionary's house to eat.

Mr. Warren asked my brother and me when we last took a bath and we both answered, "This morning, sir!" He talked in a hushed tone. After a long time, he handed the phone to the hot-faced boy, who slammed the receiver down. There was a lot of cussing as my brother and I went up to get our baskets. "Dirty Indians!" one of the others said from behind the big desk.

I remember how glad I felt as we peeled off our clothes and put on brand new bathing suits Mom got us from the J.C. Penny store. Then we took our showers, not minding the cold water, and marched triumphantly into the "big" swimming pool. I went down to the shallow end and looked at the wide expanse of green-blue, and felt like I could walk on water.

Well, this worked pretty good, going to the swimming pool on hot days. But one time Mom was late picking me up after I got out of the pool. I was standing in the shade by the dressing room, when five white boys came up and taunted me.

"Go back where you belong, savage!"

"Stay in your village, war whoop!"

"We don't want you around here, you dirty little Indian."

They began pushing me, then grabbed my towel and threw it to the ground, and began hitting and kicking me. I covered myself and swung haymakers at them. A couple of my punches connected, which added to their hostility. When one of the blond boys grabbed my arm and pulled it around behind me and added pressure, I cried out in pain.

Just then my mother drove up with the car horn blaring. The white boys saw her and began running. I tried to run after them but Mom just held me. "Never mind. They've all got small hearts to pick on you."

I just wished I had the power to walk on water!

SATURDAY MATINEES AT THE GRENADA THEATER

Another form of entertainment when we were kids was the Granada Theater, downtown at the corner of Second and Washington Streets in The Dalles. It is a small theater by today's standards, with a sloping floor and a raised stage with the movie screen occupying the whole space behind the curtains. Upstairs there is a balcony, accessible by stairs at both sides. Because the girls' restroom was also upstairs on one side, I sometimes would climb a few extra stairs to look at the balcony. It seemed mysterious to me and someplace I always wanted to sit but never had the nerve to do. It is more than a little ironic that the balcony beckoned to me and I always wanted to sit there and didn't, yet it was the only place Native people were allowed to sit.

In the 1950s, the Saturday matinee drew lots of kids. If my memory serves me well, most of the movies were westerns, with Roy Rogers, the Long Ranger and Tonto, and Hopalong Cassidy and others, replete with "cowboys and Indians" story lines. It was from these movies that we kids drew our inspiration as we played "cowboys and Indians" in the neighborhood. In retrospect, I can recall that no one wanted to be the Indians. The littlest kids had to be the Indians because the cowboys were always supposed to win. This kind of play was thought of as normal and harmless but, today, as an ethicist studying how we human beings organize ourselves to harm some of us for the benefit of others of us, I cannot help but think about how these games and the movies we watched affected our perceptions of the Native peoples in our midst. How could it not have led us to view them as other-than-us in an irredeemable way?

The only movie house in The Dalles was the Granada Theater. We always sat in the balcony. When I was really young, I just thought that Mom and Dad picked those seats because they were the "bestest seats in the house." I looked around and there were the Navajos who worked on the railroad and the Japanese who grew the crops in Dallesport.

One time, my older brother Frenchie and I were sitting on the main floor. The usher growled at us. "You Indian boys have to go up to 'Nigger Heaven' to sit." My brother Frenchie pointed to his Army uniform. "See this uniform? I fought for this country! I can sit anywhere in this country I want to!" The usher's Adam's apple on his neck bounced a couple of times. The usher spun on his heels and went marching back towards the back. The manager came down, a large man, who always jingled change in his pocket to convince himself that he was important. "You Indian boys have to go up to 'Nigger Heaven' to sit," the manager said, jingling change in his pocket. "See this uniform? I fought for this country. I can sit anywhere in this country I want to," my brother Frenchie shouted at the manager. "I'm going to call the cops!" the manager threatened. "Go ahead. Call the cops. That cop has a uniform on, I've got a uniform on. Maybe we can talk man to man," Frenchie said. That manager never called the cops and ever since Indians have always sat on the main floor of the Granada Theater.

THE DALLES HIGH SCHOOL INDIANS

Sports teams uses of "Native Americans" as mascots is under consideration all over the United States and a lesson I use in my ethics classes. I have had to tell my students, with chagrin, that my own high school was The Dalles High School Indians and, worse, the mascot image was "Chief Wahoo," a grinning cartoon caricature of an "Indian" complete with feather. The *Portland Oregonian* newspaper stopped using such names in the early 1990s but my high school and others in the state of Oregon have continued to use Native names for their teams. Early in May 2005, the Enterprise High School student body voted to quit using the "Savages" as their mascot and the school board supported this change.

In the spring of 2004, the school board in The Dalles was busy combining two school districts. In 1963, the Chenoweth School District had opened its own high school, Wahtonka, and we students who had gone to school together for years were split into two groups, the Wahtonka Eagles and The Dalles Indians. In the recent process of rejoining the two school districts, the name of the new high school and its mascot became heated topics of debate. I decided I had to enter this discussion so I wrote to the school board chair regarding my wish to have the high school stop using the name "Indians" and especially to stop using Chief Wahoo as the logo. I enclosed articles my students read in critically analyzing this debate and asked that he share my concerns and the reading material with the rest of the school board. The controversy raged on for months, with petitions both for and against the "Indians," polls of students in both high schools, public testimony from many interested townspeople and, apparently, a great deal of communication with individual board members, one of whom said he'd received more than 80 emails.

The central argument of those who wanted the school district to retain The Dalles High School Indians was to preserve a proud history. I am a fourth generation graduate of The Dalles High School and it was my expressed view that there was nothing whatsoever in the historical records encompassing the Indians in the community which was worthy of pride or preservation. To the contrary, the historical past was shameful. Several different decisions about names and mascots were made and rescinded. Only two of the board members ended up agreeing with the view that I and others held. In the end, on June 23, 2004, the school board voted to name the high school The Dalles Wahtonka Union High School. They adopted the Eagle Indian as the mascot.

My brother and I were mascots for The Dalles High School Indians basketball team. I'm not sure what all went into the arrangement of how we became mascots. I know that I can speculate that it was a way of my father and mother trying to gain some sort of acceptance with the white community in The Dalles. What I did was to wear my war bonnet and lead the team out on the court, dribble the basketball and shoot a shot at the basket, with the belief that if I made the basket, the team would win the game that night.

I got to go to Astoria, Oregon and really see the ocean as a mascot! I even got to stay in a hotel and be treated like a white boy. I remember eating steak in a cafe and not being asked to leave because I was an Indian. I believe now that people do strange things for strange reasons, looking back to my mascot days.

After the dam flooded us out, we moved to Wishram, Washington (across the river from where Celilo Village used to be). The basketball team's name was the Indians too so I was a mascot at Wishram also!

I was chosen to go to Boys' State in Washington from 1963–64. Quite an honor. Well, when I got to the campus, the rich white kids decided to make me a mascot! I was to sit cross-legged on a table on stage while they were

*learning how government laws were passed. I didn't get a chance to partic-
ipate. "Sit like an Indian," was mentioned with quite a bit of laughter from
the rich white boys.*

RACISM

Children are defenseless in terms of the social messages they receive from
family, friends, entertainment. I never noticed that "kids" mostly meant
"white kids" when it came to the swimming pool or the theater. Even though
I was raised to not judge others by the color of their skin and my parents forbade, in no uncertain terms, the use of racist words, I grew up smack dab in
the middle of toxic, cruel racism directed toward the Indians with whom I
lived. And I didn't know. How is this possible? In my classes, if I describe a
town in which people from an ethnic minority could not sit on the main floor
of the theater or swim in the swimming pool and the signs in stores said, No
Dogs, No "Coloreds," they do not hesitate to name the Jim Crow South.
When I tell them this is my hometown, The Dalles, Oregon when I was a kid,
they are shocked.

*I remember seeing the signs in the windows of most of the store in The
Dalles, Oregon. "No Dogs or Indians Allowed!" I couldn't understand it. I
was raised in a good Christian home, taught that love would overcome all,
but when we went to town the white people would "throw rocks at us with
their eyes." You can't see those rocks, but it sure hurts and the bruises last a
long time. That's what it seemed like to me when I went to town; I felt like I
didn't belong or was not good enough. I remember buying candy bars in the
alleyway at the back door of the store because we Indians were not allowed
in the store.*

Toward the end of my dad's life, after I had been teaching about the dynamics of racism for several years, I tried to very gently pry some information from him about his awareness of the racism in our hometown. I asked
about who my ancestors had hired to work for them, how they were treated,
and other leading kinds of questions. My dad sincerely and completely maintained the worldview that the Indians in The Dalles were not subjected to
racism.

*There was a vicious prejudice against Indians in the small town near the
fishing village where I grew up. The stores in The Dalles, Oregon had signs
displayed in the windows stating "NO DOGS OR INDIANS ALLOWED."*

These signs were in most of the store windows, not just a few stores. Indians were only allowed to eat in one café and that was on the east side of town where the winos, prostitutes, and bootleggers hung out.

I remember one time, it was a sunny warm late afternoon, the clouds seemed to be dropped by God on the twilight scene. I was about six years old. Me and Mom were sitting in the car in front of Johnny's Cafe. That's what we did in those days, "watching people" as Mom called it. Well, it was at that time Mom gave me instruction on which stores I could go into by myself and which store I could go into only with another adult with me. Then she pointed with her lips to the dress shop right across the street and said, "That's an 'upper crust' store. Even I don't go in there." Mom used the term "upper crust," meaning the rich people in town.

When Mom wanted her hair done, she'd have to go to the home of the beautician and she wasn't allowed into the beauty parlor. I remember that when an Indian went into a store, we'd have to wait and wait until all the white people were waited on and then the clerk would wait on us. Then when a white person came into the store, the clerk would stop waiting on us and wait on the white person. I remember we weren't allowed to try on clothes either. We would have to look at the shirt and guess if it would fit.

How it is possible I did not notice any of these wrongs? Why didn't my parents tell me about the injustices towards the Indians right 'there in our town and warn me not to ever treat another person like that? They told me explicitly to be fair and kind to African-Americans (at that time, Negroes) and Mexicans. Why is it that the wrongs most present in our everyday lives are the very ones most difficult to see? Is it because they are so ever-present everywhere that they become like the air we breathe, invisible? Is it because I am European-American, "white," so that my privileged place in my Oregon hometown meant I didn't have to notice, that those of us who do not receive the cruelty of racism, even those of us who are the perpetrators, are oblivious?

I can't go home to the small-minded society in which I couldn't find a girlfriend. I remember that I liked this white girl, and I believe she liked me. When I came back to her house, she went inside and her mom looked out the window at me. Then she said that we couldn't be together because I was an Indian. I remember walking and crying all the way from her house on the hill to downtown. Just walking and crying and feeling less than.

I can't go home
over where my

house used to stand
where my house
used to stand
there's a freeway

NOTES

1. The Dalles, Oregon is approximately 80 miles upriver, east of Portland. Celilo Falls was another 20 miles or so further upriver from The Dalles, and Wishram, Washington is approximately across the river from where Celilo once was.

Chapter Eleven

Defying Definition: Portraits of Arab Oregonians

Kera Abraham

When I was a kid in the '80s, I learned two different meanings of the word "Arab." The TV, nestled in our living room like one of the family, offered one take: Arab men were dark and foreign and shifty-eyed, with a salesman's smooth talk but prone to rage. Arab women either served their men silently, cloaked in hejabs, or popped out of genie bottles in balloony harem pants. One of my favorite flicks, *Aladdin*, featured it all: mean-lookin' guys with scimitars, greedy merchants in turbans, a bodacious princess in gauzy veils. Watching the evening news with my dad, I vaguely grasped reports of Arabs taking hostages, planting bombs and raising gas prices.

But the media's Arab didn't seem at all related to my round, worried Situ,[1] my dad's Syrian mother, who poured her love into sweet flat loaves of Arabic bread and lemony stuffed grape leaves picked fresh from Jidu's garden. Situ would smother me with kisses, her brown eyes welling with concern as she murmured, "May the Lord Jesus protect you, Inshallah." And though TV Arabs also invoked Allah, their religion was nothing like the services at my dad's Antiochian Orthodox church,[2] where a curvy woman with a cap of glossy red hair would stand in the front pew and sing hymns in Aramaic, her voice as round and smoky as the frankincense.

For years I couldn't reconcile the two meanings of Arab, and I didn't know whether I should feel proud or ashamed telling friends I was half one. As an American-born kid with a second-generation Syrian dad and a white (Irish) mom, I didn't want to seem too different from my Anglo and Jewish friends. I was a curly-haired, light-olive-skinned, hummos-eating American, content to pass as almost white for the first two decades of my life.

Until the attacks of September 11, 2001 and the ensuing War on Terror lit a match to my heritage. For the first time, I became acutely aware of my ethnicity. When newspapers carried pictures of Iraqis, I saw men that look like my uncles, women who looked like my Situ. When law-abiding Arabs in America were targeted in hate crimes and summoned *en masse* to the INS, I wondered why they were being singled out and treated like enemies. Yet I still viewed them from across a cultural gulf, knowing that while they were made vulnerable by their headscarves and turbans, their Arabic accents and their Muslim faith, I was protected by my American style, my native English and my Christian upbringing.

I wanted to understand more about this culture that both was and wasn't part of me. I leafed through literature about Arabs in America and in the Middle East. I shyly attended a few meetings of the Eugene Middle East Peace Group, conscious that I had less in common with the Arabic-speaking Muslim Yemeni than with the Jewish American college student. I did my master's project at the UO School of Journalism and Communications on Arab American identity after 9-11 and interviewed Arab Americans from across the country to gain a better understanding of what defined the demographic.

What I found was a diverse community that spills out of the rigid confines of census boxes and television screens, and I realized that none of the definitions I learned as a kid was quite accurate. Arab Americans can't be defined by language, religion or political leanings, and they don't all share a common history or a single goal. Yet they include lawmakers, entertainers, business owners, PTA parents—and me.

Before we talk about Arab Americans, let's make the terms clear. In the Middle East, Arabs are Semitic people ethnically rooted in the Arabian Peninsula—Saudi Arabia, Yemen, Bahrain, Kuwait, Oman, Qatar, and the United Arab Emirates. Arabs also make up a significant percentage of the populations of Iraq, Jordan, Lebanon, Syria, Israel, Egypt, Sudan, Libya, Algeria, Morocco and Tunisia. Iranians, Turks, Pakistanis and Indians are not Arabs.

Most Arabs in the Arab world speak Arabic and are Muslim. But in the United States, people of Arab heritage comprise a very different demographic. According to the 2000 Census, 1.2 million Arab Americans reside in the U.S., though a Zogby International poll estimates the number at closer to 3 million.[3] The states with the highest Arab American populations are Michigan, New York, Ohio, Florida and California. The Census reports that almost 10,000 people of Arab heritage live in Oregon.

Most Arab Americans are descended from two waves of immigrants: those who came to the United States before World War I (1860–1920s) and those who came after World War II (1948–1965). The former were primarily Christians from present-day Lebanon and Syria, and they generally settled on the East Coast. Their descendents—like pop singer Paula Abdul, zany composer

Frank Zappa, radio personality Casey Kasem, White House correspondent Helen Thomas, former U.S. Secretary of Health and Human Services Donna Shalala and leftie activist Ralph Nader—are largely assimilated to American culture. The latter group of immigrants consisted largely of Muslims from Egypt, Palestine and Iraq, many of them capitalists seeking economic freedom or refugees fleeing oppressive regimes. They tended to settle in the Midwest, West and South, assimilating slower while preserving the languages and traditions of their mother countries. This group includes the late Palestinian American professor Edward Said, poet Naomi Shihab Nye and Egyptian American filmmaker Jehane Noujaim.

The race question is murky for Arab Americans. In the early 1900s, when American immigration laws explicitly favored European immigrants, judges debated the official racial classification of Arabs. Between 1909 and 1915, seven court cases considered whether Syrians were white, and thus eligible for naturalization. Three judges ruled no; four ruled yes.[4] Although people of Middle Eastern heritage are now officially classified as white on the U.S. Census, Helen Samhan, Executive Director of the Arab American Institute, describes Arab Americans' peculiar status as "not quite white." Now, as the federal government profiles Arabs and Muslims in America and wages war in Iraq, Arab Americans are quickly becoming a "new minority."

According to media expert Jack Shaheen, himself of Lebanese ancestry, for the past 50 years American media have projected negative stereotypes of Arabs, leading to a general public misunderstanding of Arab Americans. Shaheen doesn't know why Arabs get such a bad rap, but he does know how it's done. He describes the causes of discrimination as connected, each inciting the next like a row of dominoes. Hollywood tends to depict Arabs as shadowy "others," like the shady characters I saw on TV as a kid. The repetition of those images creates stereotypes that lodge deep in Americans' minds, ready to be accessed when the government is ready to make Arabs and Muslims the nation's enemy *du jour*.

And yet the antidote to those stereotypes, articulated to me by writer Diana Abu-Jaber, is so childishly simple: To tell the stories of everyday Arabs and Arab Americans so that others can relate. To counter media stereotypes with depictions of Arabs as normal people. To connect as humans.

In this chapter, I will introduce you to Arab Americans who, like myself, have lived in Oregon. None of their stories alone confers The Quintessential Arab American Experience—indeed, there is no such thing—but taken together, I hope they illustrate the diversity of Oregon's Arab American community.

VIC ATIYEH, OREGON GOVERNOR, 1979–1987

Vic Atiyeh's Portland office is filled with tokens of his political career. On his desk sits a photograph of himself grinning alongside Presidents Reagan, Ford, Carter and Nixon; it's autographed by all four presidents. Another photo shows Vic's friend Liza Bill, a Native American woman from the Umatilla Confederated Tribes, standing in a tepee. A row of Japanese dolls stand in a line on a high shelf, souvenirs from his travels. On the windowpane sits a hookah from Vic's family home in Amar, Syria.

"Almost everywhere I look there's a story," Vic says, his smile radiating deep lines around dark eyes framed by square bifocals. He sits behind a thick, masculine desk headed by a nameplate reading "Governor Atiyeh," a tribute to his eight years as Oregon governor. His wife Dolores sits in a chair beside me, interjecting commentary as Vic, now 82, tells his family's story.

In the late 1800s, Vic's father George and his brother Aziz immigrated from Amar, Syria, a predominantly Christian village in the northwest of the country. They first settled in South Bethlehem, Pennsylvania, a community with a small but thriving Syrian immigrant population. Around 1900, the brothers moved to Portland and established A. Atiyeh & Brother, the oldest Oriental rug business in the Northwest. Today, Vic's nephew and his brother's son-in-law run Atiyeh Brothers Inc. facilities in Portland, Tigard and Eugene, Oregon.

George returned to Beirut in the 1920s, married Linda Asly and brought her back to Oregon. They had three children: Vic and his twin brothers Edward and Richard. Although George and Linda spoke Arabic to one another, they taught their boys to speak only English.

"Dad said, 'You're an American,'" Vic says. "As a kid, that was quite satisfactory. But once I grew up, I wished I had learned Arabic."

Vic and his brothers attended the UO for a few years until the start of World War II, when all three enlisted in the Army. But Vic was discharged before even putting on his uniform, due to a serious bone infection in his ankle. Disappointed, he called his draft board and asked to be drafted. They turned him away. Then he went to the Merchant Marines and offered his services, but no luck there either. Vic, frustrated, dropped out of university and helped his parents with the store. When his father died shortly thereafter, Vic took charge of the business, married Dolores and sired two children. When Vic's brothers returned from the war, they told him he was lucky; both had been captured by the Germans in the Battle of the Bulge and were held as POWs for several anxious months.

Vic ventured into the world of politics as a young businessman, first running for state representative in 1958. He was successful in that race and in almost every one thereafter, serving four consecutive terms in the Oregon House and Senate. In 1974 he lost his first bid for governor. But he won on the second try, and in 1979, Vic Atiyeh became America's first governor of Arabic descent. Oregonians re-elected him by a landslide in 1983.

Vic describes himself as a moderate Republican, a fiscal conservative and a practicing Episcopal Christian. He supports President George W. Bush but has reservations about the war in Iraq. "I'm not very happy with the fact that they told us that we had to go over there because of weapons of mass destruction and they're not there," he says. "But Bush is correct that Saddam Hussein was prepared to reinvent all that. He was a threat in that sense."

Vic made several trips to the Middle East in his lifetime, but the most important, he says, was in 1984, when he took a delegation to Saudi Arabia, Egypt, Syria and Israel. Although Egyptian President Hosni Mubarak, Syrian President Hafez al-Assad and Israeli Prime Minister Yitzhak Shamir all knew that Vic had Arabic heritage, he introduced himself to each of them as "a devout American" so they would know where his foremost loyalties lie.

Though intensely patriotic, Vic views the White House's treatment of Arab nations as unfair. When he finished his second term as governor in 1988, he proposed that the Unites States employ a neutral third party to mediate talks with Syria regarding the conflict in Israel. President George H. W. Bush and his chief of staff, John Sununu—also an Arab American—declined, which was a big disappointment for Vic. "My country doesn't treat Arab countries even-handedly," he says. "I'm not pro-Arab and anti-Israel. I'm saying I want even-handed treatment."

The changing environment for Arab Americans on the home front also makes Vic uncomfortable. He tells me that he opposes racial profiling "because that makes a determination that some people have got to be bad and others good. I've had some arguments, incidentally, with the FBI about picking on Arab-background folks. They started off saying that the unfortunate part is that a lot of the terrorists are Arab. That doesn't mean that all Arabs are terrorists, which is obviously what a lot of people think." He pauses. "But I'm not prepared to accept the idea that America dislikes Arabs. I don't believe that."

He points to himself as a prime example. He says he has never suffered from ethnic discrimination, though in every political speech he tells audiences that he is Syrian. "When people ask whether I've experienced discrimination, I tell them yes. I've been discriminated against—because I'm a Republican," he says with a wink. "Arabs are hard-working and very family-oriented. When you stop to think about the history of the Arabs in terms of mathematics and language, I don't think you can be anything but proud of it."

DIANA ABU-JABER, AUTHOR AND WRITING TEACHER

Diana Abu-Jaber answers the door of her yellow Miami home in a turquoise shirt and jeans. She is pretty and clean-scrubbed, looking younger than her 45 years. Her hair is pulled back into a bun with a halo of frizz induced by the Florida humidity, and her sea-green eyes are sleepy. She'd been up late last night, working on her overdue manuscript, *The Language of Baklava*, a cookbook-history about Jordanian women. She pronounces.

Baklava the Greek way: "BAK-la-va."

"Why don't you use the Arabic pronunciation, 'bak-LA-wa'?" I ask her.

"The public's not ready for 'bak-LA-wa,'" she says with an apologetic laugh.

She makes tea: mint for me, orange blossom for her. Her little dog, Yogi, runs circles around us until her husband tosses him outside. She blinks and leans her face over the steaming tea before she begins to tell her story.

Diana was born in upstate New York to a Jordanian-American, "occasionally Muslim" father and a half-Palestinian, half-Irish, Syrian Orthodox Christian mother. She moved to Oregon in 1990 to teach writing at the University of Oregon, and in 1995 she began a professorship at Portland State University. She currently spends part of the year teaching at PSU and part of the year in Miami.

Diana's fiction books, *Arabian Jazz* and *Crescent*, feature Arab American protagonists confronting universal human trials—loneliness, frustration, love. Many of her journalistic articles, published in newspapers from *L.A. Times* to *The Washington Post*, stress the common humanity of Arabs and Americans. She does all this, she says, in an effort to dispel the effects of a popular culture that depicts Arabs as caricatures: violent, greedy, sexist.

"For all the lip service we get about tolerance and diversity, Arabs are still one of the last great vilified groups," she says. "I think it's about race, because Arabs are seen as darker. I think it's about the long colonial history. I think it's about religion. It's an unholy mix of very bad impulses. It shows the very worst in human nature."

The backlash against Arab Americans after 9-11 hit Diana hard. The 2001 release of *Crescent*, which tells the story of an Iraqi-American chef's relationship with an Iraqi political refugee, coincided with the beginning of the war on Iraq. Threatening e-mails, phone calls and letters streamed in. "It was a bad, suppressing moment for my writing," she says. "This country is full of undirected anger, and it's just looking for a target. As soon as you identify yourself as one of 'them,' watch out."

Part of the problem, Diana says, is the lack of Arab American voice in mainstream media. "We don't have enough Arab Americans stepping forward and claiming their stories," she says. "And it's circular, because people don't feel like the environment is welcoming. Then the media fills in the void with all kinds of sensational stuff, and it just goes on like that. At some point, the cycle has to be broken."

Arab Americans' image woes are due largely to a lack of common identity, she explains. Americans of Arab descent come from wildly diverse geographical and cultural roots: Saudi Arabia to Morocco, Lebanon to Yemen. "It's hard to muster a response to mainstream media in any coherent way," she says. "What Arab Americans—and any immigrant group that's under siege—need to do is find a way that they can speak to the American public and keep their sense of integrity and wholeness. And it's very difficult."

Jewish Americans, by contrast, have a more clearly defined sense of self, Diana says. "The Jewish people have such an ancient history of a kind of singular stereotyping and embattlement as a people that it's created a very strong, centralized identity. And certainly, coming out of World War II, that was a crucible of pain—so powerful that it couldn't help but heighten a sense of identity, a sense of commitment, of loyalty, of ferociousness, of pride."

The Arab American demographic is particularly hard to pin politically. Diana, for example, considers herself a liberal, but her father, a Jordanian immigrant who lives in upstate New York, votes Republican. "Any Arab-American who has regular interactions with the American mainstream has to confront the question of who they identify with at some point," she says. "When we see people waving the flags on the front lawn, who does that include? The Republicans claim it for themselves. That's the problem. At times like this, the flag is made into a military symbol. It's like the rubber bullets and the big batons are right behind those big old flags."

That contradiction created a sort of damned-if-you-do, damned-if-you-don't scenario after 9-11, Diana explains. Conservative Arab Americans were shoved to the margins when they objected to domestic profiling of Arabs and Muslims and the bullying of Arab nations, but liberalism carried even more frightening risks, especially for immigrants. "It's scary to question the mainstream," she says. "You have to develop a thick skin. You have to be willing to hear resistance and expose yourself to a lot of free-floating anger."

Still, Diana says, Arab Americans need to take that risk if they hope to debunk the media stereotype. They need to claim their heritage, speak out and move on; to become more visible as neighbors and activists, church and mosque members, teachers and parents. "My agenda is to constantly be humanizing, constantly be making real," she says. "There's that E. M. Forester quote, 'Only connect.' And at the most basic level, that is what I fundamentally believe. That we all have to only connect."

WAEL WAHBEH, FORMER PORTLAND AND
EUGENE RESIDENT, NOW LIVING IN JERUSALEM

Compared with the Arab immigrants of the 1900s, those who came to the U.S. after 9-11 found it immeasurably harder to gain U.S. citizenship. Wael Wahbeh, a 30-year-old Palestinian Muslim with Israeli citizenship, lived in Oregon for seven years while waiting for immigration authorities to issue him a Green Card. He finally lost hope in March 2005 and returned to Jerusalem with his 10-year-old, American-born daughter.

We meet at a coffee shop in Eugene. Wael is handsome and somber, with intent dark eyes, full lips and a shaved head. He buys a chocolate éclair, I buy a bran muffin, and we sit down to talk. He is hesitant to speak at first, either wary of me or shy or both. But after we chat for awhile, he warms up and tells me his story:

Wael was born in Kuwait to Palestinian parents. When his father died, the Kuwaiti government confiscated the family's possessions and forced them out of the country. Wael, his mother and three sisters moved to Jerusalem when he was eight years old. The Palestinian uprising started when Wael was 13, shadowing his life through high school.

Israeli soldiers arrested Wael when he was 17, accusing him of throwing a glass bottle at a Jewish bus. He says he didn't do it; he had just been looking at shoes through a store window after basketball practice. But the soldiers chased him down, he tells me, hit him with their M-16s, dragged him down the street and beat him at a military camp. After 59 days of intense interrogation, during which Wael maintained his innocence, he was released. But the incident left Wael bitter. He wanted out of Israel.

Around that time, a Jewish American scholar named Diane Baxter moved into the Wahbeh house. She had come to Israel to study Palestinian women for her Ph.D. thesis, and Wahbeh's mother hosted her in Jerusalem. "Her being American and Jewish opened my eyes to a lot of things, and I liked the possibility of people living together peacefully in one country," Wael says. "The dream of America—she really sold it to me."

In 1991, Wael came to the United States to attend college in North Carolina. He met and married an American woman, and his daughter was born in 1994. Wael and his wife divorced in 1995, and he returned to Jerusalem for several years. But he missed his daughter terribly, and in 1998 he returned to the United States, this time to Portland, Oregon. He re-married and worked as a technician for a wireless systems company, winning custody of his daughter in September 2004, but his second marriage failed soon after. Wael moved to Eugene, staying with his old friend Diane Baxter and her husband Shaul Cohen, both UO professors, before returning to Israel.

Wael loved the Northwest—particularly Oregon—but he felt like an outsider. He offers an example: During his job interview at a technology corporation, a manager asked him his nationality. When Wael replied that he was a Palestinian Muslim with Israeli citizenship, the manager eyed him suspiciously.

"Is that a problem?" Wael asked.

"As long as you don't come in one morning and start shooting everybody, I don't have a problem with you working here," the man replied.

Another time at a UO frat party, a college student mistakenly assumed that because Wael had an Israeli passport, he was Jewish. "I support you so much," the kid said. "We should throw all those Arabs in the ocean." Wael simply turned on his heel and left the party.

Incidents like that gave Wael this impression that Oregonians generally lack multicultural exposure. "A lot of people feel like they have to act differently because I'm from the Middle East," he says. "They start saying stupid stuff, like they know somebody who's dark, or they work with someone who's black, or they rode in a taxi where the guy had a turban on his head. It's as if they try to fill in the blanks themselves, convince themselves that we're different. Even women become more perceptive to everything they think a Middle Eastern man would do, whether it's violence or disrespecting women's rights. That's profiling."

The final insult came when Wael received word that after two and a half years waiting for a Green Card, the process would be delayed further by a background check. "It's just harassment, basically," he says. "There is no reason for the delay. I didn't do anything that requires all this attention. I feel unwelcome in this country. I'm just getting tired of it."

With his second divorce pending, and without citizenship papers, Wael's choice became clear. Shortly after our interview, he moved back to Israel with his daughter—but he hopes she'll return to the U.S. for college. "I don't want to destroy any bridges," he says. "We're not abandoning the country for good. I just want my daughter to grow up in Israel for the next eight years. After that, when she comes back to America, she'll be much stronger."

IBRAHIM AND MAHA HAMIDE, EUGENE RESTAURANT OWNERS

After living for almost 40 years in Eugene, Ibrahim Hamide—or Ib, as he is locally known—has become a small-city celebrity of sorts. His restaurant, Café Soriah, sweeps several categories in *Eugene Weekly*'s reader polls every year; Ib himself won a first-place award for Best Peace Activist in 2003. Ib, a Palestinian, has been active in local peace organizations for more than 25 years. He co-founded the Eugene Middle East Peace Group with his friend Alon Raab, an Israeli professor of Judaic Studies at the University of Oregon, and he teaches community members about Arab and Muslim cultures in his roles as a human rights commissioner and a cultural competency trainer for police officers.

I meet with Ib and his wife, Maha, at Café Soriah on a cloudy January day. Maha is curvy and classy, with curly black hair and lush brown eyes. She talks fast, her English lilted by her Arabic accent, and laughs often. Ib looks especially long and angular next to her, his narrow face etched with smile lines, his voice low and even, his English unaccented. Each listens attentively while the other speaks, and together they tell their story.

. Ib was born in 1950 in Bethlehem, a Palestinian territory on the West Bank, and grew up in an atmosphere of civil unrest. At age 18 he ventured to the United States to study at the UO, but had no intentions of staying. "I came here with a very typical foreign student story: Get a degree, go back home and help your folks," he says.

What prevented him from going back home was the Israeli occupation of the West Bank. Instead of returning to a war zone, Ib got a job managing a restaurant. He married an American woman and they had two children. "Raising a family and working such long hours basically butted school out of the equation, and life got progressively more busy," he says. "All the while, my home never really left my heart. I was always interested in politics and the reconciliation of that problem," he says, referring to the Israeli-Palestinian conflict.

In 1982 Ib opened his first restaurant, Casa Blanca, in downtown Eugene; soon after, he launched the Mediterranean Café. His kids grew up, and he and his first wife divorced. He might have entertained thoughts of going back to Palestine then, but he still had family in the U.S.: an older brother, a college professor in Washington, and a younger brother, a businessman in Los Angeles.

Ib and his older brother secured citizenship, but his younger brother is currently facing deportation hearings. "The federal government accused him of all kinds of things," Ib says mournfully. "Trying to overthrow the United States government—you name it. But he was just teaching kids how to do the *dubke*, a Palestinian dance, and also collecting money and buying blankets and medicine for refugees in southern Lebanon. He has won every trial that has come up. His lawsuit is very famous."

Ib's life started anew when he met Maha in mid-1996. Maha, who grew up in Jordan, came to the U.S. in 1985, when she was 23. She was a worldly young woman, having already studied in England and France, and she took classes in art and dance at Portland State University. Like Ib, she had come to America with no plans to stay; but when she visited the UO from Portland to perform with a Palestinian dance troupe, she met Ib. They married in 1997 and she moved to Eugene.

9-11 changed things, including people's perceptions of the Hamides. Maha says that her friends have been harassed for wearing headscarves or talking with Arabic accents, and she feels that some people are more wary of her. "I have been asked a lot more questions, like 'What's your religion?'" Maha says. "I almost have to excuse myself when I say Muslim. Like, 'I'm a Muslim, but I don't practice as much.'"

"I'm sorry I'm a Muslim," Ib chimes in sarcastically. "I'm seeking treatment."

"I am getting a prescription for it!" Maha says, laughing.

Maha and Ib have a four-year-old daughter, Dalia, who they adopted as a baby from Jordan. "She's cute, and wild to boot," Ib says with a gentle smile. "She's got me wrapped around her little finger. Any little finger she chooses."

Maha and Ib are trying to teach Dalia Arabic. They want her to maintain a sense of connection to her roots even as she grows up American. "We can take the best from the Arabic culture and the best from here, but we don't have to take either completely," Maha says. "For me, being from the Middle East, a lot of things in American culture I find too loose. There's not enough family ties. Sometimes we feel a bit lost, but at the same time I think it's a blessing that we can have the best of both worlds."

Maha feels that she is constantly trying to defend herself against stereotypes of Middle Easterners—especially the misconception that Arab women are oppressed and weak. "There are a lot of people who think that for Muslims in the Middle East, the man has a lot more power than the woman. It's not really true. In real Islam, women have a lot more respect than people think. Inside the house, my grandmothers in Jordan have the final word. They run the household."

Maha purses her lips and ticks off the common stereotypes of Arabs. "Arab men are violent, Arab men are womanizers, Arabs are rich, Arab women are abused, men make all the decisions," she says wearily, rolling her eyes.

"Generalizations are for the lazy person who doesn't want to look further," Ib offers. "This country still does not pay women for the same job as much as they do men. Just think about that. This is the greatest, most liberal country, the one that points fingers at other countries for not treating their women right, and yet we don't treat our women right. So it's not an Arab issue, it's not a Muslim issue, it's a world issue."

Ib gripes that most Americans were woefully ignorant about the Arab world when the U.S. invaded Iraq in March 2003. "People had to learn, 'Oh,

Iraq. That's a country in the Middle East. What kind of people are in Iraq? Arabs, I think. Well, no, they're Iraqis. What's the difference?'" He throws up his hands. "The people who have minds based on logic and process are getting more educated. The people who base their knowledge on fear are getting worse. They close their minds and they say, 'Don't confuse me with facts. Arabs are out there, they're bad, they're after us and that's that.' You see; fear is illogical."

After 9-11, Ib and other Eugene-area Arabs and Muslims met with city officials—the police chief, the mayor, the school superintendent—asking for help and protection. The climate of fear was so palpable that Ib got nervous on his weekly visits to the local mosque. "People who are fearful and ignorant are dangerous," he says. "Oftentimes they cannot contain their anger. They lash out. The acts of prejudice and violence against Muslims, according to the Council on American-Islamic Relations, went up 3,000 percent after 9-11."

Ib excuses himself to pick up Dalia from preschool, and Maha dispels the tension in the air with a smile as soft and warm as her pink sweater. "To tell you the truth, Oregon is one of the nicest places I've been," she says. "After 9-11, here at the restaurant, we had a counter covered with bouquets of flowers and notes saying, 'We still love you. We know you had nothing to do with it.' People came to the restaurant to show their support.

"It's funny," she continues. "When I'm here, I refer to Jordan as home. When I'm in Jordan, I refer to the United States as home. If anyone says something negative about the U.S., we jump in and we start defending. Suddenly, patriotism! This is a great place to be, and if you're willing to work, you can do something here."

After doing these interviews, I concluded that Diana Abu-Jaber was right: the Arab American demographic defies definition. The six Arab Oregonians introduced in this chapter, including myself, have almost nothing in common. Certainly not language; four are bilingual, three speak English as a second language, two speak only English. Not religion; we come from Muslim, Christian and mixed-faith families. Not citizenship; Three are American-born, two naturalized, one denied citizenship. Our politics and philosophies span the mainstream spectrum.

That lack of common identity makes the domestic "War on Terror" all the more confusing. After years of ignorance and gross stereotyping, American media are now focusing on Arab Americans with a mixture of curiosity and animosity, wondering for perhaps first time who we are and if we pose a threat. Some assimilated Arab Americans, like me and Vic Atiyeh, have the choice of remaining invisible if our names are sufficiently Anglo, if our skin is sufficiently light. But as we pass, the "other" Arabs in America, like Wael Wahbeh and Maha Hamide—practicing Muslims, immigrants, speakers of English as a second language—become all the more conspicuous. They're approached with ignorance, made to feel unwelcome, or worse, viewed as a threat.

Writing this chapter was hard for me. Not the research or the interviews so much as the personal narrative about my heritage, the laying bare of something private and vulnerable. I thought about editing myself out entirely, leaving those five interviewees dancing the *dubke* without me, but then I had to challenge myself: What am I afraid of?

My Arab pride comes like that, in defensive jabs. Then it retreats behind my all-American background, my inner child who doesn't want to be "other." But I've discovered why I feel compelled to out myself, to expose the Arab American journalists, governors, business owners and neighbors among us. It reveals our common humanity, our shared sense of patriotism and frustration. It allows us to connect, as Diana Abu-Jaber said. And that may be our best hope for racial harmony, for ending all wars, right there, so simply stated: To connect. To only connect.

NOTES

1. "Situ" was my paternal family's baby-word for grandmother, "Jidu" for grandfather. If it were proper Arabic it would be "Siti" and "Jadi," but my siblings and I are a few generations removed from the mother tongue, and my grandmother never corrected us.

2. The Antiochian Orthodox Church is said to be the first Christian church established by St. Peter the Apostle in 34 AD. Today, most members of Antiochian Orthodox churches in the U.S. are of Syrian, Lebanese, Palestinian and Iraqi ancestry. By tradition, the liturgy is often in Aramaic, an ancient Semitic language related to both Arabic and Hebrew. It is believed that Jesus spoke Aramaic.

3. Zogby attributes the discrepancy to an undercount of Arab Americans on the Census due to form-shy immigrants and assimilated citizens who don't identify as Arabs.

4. The seven cases referred to here are: In re Najour, 174 F. 735 (*N.D.Ga.* 1909); In re Mudari, 176 F. 465 (C.C.D.Mass. 1910); In re Ellis, 179 F. 1003 (D.Or. 1910); Dow v. United States, 226 F. 145 (4th Cir. 1915); Shahid, supra, 205 F. 8121913; Ex parte Dow, 211 F. 486 (E.D.S.C. 1914); In re Dow, 213 F. 355 (E.D.S.C. 1914). In the Najour, Mudari, Ellis and Dow (1915) cases, judges rules that the Syrian defendants were white; in the Shahid and two Dow (1914) cases, judges ruled that they were not white. While Syrians, along with Armenians and Asian Indians, were 'scientifically'

acknowledged to be Caucasians, the debate was over whether or not they were also white. In the Najour opinion, District Judge Newman opined: "I consider the Syrians as belonging to . . . what the world recognizes, as the white race." But in the Shahid case, District Judge Smith rejected the equation of white and Caucasian, ruling that Syrians (as well as Hindus and Malays) are not white. In *White by law: the legal construction of race*, Ian Haney López writes, "Syrians and Asian Indians . . . were between 'white' and 'yellow.' These people became White or non-White according to what the courts believed about them" (103).

Part VI

POLITICS AND SOCIAL CONTROL

Chapter Twelve

"Political History, Political Science, and Oregon Politics: Race and Ethnicity"

Robert C. Dash

Oregon's reputation among political scientists has been, for the longest time, that of progressive politics. To illustrate, Daniel Elazar's particularly influential *American Federalism: A View from the States*[1] categorized Oregon's political culture as "moralistic," by which Elazar meant that politics in the state centers on the public good and is devoted to the advancement of the public interest. Politics are seen and are practiced as a means by which to improve society, and public service represents a commitment to selflessly promote the public good. Elazar's work, like that of many others, was silent on the role of race and ethnicity in Oregon. And even now when racism is widely acknowledged to have occurred, it is generally viewed as somehow marginal to the state's progressive political history, more of a footnote or an aside than integral to the state's political history.[2]

A Tocquevillian notion of political development has dominated analyses of Oregon political history and culture. Alexis de Tocqueville's view of U.S. political history involves the working out of deeply embedded liberal or republican traditions that were promoted in its founding, and when illiberal and undemocratic beliefs and practices appear they are ultimately destined to retreat because of their lack of rational defenses, according to Rogers M. Smith.[3] Smith acknowledges that Tocqueville's thesis captures some important fundamental truths about U.S. politics and society, but he also strongly argues that the thesis fails to take into account inegalitarian ideas and conditions that have been integral to U.S. politics. These have reflected deeply entrenched ascriptive systems of unequal status supported by distinctive ideological justifications. Rather than a single tradition of liberal or republican democracy, the political history of the United States has constituted an interaction of political traditions—both liberal and illiberal—that have confronted and conflicted with each other.[4]

This chapter suggests, with regard to race and ethnicity, that *illiberalism* has been central, not marginal, to Oregon's political history. Moreover, while formal, legal, and ascriptive hierarchical systems of race and ethnicity are now in the past, they reverberate in significant ways in contemporary politics and social practice. Furthermore, with the recent dramatic rise in the racial and ethnic portion of Oregon's population, a trend that promises to continue in the foreseeable future, the political significance of race will not lessen.

This chapter selectively traces the role of race in the state's political history. It then points to some important contemporary dimensions of race and ethnicity that are significant in discussing contemporary Oregon's politics, and finally it offers some preliminary thoughts regarding the future trajectory of race and ethnicity in the state's politics.[5]

RACE AND ETHNICITY IN OREGON'S POLITICAL HISTORY
NATIVE AMERICANS

Before the onset of Euro-American colonial settlement, many diverse and distinct Native American groups lived in the region of the Pacific Northwest (PNW) that would eventually become the state of Oregon. The pre-contact Native American population in Oregon is estimated at 45,000[6]; the U.S. Census Bureau estimates the current Native American population as slightly below 40,000.[7] Thus, the Native American population still has not recovered demographically from the initial contact with Euro-Americans that began early in the 1800s with land exploration and escalated when thousands of white settlers arrived from the Midwest seeking land and other resources beginning in the 1840s. While the ruinous demographic decline of the Native American population caused by disease and violence can be statistically estimated, the cultural impact of Euro-American exploration and initial settlement cannot be quantified; it was, however, equally catastrophic.

The expanding encroachment by whites on Native American lands and the extension of federal control through Indian boarding schools (such as the Chemawa Indian School near Salem) and Indian agents contributed to the continued deterioration in the Native American population's physical and cultural circumstances throughout the nineteenth and into the twentieth centuries.[8] In 1887, the General Allotment Act (Dawes Act) allowed Indian reservations to be divided into smaller allotments for assignment to tribal members: "The disastrous effects of land allotment were felt at every reservation in Oregon."[9] The broader aim of the policy was to completely remold the Native American's conception of life and fully assimilate them into U.S. society. This entailed both the eradication of their cultures and values and their replacement with those of the dominant society, and an aggressive reservation land reduction program.[10]

Responding to the distinguished service of Native Americans in the First World War, Congress passed the Indian Citizenship Act in 1924. Prior to its passage, all reservation Indians in Oregon who had not yet been granted citizenship and all non-reservation Indians who could not prove that they had abandoned their tribal relations were barred from the polls.[11] In 1934, the Indian Reorganization Act (IRA) ended the allotting of Native American lands. Only the Grand Ronde and Warm Springs reservations in Oregon accepted the IRA; the former reservation gained little land under the act, but the latter reservation fared better in that regard.[12]

The internal fragmentation of reservation tribes often resulted from their attempts to adjust to the many challenges that federal policy forced upon them.[13] One result of this internal splintering of tribes was that an English-speaking, bicultural, multi-tribal American Indian population developed off-reservation in the twentieth century. The Second World War stimulated an urbanization process as Indians volunteered and were drafted into the military and others left reservations for wartime urban industrial jobs. Post-war programs for job training and urban relocation were specifically designed to reduce reservation populations during the "termination" era of federal Indian policy, and these provided a further impetus to the reservation-urban Indian population stream.[14]

In 1953, Congress passed a resolution that called for the termination of federal supervision and control over many Native American tribes, and in 1954 Oregon Governor Douglas McKay resigned to become the U.S. Secretary of the Interior and he immediately implemented the termination policy. "Terminated tribes lost all federal recognition, their status as wards of the federal government, and all other federal aid, benefits, and legal responsibilities. Tribally held lands lost their reservation status, were taken out of trust, and were subjected to local tax."[15] The termination policy affected 62 Native American tribes from Western Oregon and led to another devastating round in the loss of lands and resources. Terminated tribes were placed under the direct civil jurisdiction of the state and local governments, which now had authority over their social and economic lives. "[They] were being assimilated into the state body politic."[16]

In the 1950s and 1960s, the modern civil rights movement and the federal legislation it encouraged and Lyndon Johnson's Great Society and War on Poverty programs ended the assimilationist thrust of federal Indian policy. One result was the political mobilization of urban Indians that was marked by the rapid growth of political organizations, newspapers, and community programs. The possibility of pan-Indian ethnicity emerged. Also, greater access to material incentives through affirmative action and minority set-aside programs increased federal spending on Indian affairs, and the settlement of land claims during the 1970s and 1980s occurred.[17]

In Portland, divergent organizational approaches marked the efforts to organize Native Americans. Native American migrants in the 1940s and 1950s had tended to form groups that cultivated an urban Indian community, culture, and identity that complemented their entry into mainstream society; the later generation was influenced by the more radical social protest and identity politics of the 1960s and 1970s. Conflict inevitably arose over competition for resources, especially during the Great Society era of expanding federal grants to community organizations.[18]

In 1984, Oregon voters approved a state lottery that soon grew into a major industry providing needed revenue to fund government programs; and in 1988, the federal Indian Gaming Regulatory Act decreed that states could not prevent Native American tribes from offering whatever games the states permitted. The introduction of gambling to nine of Oregon's tribes has represented a significant change in their economic fortunes as they now compete with the state, and with one another, for a growing revenue stream. The tribal casinos now generate more than $1 billion to Oregon's economy yearly, yield $189 million in profits (in 2003), and sustain 5,300 casino-related jobs and, indirectly, thousands of other jobs.[19]

The development of the gaming industry is the most significant political, as well as economic, change for Oregon's tribes since the termination process of the 1950s. PNW tribes have historically directed their lobbying and campaign contributions to federal officials and office seekers, since the federal government was the primary overseer of most tribal assistance programs. Now their attention is directed overwhelmingly to maintaining the Indian Gaming Regulatory Act that has allowed the growth of the industry.[20] The Cow Creeks, the largest donor among tribes in Oregon to federal campaigns in 2004, contributed $210,000.[21]

State races, however, are now receiving increasing political attention from tribes in the PNW. The tribes' contributions to Oregon and Washington state races surged from $8,800 in 1994 to more than $400,000 in 2002, and provided key support to (Democrat) Ted Kulongoski's successful race for governor in Oregon that year.[22] Since opening its highly successful Spirit Mountain Casino in 1996, the Confederated Tribes of Grande Ronde has become an especially influential player in electoral politics. It gave, for example, $93,000 to state candidates during the 2000 electoral season, more than all other tribes in Oregon combined, and $120,000 in 2002.[23]

While the increasingly significant financial contributions of some tribes in Oregon are politically very important in the state, their political influence is tied directly to the economic health of the casinos, and competition from state gaming continues to threaten the overall take by the Indian casinos. Annual casino revenue increases have slowed recently.[24] Oregon's Native American gambling industry could surge once again, however, if the state grants the construction of more casinos, especially near urban areas. A proposal by the Confederated Tribes of Warm Springs to shut down their isolated, rural reservation casino and to locate a new casino in the scenic Colombia River Gorge within easy driving distance of Portland has drawn a mixed response from the political class of the state[25] and a sharply hostile response from the Confederated Tribes of Grande Ronde. If granted by the governor, the Columbia River Gorge casino will inevitably draw off some of the Portland clientele from the highly successful Grande Ronde casino and thus they have waged a vigorous campaign against the proposal. The dispute over the proposed new casino reflects the central importance of casino revenues to Native American groups, and the increasingly tangled nature of their relations with one another and with political parties and politicians in the state.[26]

While revenues from gaming have marked a profound economic change for the tribes who run casinos in the state, the many problems that plague reservations are by no means solved by the influx of gaming revenues. For example, while gaming provides $2.5 million annually to the Confederated Tribes of Warm Springs, that has been more than offset by the decline in its lumber products industry. Total revenues for the reservation have fallen from approximately $38 million in the mid-1990s to an estimated $25 million ten years later. One of four tribal members on the reservation are out of work, with unemployment approaching 50 percent in the winter; one out of three children lives below the poverty line, twice the rate of children across the state; and child mortality rates run high.[27]

Despite the long history of formal and informal disenfranchisement and, more broadly, their political victimization by state and national politics, Native Americans have been registering and voting in record numbers in recent years across the country. This trend, combined with a tribal population growth rate that far exceeds that of the country as a whole, potentially promises to give Native Americans some greater political clout in certain future key races.[28] In the PNW, Washington's tribes have been fielding Native American candidates, starting voter registration drives, and financing attack ads for a number of years, while Oregon tribes largely limited their state political involvement to financial contributions until recently.[29] Oregon's last prominent Native American legislator was Jackie Taylor of the Potowatomi tribe, who left office in 2001. Created by Washington tribes in 1999, the First American Education Project is now funded by tribes across the country, including several in Oregon. It could help to spark the same level of political activism in

Oregon races that it did in the 2000 senatorial race in Washington. Also, the Native American Leadership Institute, located in Ashland, has created a voter registration, education, and get-out-the-vote project that focuses on selected counties in the state.[30]

AFRICAN AMERICANS

Even before statehood was achieved, the 1844 Oregon provisional government passed measures that excluded African Americans, slave or free, from the state. This status was reaffirmed when Oregon was made a part of the United States in 1849 and again when statehood was gained in 1859. Through the end of the nineteenth and well into the twentieth centuries, legal barriers and popular sentiment prevented African American and other non-white groups from voting or owning land in the state.[31] Only in 1927 was the Oregon State Constitution finally amended to remove the clause denying blacks the right to vote.

Unlike other migrant groups arriving in the PNW following the Civil War, African Americans generally settled initially in cities where they created enduring communities. The region's first permanent black community was established in Portland in the 1860s by a number of artisans and unskilled laborers. The level of relative economic opportunity that was open to African Americans allowed a stable if slow-growing black community to take hold there.[32] Many early African American settlers were single men, but families began to settle in the region by the late nineteenth century.[33] In 1900, Portland's 775 African Americans constituted 65 percent of the total Oregon African American population. Originally located west of the Willamette River, the community was displaced by an expanding industrial district and was relocated to the river's east bank in the 1890s where it has since constituted the historical core of Portland's black community.[34]

Portland's African Americans faced segregation barriers such as an 1867 decision that prohibited black children from attending public schools, a decision that was reversed only in 1880. As early as 1893, African Americans were organizing to pressure the state legislature to overturn laws that banned racial intermarriage and blocked access by minorities to public accommodations. African Americans in Portland defended their political or civil interests through formal organizations as well as ad hoc groups. As was the case elsewhere, African American churches incubated leadership and often helped to catalyze black community fraternal and civic organizations. In Portland, several African American artisans and unskilled laborers founded one of the first black churches in 1862, a small multi-denominational congregation called the "People's Church."[35] The founding of the Portland branch of the National Association for the Advancement of Colored People (NAACP) in 1914 was signaled in the organizational response by the state's African American population to the established racial order. Other significant political actors from the community were lawyers, fraternal orders, civic and social clubs, newspapers and other businesses, the Urban League, and the Afro-American League of Portland, a civil rights and self-help organization that was influenced by Booker T. Washington's (conservative) approach to change.[36]

Most African Americans in the state voted Republican after suffrage was extended to them in 1927. With small numbers, their vote was only influential in closely contested local races. Only occasionally did individual African Americans seek electoral office; mostly the African American vote was cast in favor of a white office seeker who offered either symbolic political or material support to the black community. In general, however, African Americans received little in terms of legislative consideration or political result for their electoral participation. One explanation for their continued diligence in voting despite the mean payoff they received was the knowledge that the vote was still being systematically denied to African Americans throughout the Jim Crow South.[37]

Oregon was one of the states in the West in the 1920s where the Klu Klux Klan was strongest. It found fertile ground in a population that was composed of more than 80 percent white and U.S.-born and 90 percent Protestant. In two years, beginning in 1921, the KKK recruited 14,000 members in the state, giving it perhaps the highest per-capita membership in the country, a membership that included elected and police officials and others from "respectable society."[38] The actions of the Klan were aimed not only, or even primarily, at African Americans, but rather at "outsiders" in general and especially Catholics and Jews whose presence in the state challenged the "traditional way of life" that the Klan was dedicated to maintaining.[39] While the influence of the Klan on the state's politics would fade by the end of the 1920s, organized racist groups have continued to haunt Oregon.[40]

Fewer than 2,000 African Americans resided in Portland in 1940 out of a total population of approximately 340,000, but an estimated twenty-three thousand were to arrive in Portland during the Second World War as the city was transformed into a hub of the industrial war machine. Seeking work in the region's war industries, African Americans flocked to the city from the South and Midwest. For the first time, African Americans were the largest and most visible minority group in the city. The response of much of the Euro-American population was, predictably, negative. While sympathetic whites joined the NAACP and promoted harmony among the races, deeply engrained racist social and business practices supported the existing system of social segregation and political subordination. Nevertheless, the Second World War was a watershed event in that the African American community became more politically, economically, and socially active than at any time in Oregon's history.[41]

While the modern African American civil rights movement of Oregon never garnered the national attention of larger cities, the 1960s through the 1980s was a period of heightened political activism and organizing directed against the established system that obstructed the full development of the black community. The Black Panther Party in Portland and Eugene, for example, opened free medical and dental clinics and organized free breakfast programs for schoolchildren.[42] Since the high point of the social protest movements of the 1960s and 1970s, the African American community has achieved substantial footing in state politics, with several being elected to the state legislature and in one instance, to statewide public office.[43]

ASIAN AMERICANS

From the mid-nineteenth century, the discovery of gold, the steady expending of the agricultural and fishery economies, and the arrival of the Northern Pacific railroad in Portland in 1883 drew to the state, among other groups, Chinese. Drawn initially to California after the Gold Rush of 1849, regular steamer service from San Francisco to Portland beginning in 1851 facilitated the entry of Chinese into Oregon following the discovery of gold in the southern portions of the state that same year. Most Chinese initially settled in rural areas, but racial violence and legal restrictions perpetuated by whites seeking work in the state resulted in the rapid shift of Chinese to Portland, the state's largest city and the county seat of the state's most populated county, Multnomah. While only 17.5 percent of the Chinese lived in Multnomah County in 1880, the percentage had increased to 75.4 percent by 1890.[44]

Constituting the largest non-white group (5 percent) of the population in the state in 1880, the number of Chinese declined thereafter as a result of organized anti-Chinese efforts on the West Coast and the enactment in 1882 of the national Chinese Exclusion Act. They were replaced in the last two decades of the twentieth century as the largest Asian population by Japanese, who grew from just twenty-five in the 1890 census to 2,522 in the 1900 census, of whom 1,191 resided in Portland.[45] Young Japanese men were imported for what was expected to be temporary work on the railroads, in the forests, and in the canneries, but later many decided to become permanent U.S. residents and became self-employed, often in agriculture. As brides from Japan joined the men who had arrived earlier, the state's Japanese American population grew to 4,151 by 1920 with the largest concentrations in Hood River, Astoria, and in or near Portland. Japanese Americans owned just 1 percent of the state's total acreage, but by 1923 the Klan-dominated Legislature passed an Alien Land law that barred Japanese land ownership.[46]

In response to the many challenges of being immigrants in a generally unwelcoming state, the Japanese developed mutual support associations, many of which consolidated under an umbrella organization, the Japanese Association of Oregon, in 1928. The JAO offered community leadership and helped to foster the growth of the Portland Japanese American Citizens League. This organization worked for Japanese American integration into mainstream religious, civic, and recreational organizations, and it also addressed racial discrimination and citizenship rights.[47]

Japanese and Japanese Americans constituted the state's largest non-white group in 1940, but the federal internment policy of 1942 totally uprooted the community from the state. The ending of the internment policy in 1945 did not result in the reestablishment of the original Japanese communities in Oregon. Many Japanese rebuilt their lives elsewhere, and those who returned to Oregon often faced bitter legal struggles in recovering homes, farms, and businesses that had been taken over by whites. A particularly spirited reaction against the return of the Japanese came from some in farming communities who wanted to limit competition by enacting restrictive alien land laws. Those laws were struck down by judicial decisions or repealed by the state legislature by the end of the 1940s.[48]

The Japanese who did return to Oregon largely moved into integrated communities and built new forms of community-based institutions and organizations, including mainstream advocacy and service groups, and grassroots organizations that challenged fundamental inequalities. Citizenship was made available to Japanese-born Americans, and racial discrimination in employment officially ended.[49] A campaign to redress the Japanese Americans incarcerated during World War II, combining grassroots protest and congressional lobbying, resulted in federal legislation in the 1980s that provided for both an official apology and symbolic monetary compensation.[50]

The Asian American and Pacific Islander (AAPI) population of the state is now much more diverse than in the immediate post-Second World War era. The five largest AAPI populations in the state are in descending order Chinese, Vietnamese, Korean, Japanese, and Filipino; and the most rapidly growing communities are the Hmong, Asian Indian, Pacific Islander, Vietnamese, and Thai.[51]

LATINOS

Mexicans worked in the state as miners and muleteers in the mid-nineteenth century and as *vaqueros* in the last quarter of the same century. The short life

of the state's mining economy, the displacement of mule trains by freight
wagons, the strong anti-Mexican sentiment that carried over from the U.S.-
Mexican War, and the federal land donation acts that precluded Mexicans
from acquiring land caused them to move elsewhere during the nineteenth
century.[52] Federal, state, and local policies during the 1930s depression reinforced the drive to move Mexicans (and sometimes Mexican Americans) on
the West coast into Mexico, but the federal "Bracero" program, instituted in
1942, reversed that flow.[53] Over 15,000 Mexicans worked in Oregon's agricultural fields, packing sheds, and in other economic activities during the
Second World War. The Mexican presence would shrink immediately following the termination of the Bracero program in the state in 1947, but the program had the long-term effect of establishing permanent patterns of migration
from Mexico and U.S. Southwest to the PNW. Beginning in the 1950s, thousands of Mexican American and Mexican migrants working the western and
northwest migrant trails eventually became the backbone of the region's temporary agricultural labor force. Many south Texan migrants settled out in Oregon, particularly in the Willamette Valley and along the Oregon-Idaho border
in those years. Beginning in the 1960s, increasing numbers of Mexicans arrived either directly from the "traditional" sending states in central and north-
central Mexico, or indirectly after working California harvests. Then in the
1980s, large numbers of Mexican migrants from a more diverse range of
states in Mexico continued the movement northward. This latter wave of migrants has included very significant numbers of indigenous ethnic workers.
Mexican laborers, with some Central Americans, now comprise the state's
temporary migrant agricultural work force almost wholly; nearly half of that
labor force is composed of Mexican indigenous groups. It is also estimated
that more than half of that workforce does not possess legal immigration documentation, and this has become a highly charged political issue in Oregon as
it has in other states. In recent decades, Latinos have moved into a wide range
of other occupations in the state. Of the total Latino population currently in
the state, it is estimated that roughly three-fourths of it is composed of individuals of Mexican descent.[54]

CONTEMPORARY RACE AND POLITICS

A hierarchical structure of racial domination, exclusion, and oppression characterized Oregon from the early nineteenth century into the 1950s. The effects of the structure varied somewhat by minority group, depending on a
wide range of circumstances—economic, cultural, and geographic—but the
overall impact on all minority groups was, at a minimum, deeply burden-

some. Racial minorities were not considered citizens of the state for the longest time, and when they were admitted to citizenship they were assigned to subordinate positions in the political and social order. While dissenting voices were frequent and sometimes many and those voices often included Euro Americans as well as people of color, the enduring system of oppressive laws, discriminatory social practices, and justificatory ideologies worked to the political benefit of the dominant population and against the interests of people of color.

Throughout that long period of racial oppression, peoples of color dealt with the daily burden of discrimination through a variety of means, including organizing and protesting, enduring in silence, and sometimes escaping to what they hoped to be more enlightened states. The first definitive, enduring break in the racist structure occurred with the Second World War, which produced significant, if short lived, demographic change in the state and major civil rights legislation at the national and state levels after the war. The years immediately following the Second World War saw the ending of the systematic legal barriers that had been constructed against the social, economic, and political inclusion of racial minorities in Oregon. A state fair employment law was passed in 1949, followed by a public accommodation law in 1953 and fair housing laws in 1957 and 1959. The overturning of legal structures that excluded or subordinated minorities is attributable to the crucial participation of racial minorities in the war effort, both at home and abroad; changing public policies and judicial decisions at the national level and enlightened political leadership at the state level; and the long, sustained organizing efforts by many in the minority communities to politically challenge the barriers they confronted in the state.

In 1965, a second major transformation was introduced into the state with passage of the national Immigration Act. The Act repealed national quotas that had expressly favored Western European immigrants since the 1920s and provided for family reunification. With the lifting of national quotas, an unprecedented level of immigration from Asia ensued, and the provision for family reunification stimulated an unanticipated level of immigration from Latin America. According to 2003 estimates, the fraction of foreign born in Oregon, while below the national average, stood at a significant 8.5 percent.[55] From 2000 to 2003, ethnic and racial minorities, many of them immigrants, made up about 60 percent of the state's added residents, with the Latino population growing 18.5 percent and the AAPI population growing more than 16 percent. The immigrant population from Latin America constitutes 45 percent of the total foreign born in the state, while Asians constitute 27 percent: together, the two groups now contribute three out of every four to Oregon's foreign born population.[56] While the growth in the Latino population is occurring throughout the state, Asian growth is concentrated in the state's three largest metropolitan areas, Portland, Salem, and Eugene.

After a century and a half during which the state's white population never dipped below 90 percent and was often in the high nineties, the U.S. Census Bureau estimates are that 87.8 percent of Oregon's population is white; 1.7 percent is African American; 1.1 percent is Native American; 3.5 percent is AAPI; and 9.3 percent is Latino (of any race).[57] The political significance of the changing demographic landscape of the state is not, however, as straightforward as the changing numbers. Political participation and influence require affirmative steps based on interest, attention, knowledge, time, energy, and a sense of efficacy. Individuals and groups, due to a variety of factors, do not share equally in those attributes.

As Table 12.1 illustrates, voter registration rates as a percentage of the total populations of the four minority groups at the national level lag behind white rates, and the rates of Latinos and Asians lag badly. The large non-U.S. citizen portion of the latter two groups, roughly 4 out of 10, who cannot legally register to vote, explains a good deal but not all of the difference in their registration rates. For U.S. citizens, there was still a substantial 20 percent point difference between the registration of whites and Asians and a 14 percent gap between whites and Latinos. Native Americans and Blacks lie between those two positions.

Regarding the voting rates (turnout) for total group populations, a similar pattern emerges. The voting rate for whites is more than double that of Asians and Latinos, with, again, Native Americans and Blacks falling between the two extreme positions. What emerges most strikingly, however, is the comparative group voting rates of those who have registered. Whites retain only a slim 2 percent point margin over blacks and Asian, with Latinos and Native

Table 12.1. Percentage Distribution of National Voting and Registration in the 1998 Election by Race

	Asian	Latino	Indian	Black	White
Citizenship	59%	61%	98%	96%	98%
Registration					
of total population	29	34	57	61	68
of citizens	49	55	58	64	69
Voting					
of total population	19	20	35	40	47
of registered	66	60	61	66	68

Source: Pei-te Lien, Christian Collet, Janelle Wong, and S. Karthick Ramakrishnan, "Asian Pacific-American Public Opinion and Political Participation," *PS: Political Science and Politics*, Vol. 34, No. 3 (September 2001), 625-630, excerpted from Table 1 Percentage Distribution of Voting and Registration in the Elections of 1990-1998 by Race, 626.

Americans notably trailing those groups but not by exceedingly large margins. Thus, political participation rates vary substantially among racial groups, but when citizenship is held constant a good deal of that variation disappears.

As pointed out above, the Latino and AAPI communities in Oregon contain large numbers of immigrants. There is substantial variation within each racial/ethnic group and across both groups in terms of citizenship status, nativity, length of stay in the state, immigrant generation and English-language skills.[58] For example, while the Mexican-descent population numerically dominates the Latino population in the state, the AAPI community is much more diverse in terms of national origin. But both groups—Latinos and AAPI immigrants—share a lack of familiarity with the U.S. political system, and many immigrants in both groups come from countries where they prudently learned to avoid involvement in politics. These are barriers that some immigrants surmount rather easily, but others find more daunting. Still, it is a constant among naturalized citizens of both groups that those who have a longer length of time at their current residence and in the United States, are older, and have more education and higher income are more likely to register and vote. *Much like the broader citizen population, those immigrants who are most established in society are also most likely to register and vote.*[59] The region of origin is not significantly related to voting and registration among naturalized citizens, once duration in the United States is taken into account.[60]

Another way to examine political activism is to look at the extent of participation beyond registration and voting, to look for example at campaign donations and membership in associations. Individuals in the AAPI community generally give campaign donations at lower rates than whites and blacks. When they do make donations, they typically prefer candidates of shared ancestry who have little chance of winning and are likely to reside outside of the donors' districts. This pattern illustrates the strength of ethnic identity in shaping AAPI political behavior.[61]

Japanese Americans in particular participate heavily in ethnic voluntary associations, even when they leave highly concentrated urban ethnic enclaves. They are more likely than other racial groups to combine high levels of structural assimilation and high levels of ethnic group membership retention. This situation is basically at odds with the traditional assimilationist perspective, which implies that as members of an ethnic group become structurally assimilated, they will give up their ethnic ties. Putting resources into the ethnic community does not preclude putting resources into relations with persons in the larger society.[62]

Political parties serve as the main conduit for political activation and recruitment, and the two major political parties in the state have discovered the

"Latino vote" in recent electoral cycles as that group's demographic and political visibility has risen significantly. During the 2002 gubernatorial race in Oregon, for example, Kevin Mannix, the Republican candidate who spent much of his childhood in South America, often spoke Spanish on the campaign trail, and in 2004 his party launched a significant "get-out-the-vote" effort aimed at Latinos. The Democratic National Committee has expended an even greater effort in its Latino voter outreach effort in Oregon in recent elections. Additionally, other activist and non-partisan groups have been working to increase Latino voter registration and turnout. Despite these efforts, the electoral impact of Latinos lags badly in the state. As pointed out above, the lack of citizenship among Latinos is the overriding factor in explaining this pattern. For example, of the 48,714 Latinos that the 2000 U.S. Census identified in Marion County, 26,783, or 55 percent, were not citizens. Beyond the lack of citizenship, Latinos are disproportionately younger than other groups, and the lowest level of electoral participation corresponds to the youngest cohort; foreign-born Latino immigrants move more frequently than those who are native-born; and language barriers still remain for many Latinos, as they do for many in the AAPI population.[63]

Yet, despite the many obstacles to their increased political participation, it is estimated that there was from 2000 to 2004 an increase of about 14,000 registered Latinos in the state, to 56,000. About 45 percent of them registered as Democrats, 21 percent as Republicans, and 32 percent as independent. Nearly four times as many Oregon Latinos voted in the 2004 presidential elections, about 45,000 or about 2.5 percent of the total vote, as did in the 2000 election.[64] Beyond the increases in registration and voting among Latinos, the rapidly increasing share of the state's population that they represent, the aging of the group, and the increasing share of naturalized and native citizens among them promises a greater future political role for Latinos, as it does for Asians, even if their participation rates continue to compare unfavorably—which is by no means a foregone conclusion—with those of other groups.[65]

Neither the Republican nor Democratic parties has yet had notable success in putting Latino candidates in office. Rocky Barrilla in the 1980s and Susan Castillo (both Democrats) in the 1990s and early 2000s were in the state legislature, the latter then winning the office of state schools superintendent in 2002. Encouragingly for Republicans, Billy Dalto is the first Latino in the legislature from that party and is now serving his second term. On the other hand, a Latino candidate lost in the 2004 Democratic primary for the newly created 22nd House District that incorporated the heavily Latino populated area of northeast Salem with Woodburn, which has a majority Latino population. The 22nd House District was a product of the redistricting plan controlled by the Democratic Party based on the 2000 census, and it was intended by its architects to create a "safe" district for Latino candidates and to cement that group's loyalty to the party.[66] While the Democratic strategy initially failed, in the long term and with a continuation of current demographic patterns, having the opportunity to elect a Latino could be empowering for Latino voters in the 22nd House District and symbolically important throughout the state.[67]

Overall in the state, all racial and ethnic groups are under-represented by elected and appointed officials. Among city councils and mayors, minorities are significantly under-represented; when taken as a whole statewide and primarily because of the contribution of two large urban counties, county commissions reflect some greater degree of racial and ethnic parity with the general population; and at the state level, with the exception of Latinos, elected and appointed officials more closely reflect the racial makeup of the population.[68]

CONCLUDING OBSERVATIONS

Grant McConnell famously argued in the 1960s that "Policies generally adhering to maintenance of the status quo and favoring the concrete interests of existing elites will tend to be associated with organizations based on small units; alternatively, large units will more probably produce policies favoring change directed to the general, diffuse, and widely shared interests of a broad segment of the population."[69] McConnell's proposition suggests that racial and ethnic groups trying to influence the public policy agenda and seeking to gain elected and appointed representation in Oregon will likely find more initial success in large governmental units—the more populated cities and counties and at the state level—than in small governmental units. Because the AAPI and African American populations particularly tend to reside in the state's largest metropolitan areas—Portland, Salem, and Eugene—they are somewhat more advantageously positioned than Latinos and Native Americans in this regard.

Partial and anecdotal evidence seems to at least partially sustain McConnell's proposition. While not yet finding much success at the local level, the AAPI community, for example, was over represented in comparison to their proportion of the state's population for at least one state legislative cycle in recent Oregon history;[70] David Wu, a Chinese American Democrat, has represented Oregon's 1st Congressional District from 1999 to the present; and Korean Americans using a "crossover" strategy have had recent success in running for state electoral office in Oregon and Washington.[71] Likewise,

African Americans from the Portland region have had notable success in winning state legislative races (although the failure to yet gain a seat on the Portland City Commission weakens the proposition regarding success in more populated local-level jurisdictions) and gaining influential positions in the legislature.[72] The still-strong attachment of African Americans to the Democratic Party and the firm hold of that party on the Portland metropolitan area suggests that region will continue to serve as the most effective conduit for African American candidates to the legislature and broader African American political influence.

While demography is not politically determinant, projected demographic trends in Oregon strongly suggest that African Americans, because of their relatively slow population growth in comparison to AAPI and Latino populations, will necessarily face the task of developing stronger coalitional politics with the two groups or finding their influence slipping in comparison.[73] Also, Native Americans, the smallest of the racial groups in the state, present a complex mosaic of rural and urban Indians, reservation and non-reservation Indians, casino and non-casino reservations, and dozens of groups with distinctive cultural traditions. Neither political party has made particularly strong attempts to fully integrate Native Americans as political actors. It is currently not clear whether, given the tremendous future growth of the Latino and AAPI populations, the political parties will see it in their self-interest to become more invested in such an effort. While a handful of Native American reservations have become key political players in the state because of the wealth-generating power of their casinos, it is not certain that their influence will be sufficient to generate broadly sustained political attention to Native Americans' concerns throughout the state.

While politics in Oregon cannot be comprehended only through the prism of race, this chapter has argued that the state's politics cannot be adequately understood if race is not integral to the analysis. The state's political history sustains this proposition; future transformations in the state's racial and ethnic landscape will confirm it.

NOTES

1. Published in 1966.

2. To illustrate, there is no chapter (nor index entry) on race or ethnicity in a very recent and otherwise thorough overview of Oregon politics and government in Richard A. Clucas, Mark Henkels, and Brent S. Steel, eds., *Oregon Politics and Government: Progressive versus Conservative Populists* (University of Nebraska Press, 2005).

3. Rogers M. Smith, "Beyond Tocqueville, Myrdal, and Hartz: The Multiple Traditions in America," *American Political Science Review* 87:3 (Sept. 1993): 549–566.

4. Smith, "Beyond Tocqueville," 549–550.

5. This chapter does not address the many conceptual issues regarding the meanings of race and ethnicity, nor does it contend with the issue of which groups legitimately qualify as racial or ethnic "minorities." I simply consider that the systematic and historic oppression of Asians, Latinos, African Americans, and Native Americans in Oregon *as groups* was uniquely different from the treatment of other populations and that distinction qualifies them as the appropriate subject of this chapter.

6. Jeff Zucker, Kay Hummel, and Bob Hogfoss, *Oregon Indians: Culture, History, and Current Affairs: An Atlas and Introduction* (Portland: The Press of the Oregon Historical Society, 1983): 145.

7. U.S. Census Bureau, Amer. Fact Finder, "Fact Sheet: Oregon," retrieved 5 July 2005, <http://factfinder.census.gov/servlet/ACSSAFFFacts?_event=Search&geo_id =01000US&_geoContext=01000US&_street=&_county=&_cityTown=&_state=040 00US41&_zip=&_lang=en&_sse=on&ActiveGeoDiv=geoSelect&_useEV=&pctxt =fph&pgsl=010>. This figure includes an estimated 40 percent who are affiliated with non-Oregon tribes.

8. David Peterson del Mar, *Oregon's Promise: An Interpretive History* (Corvallis: Oregon State University Press, 2003): 108–112.

9. Jeff Zucker, Kay Hummel, and Bob Hogfoss, *Oregon Indians: Culture, History, and Current Affairs: An Atlas and Introduction* (Portland: The Press of the Oregon Historical Society, 1983): 74.

10. Cary C. Collins, "Through the Lens of Assimilation: Edwin L. Chalcraft and Chemawa Indian School," *Oregon Historical Quarterly* 98:4 (Winter 1997–8): 392.

11. Suzanne E. Evans, *Encyclopedia of North American Indians*, retrieved 16 July 2005, <http://college.hmco.com/history/readerscomp/naind/html/na_041800_voting .htm>

12. Jeff Zucker, Kay Hummel, and Bob Hogfoss, *Oregon Indians: Culture, History, and Current Affairs: An Atlas and Introduction* (Portland: The Press of the Oregon Historical Society, 1983): 75–76.

13. Patrick Haynal, "Termination and Tribal Survival: The Klamath Tribes of Oregon," *Oregon Historical Quarterly* 101:3 (Fall 2000): 272.

14. Joane Nagel "American Indian Ethnic Renewal: Politics and the Resurgence of Identity," *American Sociological Review* 60:6 (Dec. 1995): 954.

15. Patrick Haynal, "Termination and Tribal Survival: The Klamath Tribes of Oregon," *Oregon Historical Quarterly* 101:3 (Fall 2000): 274.

16. Haynal, "Termination," 284.

17. Joane Nagel "American Indian Ethnic Renewal: Politics and the Resurgence of Identity," *American Sociological Review* 60:6 (Dec. 1995): 955–956.

18. Nicolas G. Rosenthal, "Repositioning Indianness: Native American Organizations in Portland, Oregon, 1959–1975," *Pacific Historical Review* 71:3 (Aug. 2002): 415–417.

19. Jeff Mapes, "Tribes Press Case on Gaming," *Oregonian*, 8 Mar. 2005.

20. "Plan for Off-Reservation Casino Causes Stir in Oregon," *Los Angeles Times*, 30 May 2005.

21. Jeff Kosseff, "Tribes Buy into Political Process," *Oregonian,* 9 May 2005.

22. Jim Lynch, "Tribes Invest Record Cash in State Politics," *Oregonian*, 15 Jan. 2003.

23. Lynch, "Tribes Invest"; and Jeff Mapes, "Grand Ronde Endorse Candidates," *Oregonian*, 16 Jan. 2002.

24. Jim Lynch, "Tribes Invest Record Cash in State Politics," *Oregonian*, 15 Jan. 2003.

25. Lynch, "Tribes Invest." As an illustration of the sometimes divergent interests of different racial groups in the state, U.S. Representative David Wu, a Chinese-American and Democrat, has been one of the most impassioned opponents to off-reservation gaming in the Columbia Gorge, declaring, "We should not sacrifice our national treasures, our communities or our souls upon the altar of Indian casino gambling." See "Plan for Off-Reservation Casino Causes Stir in Oregon," *Los Angeles Times*, 30 May 2005.

26. Governor Kulongoski's willingness to entertain the possibility of the new casino has severely strained relations with the Confederated Tribes of the Grand Ronde and resulted in the Grand Ronde spending nearly $1 million during the 2006 gubernatorial primary race on television ads attacking him and one of the Republican candidates for their support of the new casino. The decision by the Grande Ronde leadership decision to undertake this political attack campaign also caused fissures within its community. See Harry Esteve, "Tribe Takes Gamble in Turf War," *Oregonian*, 25 June 2006.

27. Brent Walth, "A Reservation's Reckoning: Ballot Marks a Crossroads," *Oregonian*, 28 Mar. 2004.

28. Brad Knickerbocker, "Gains on the Reservations," *The Christian Science Monitor*, 15 Feb. 2005.

29. For example, an estimated 10,000 new Native American voters registered in anticipation of the 2000 U.S. Senate race in Washington, thereby contributing to the defeat of Senator Slate Gorton who had an often-adversarial relationship with tribes. See Nicole Adams, "Getting Out the Vote in Indian Country," *Winds of Change* 20:2 (Spring 2005), retrieved 16 July 2005, <http://www.wocmag.org/2004/summer/education2.html>.

30. Adams, "Getting out the Vote"; and Jim Lynch, "Tribes Invest."

31. Other laws required that Blacks be whipped twice a year unless they left the territory and, when that measure was deemed too harsh, its provisions for punishment were reduced to forced labor; and Blacks (as well as Chinese, Hawaiians, and people of mixed ethnic heritage) were required to pay an annual tax of $5, and if they could not pay the tax the law empowered the state to press them into service maintaining roads. Furthermore, interracial marriage was banned in the state. See End of the Oregon Trail Interpretive Center, "Timeline of Black History in the Pacific Northwest," retrieved 23 June 2005, <http://www.endoftheoregontrail.org/blaktime.html>.

32. Quintard Taylor, "The Emergence of Black Communities in the Pacific Northwest, 1865–1910," *The Journal of Negro History* 64:4 (Autumn 1979): 342.

33. Mario Compean, "African Americans in the Columbia River Basin—Historical Overview," retrieved 16 July 2005 from <http://www.vancouver.wsu.edu/crbeha/aa/aa.htm>.

34. Taylor, "The Emergence of Black Communities," 343–344.

35. Compean "African Americans in the Columbia River Basin."

36. Elizabeth McLagan, *A Peculiar Paradise: a History of Blacks in Oregon, 1788–1940* (Portland: The Georgian Press, 1980): 157–164; and Taylor, "The Emergence of Black Communities," 343–344.

37. Taylor, "The Emergence of Black Communities," 347–349.

38. "An Oregon Century: Roaring with the 1920s," *Oregonian*, 22 Dec. 1999.

39. McLagan, *A Peculiar Paradise,"* 135–142; and David Peterson del Mar, *Oregon's Promise: An Interpretive History* (Corvallis: Oregon State University Press, 2003): 172–175.

40. The Southern Poverty Law Center tracks hate groups across the country and while some more-populous states and the South generally have more such groups, the PNW has significant numbers of neo-Nazi, Christian Identity, and racist skinhead followers. See "Racism Flaring, Northwest Fights Back," *Christian Science Monitor*, 26 Apr. 2004; retrieved 21 June 2005, from LexisNexis, <http://library.willamette.edu:2070/universe/document>.

41. Rudy Pearson, "'A Menace to the Neighborhood': Housing and African Americans in Portland, 1941–1945," *Oregon Historical Quarterly* 102:2 (Summer 2001): 159–161, 172.

42. "An Oregon Century: Rebelling in the 1960s," *Oregonian*, 28 Dec. 1999; and Jaja Anderson, "Short History of the Black Panther Party in the Eugene, Oregon Chapter," *It's About Time: Black Panther Party and Alumni*, <http://www.itsabouttimebpp.com/Chapter_History/Eugene_Oregon_Chapter.html>. Retrieved 18 July 2005.

43. After serving several years in the state legislature, Jim Hill was the State Treasurer from 1993 to 2001. The African-American Legislative Roundtable was formed in 1993 to involve more blacks in the legislative process, bringing together black organizations to discuss legislative issues and their potential impact on minority communities, lobbying state government on issues that concerned the black community, and grooming community members for public service. See Kenneth Terrell, "Pursuing a Place in Power," *Oregonian*, 16 June 1996.

44. Fred DeWolfe, "Portlander John Reed Remembers Lee Sing, His Family's Chinese Servant," *Oregon Historical Quarterly* 97:3 (Fall 1996): 361–364.

45. Daniel P. Johnson, "Anti-Japanese Legislation in Oregon, 1917–1923," *Oregon Historical Quarterly* 97:2 (Summer 1996): 178.

46. Johnson, "Anti-Japanese Legislation;" and "An Oregon Century: Roaring with the 1920s," *Oregonian*, 22 Dec.1999.

47. Mary K. Gayne, "Japanese Americans at the Portland YWCA," *Journal of Women's History* 15:3 (Sept. 2003), retrieved 21 June 2005 from LexisNexis, http://library.willamette.edu:2070.

48. Amy K. Buck, "Alien Land Laws in Oregon, 1923–1949," in "The Japanese American Experience," *Willamette Journal of the Liberal Arts* Supplemental Series 7 (Salem, Oreg.: Willamette University, 2000): 65–73.

49. Peterson del Mar, *Oregon's Promise*, 224.

50. Kim Geron, Enrique de la Cruz, Leland T. Saito, and Jaideep Singh, "Asian Pacific Americans' Social Movements and Interest Groups," *PS: Political Science and Politics* 34:3 (Sept. 2001): 619.

51. "Oregon: Asian Americans, Native Hawaiians, and Pacific Islanders," Association of Asian Pacific Community Health Organizations, retrieved 2 July 2005 from <http://www.aapcho.org/site/aapcho/content.php?type=1&id=9708>.

52. Erasmo Gamboa, "Mexican Mule Packers and Oregon's Second Regiment Mounted Volunteers, 1855–1856," *Oregon Historical Quarterly* 92:1 (Spring 1991): 41.

53. The definitive work on the Bracero program in the PNW is Erasmo Gamboa, *Mexican Labor and World War II: Braceros in the Pacific Northwest, 1942–1947* (Austin: University of Texas Press, 1990).

54. U.S. Census Bureau, American FactFinder, "Profile of General Demographic Characteristics: 2000," retrieved 19 July 2005 from <http://factfinder.census.gov/servlet/QTTable?_bm=y&-geo_id=04000US41&-qr_name=DEC_2000_SF1_U_DP1&-ds_name=DEC_2000_SF1_U&-_lang=en&-redoLog=false&-_sse=on>.

55. Ainoura Oussenbec, "Immigrants in the State and Nation," *Oregon Labor Market Information System*, 7 July 2004, retrieved 5 July 2005 from <http://olmis.emp.state.or.us/olmisj/ArticleReader?itemid=00003753>.

56. Estimates from the U.S. Census Bureau, American Factfinder, "Oregon Selected Social Characteristics: 2003," retrieved 15 July 2005 from <http://factfinder.census.gov/servlet/ADPTable?_bm=y&-geo_id=04000US41&-qr_name=ACS_2003_EST_G00_DP2&-ds_name=ACS_2003_EST_G00_&-redoLog=false&-_scrollToRow=89&-format>.

57. Some "other race" is recorded at 3.1 percent. U.S. Census Bureau, American FactFinder, "Oregon 2003 Community Survey Data Profile Highlights," retrieved 5 July 2005, http://factfinder.census.gov/servlet/ACSSAFFFacts?_event=&geo_id=04000US41&_geoContext=01000US%7C04000US41&_street=&_county=&_cityTown=&_state=04000US41&_zip=&_lang=en&_sse=on&ActiveGeoDiv=&_useEV=&pctxt=fph&pgsl=040. Many observers have long believed that census data undercounts racial and ethnic minorities and so these percentages may be more reliable as expressions of trends than as accurate reflections of current populations.

58. Pei-te Lien, Christian Collet, Janelle Wong and S. Karthick Ramakrishnan, "Asian Pacific-American Public Opinion and Political Participation," *PS: Political Science and Politics* 34:3 (Sept. 2001): 628.

59. Loretta E. Bass and Lynne M. Casper, "Are There differences in Registration and Voting Behavior Between Naturalized and Native-born Americans," Population Division, U.S. Bureau of the Census, Feb. 1999, retrieved 7 July 2005 from <http://www.census.gov/population/www/documentation/twps0028/twps0028.html>.

60. Japanese Americans, for instance, are the only Asian American group in which a majority has been born in the U.S. and they are the most likely to register and to vote. Vietnamese and Korean Americans, more recent immigrant groups, rank consistently among the lowest to register and vote. See Pei-te Lien et al., "Asian Pacific-American Public Opinion" 2001, 625–630.

61. Lien, Collet, Wong and Ramakrishnan, "Asian Pacific-American Public Opinion," 626.

62. Stephen S. Fugita and David J. O'Brien, "Structural Assimilation, Ethnic Group Membership, and Political Participation among Japanese Americans: A Research Note." *Social Forces* 63, no. 4 (June 1985): 986–988.

63. Alex Davis, "Hispanic Vote Surges to the Forefront," *Statesman Journal*, 3 Nov. 2002.

64. The state does not track registration or voting by race or ethnicity. These figures come from the Democratic Party's use of databases of Latino surnames, an admittedly inexact approach to identifying Latinos. See: Angie Chuang, "The State's Latino Voting Draws National Attention," *Oregonian*, 16 Apr. 2005; and "Courting Latino Voters, A Norm, Not Novelty," *Oregonian*, 28 Oct. 2004; Alex Davis, "Oregon Parties Step Up Courting Hispanic Voters," *Statesman Journal*, 3 Nov. 2002; and Gabriela Rico, "Latino Vote is Swinging to Right," *Statesman Journal*, 16 Nov. 2004.

65. At the same time, it must be noted that years after major voting rights laws were passed at the national level, potential threats to the integrity of the process may still remain for minority groups. For example, the Oregon House of Representatives approved a Republican-backed measure in 2005 that would require people registering for the first time to show proof of citizenship. Backers of the measure argued that it would help prevent illegal immigrants from fraudulently registering and voting; opponents argued that there is little or no evidence that such fraud is occurring and that the bill would create needless barriers to voting. See Brad Cain, "Hispanic Group Objects to Voter Bill," *Statesman Journal*, 19 June 2005.

66. See Robert C. Dash, "Latinos, Political Change, and Electoral Mobilization in Oregon," *Latino(a) Research Review* 5:2–3 (Fall/Winter 2003): 16–39.

67. Matt A. Barreto, Gary M. Segura, and Nathan D. Woods, "The Mobilizing Effect of Majority-Minority Districts on Latino Turnout," *American Political Science Review* 98:1 (Feb. 2004): 74.

68. One and one-tenths of a percent of Oregon's local elected officials—city council members, mayors, and county commissioners—are Latinos, 0.8 percent are Native American, and 0.3 percent are African American and Asian American each. Assigning greater weight to larger urban counties with more diverse populations makes the local statistics more representative of the overall population. At the state level, 2.9 percent of elected and appointed are Latino, 3.2 percent are African American, 1.8 percent are Asian American, and 1.9 percent are Native American. See Bradley Basson and Rita Conrad, "Elected and Appointed Officials in Oregon: A Report on Race, Ethnicity and Gender Parity," Oregon Progress Board, July 2002.

69. Grant McConnell, *Private Power and American Democracy* (New York: Random House, 1966), 114. With a colleague, I developed a case study that suggests that McConnell's thesis applies to small government units in Oregon. Towns and small counties are likely to be characterized by a mobilization of bias—established assumptions, procedures and distributions of access and prerogative—that tends to be quite exclusionary and alien to racial and ethnic equality. See the analysis by Robert C. Dash and Robert H. Hawkinson, "Mexicans and 'Business as Usual:' Small Town Politics in Oregon," *Aztlán: A Journal of Chicano Studies* 26:2 (Fall 2001): 87–124.

For a discussion of the concept of the mobilization of bias, see E.E. Schattschneider, *The Semi-Sovereign People: A Realist View of Democracy in America* (New York: Holt, Rinehart and Winston, 1960), 71.

70. Stanford Chen, "In Oregon and Washington, Asian-Americans Join Politics," *Oregonian*, 3 Jan. 1993, retrieved 20 June 2005, <http://library.willamette.edu:2057>.

71. James S. Lai, Wendy K. Tam Cho, Thomas P. Kim and Okiyoshi Takeda, "Asian Pacific-American Campaigns, Elections, and Elected Officials," *PS: Political Science and Politics* 34:3 (Sept. 2001): 611–612. At the same time, AAPI individuals vary greatly by nationality, religion, language, culture, class position, and political ideology. More so than blacks, who are highly Democratic in party orientation and Latinos, who lean Democratic as a group, the AAPI population varies substantially in terms of party identification. As groups, South Asian, Korean, Filipino, and Japanese are more likely than Chinese or Vietnamese to identify as Democratic. Lien, Collet, Wong and Ramakrishnan. "Asian Pacific-American Public Opinion," 629.

72. Margaret Carter from Portland, as a case in point, was the first black woman to win election to the state House of Representatives. She served seven terms, rising in the leadership ranks of the Democratic Party before leaving the legislature to become the chief executive officer of the Portland area National Urban League.

73. Politically influential African Americans, for example, were opposed to the creation of the new 22nd House District that was designed by the Democratic Party in 2000, because it was perceived to negatively affect existing "Black" districts in the Portland area. The redistricting process went forward nonetheless, and this type of political disagreement will grow along with future demographic changes in the state.

BIBLIOGRAPHY

Adams, Nicole. "Getting Out the Vote in Indian Country," *Winds of Change* 20:2 (Spring 2005). Retrieved 16 July 2005, <http://www.wocmag.org/2004/summer/education2.html>.

Anderson, Jaja. "Short History of the Black Panther Party in the Eugene, Oregon Chapter," *It's about Time: Black Panther Party and Alumni*. Retrieved 18 July 2005, http://www.itsabouttimebpp.com/Chapter_History/Eugene_Oregon_Chapter.html>.

Association of Asian Pacific Community Health Organization. "Oregon: Asian Americans, Native Hawaiians, and Pacific Islanders." Retrieved 2 July 2005, http://www.aapcho.org/site/aapcho/content.php?type=1&id=9708>.

Barreto, Matt A., Gary M. Segura, and Nathan D. Woods, "The Mobilizing Effect of Majority-Minority Districts on Latino Turnout," *American Political Science Review* 98, no. 1 (Feb. 2004): 65–75.

Basson, Bradley and Rita Conrad, Oregon Progress Board "Elected and Appointed Officials in Oregon: A Report on Race, Ethnicity and Gender Parity." Salem, July 2002.

Buck, Amy K. "Alien Land Laws in Oregon, 1923–1949." Pp. 65–73 in *The Japanese American Experience*, Supplemental Series 7 of the *Willamette Journal of the Liberal Arts*, edited by Jennifer Jopp. Salem, Oreg.: Willamette University, 2000.

Collins, Cary C. "Through the Lens of Assimilation: Edwin L. Chalcraft and Chemawa Indian School." *Oregon Historical Quarterly* 98, no. 4 (Winter 1997–98): 390–425.

Clucas, Richard A., Mark Henkels, and Brent S. Steel, eds. *Oregon Politics and Government: Progressive versus Conservative Populists*. Lincoln: University of Nebraska Press, 2005.

Compean, Mario. "African Americans in the Columbia River Basin—Historical Overview." Retrieved July 16, 2005 from <http://www.vancouver.wsu.edu/crbeha/aa/aa.htm>.

Dash, Robert C. "Latinos, Political Change, and Electoral Mobilization in Oregon," *Latino(a) Research Review* 5, nos. 2–3 (Fall/Winter 2003): 16–39.

Dash, Robert C. and Robert H. Hawkinson, "Mexicans and 'Business as Usual:' Small Town Politics in Oregon," *Aztlán: A Journal of Chicano Studies* 26, no. 2 (Fall 2001): 87–124.

DeWolfe, Fred. "Portlander John Reed Remembers Lee Sing, His Family's Chinese Servant." *Oregon Historical Quarterly* 97, no. 3 (Fall 1996): 356–371.

End of the Oregon Trail Interpretive Center, "Timeline of Black History in the Pacific Northwest." Retrieved 23 June 2005, <http://www.endoftheoregontrail.org/blaktime.html>.

Evans, Suzanne E. *Encyclopedia of North American Indians*. Retrieved 16 July 2005, <http://college.hmco.com/history/readerscomp/naind/html/na_041800_voting.htm>.

Fugita, Stephen S. and David J. O'Brien. "Structural Assimilation, Ethnic Group Membership and Political Participation Among Japanese Americans: A Research Note." *Social Forces* 63, no. 4 (June 1985): 986–995.

Gamboa, Erasmo. "Mexican Mule Packers and Oregon's Second Regiment Mounted Volunteers, 1855–1856." *Oregon Historical Quarterly* 92, no. 1 (Spring 1991): 41–59.

———. *Mexican Labor and World War II: Braceros in the Pacific Northwest, 1942–1947* (Austin: University of Texas Press, 1990).

Gayne, Mary K. "Japanese Americans at the Portland YWCA." *Journal of Women's History* 15, no. 3 (2003). Retrieved 21 June 2005, <http://library.willamette.edu:2070>.

Geron, Kim, Enrique de la Cruz, Leland T. Saito, and Jaideep Singh. "Asian Pacific Americans' Social Movements and Interest Groups," *PS: Political Science and Politics* 34, no. 3 (Sept. 2001): 619–624.

Haynal, Patrick. "Termination and Tribal Survival: The Klamath Tribes of Oregon." *Oregon Historical Quarterly* 101, no. 3 (Fall 2000): 270–301.

Jackson, Byran O. "The Effects of Racial Group Consciousness on Political Mobilization in American Cities" *Western Political Quarterly* 40, no. 4 (Dec. 1987): 631–646.

Johnson, Daniel P. "Anti-Japanese Legislation in Oregon, 1917–1923." *Oregon Historical Quarterly* 97, no. 2 (Summer 1996): 176–210.

Lai, James S., Wendy K. Tam Cho, Thomas P. Kim and Okiyoshi Takeda. "Asian Pacific-American Campaigns, Elections, and Elected Officials," *PS: Political Science and Politics* 34, no. 3 (Sept. 2001): 611–617.

Lien, Pei-te, Christian Collet, Janelle Wong and S. Karthick Ramakrishnan. "Asian Pacific-American Public Opinion and Political Participation." *PS: Political Science and Politics* 34, no. 3 (Sept. 2001): 625–630.

McConnell, Grant. *Private Power and American Democracy*. New York: Random House, 1966.

McLagan, Elizabeth. *A Peculiar Paradise: a History of Blacks in Oregon, 1788–1940*. Portland: The Georgian Press, 1980.

Nagel, Joane. "American Indian Ethnic Renewal: Politics and the Resurgence of Identity." *American Sociological Review* 60, no. 6 (Dec. 1995): 947–965.

Oussenbec, Ainoura. "Immigrants in the State and Nation," *Oregon Labor Market Information System*, 7 July 2004. Retrieved 5 July 2005, <http://olmis.emp.state.or.us/olmisj/ArticleReader?itemid=00003753>.

Pearson, Rudy. "A Menace to the Neighborhood': Housing and African Americans in Portland, 1941–1945." *Oregon Historical Quarterly* 102, no. 2 (Summer 2001):158–179.

Peterson del Mar, David. *Oregon's Promise: An Interpretive History*. Corvallis: Oregon State University Press, 2003.

Rosenthal, Nicolas G. "Repositioning Indianness: Native American Organizations in Portland, Oregon, 1959–1975." *Pacific Historical Review* 71, no. 3 (Aug. 2002): 415–438.

Schattschneider, E.E. *The Semi-Sovereign People: A Realist View of Democracy in America*. New York: Holt, Rinehart and Winston, 1960.

Smith, Rogers M. "Beyond Tocqueville, Myrdal, and Hartz: The Multiple Traditions in America." *American Political Science Review* 87, no. 3 (Sept.1993): 549–566.

Taylor, Quintard. "The Emergence of Black Communities in the Pacific Northwest: 1865–1910." *The Journal of Negro History* 64, no. 4 (Autumn 1979): 342–354.

Zucker, Jeff, Kay Hummel, and Bob Hogfoss. *Oregon Indians: Culture, History, and Current Affairs: An Atlas and Introduction*. Portland: The Press of the Oregon Historical Society, 1983.

Newspapers

The Christian Science Monitor
Los Angeles Times
Oregonian (Portland)
Statesman Journal (Salem)

Chapter Thirteen

"Made on the Inside," Destruction on the Outside: Race, Oregon and the Prison Industrial Complex

David J. Leonard and Jessica Hulst

In the midst of a state budget crisis that has led to hospital closures, shorter school years, and a systematic gutting of the social welfare system, the Oregon prison system has actually grown. Given the political importance, if not necessity, of appearing strong on crime and punishment, and the economic profitability of a prison system, this development is not surprising. Yet, Benjamin D. de Haan, the state's interim director of the Department of Corrections, requested that the legislature agree to close five prisons and release 3,000 prisoners because of a potential budget shortfall. Thanks to thirty years of anti-crime, pro-prison legislation, Oregon's prisons are bursting at the seams. In 1994, Ballot Measure 11 resulted in stiffer sentences that lengthened the average prison stay to 40 months from 16 months. As of 2003, the state now incarcerates 12,000 prisoners, costing $500 million a year. "We're building prisons as quickly as possible, but we can't keep up," Dr. de Haan said. "We're going to have to contract for beds in county jails and just crowd them into existing institutions."[1] Despite requests and the budget crisis, Ted Kulongoski, the 2002 elected Democratic governor of Oregon, rejected this proposal; instead, he increased the budget of the prison system, choosing to expand the prison industrial complex over social welfare and community empowerment.

While exploring the racialized consequences of the prison industrial complex through the history of Oregon, we examine four particular issues concerning the Oregon prison system within this chapter: (1) We document the economic and political contexts that have given rise to a system of mass incarceration within Oregon, providing a historical foundation for our examination of the impact of Oregon's prison industrial complex on its communities of color. (2) We discuss the complex nature of the Oregon prison system, what is known as the prison industrial complex. Whether through chronicling the Federal Omnibus Crime Control and Safe Streets Act of 1968, which provided federal dollars to "clean up" the streets of Portland, or Ballot Measure 11 (1994), which mandated longer prison sentences, it is crucial to understand the historical context and mechanism that propelled a movement of mass incarceration throughout Oregon. While Oregon does not currently operate private prisons (although a movement for such a practice continues to grow), it is crucial to comprehend the economic contexts (interests) associated with a prison system that increasingly relies on private prisons and benefits economically from prison labor, especially given the passage of Measure 49. The passage of Measure 49 in 1997 required all eligible Oregon inmates to work, and it also required that business partnerships were formed between Oregon's corrections department and private corporations. (3) This chapter specifically interrogates the history of the prison industrial complex within Oregon, illustrating how policy shifts and state initiatives have resulted in a drastic increase in the state's prison population. With this in mind, we focus our attention on the impact of the prison industrial complex on communities of color. In terms of both disproportionate levels of incarceration and the corresponding effects on families/communities of color and the under-funding of public services, Oregon's system of mass incarceration has historically been detrimental to communities of color. (4) We will also examine the function of the criminal justice system, its unequal application through recent Oregon history, and the connections between fear, capitalism, race and institutions of policing. Rather than only focusing our attention on processes of subjugation, we will equally examine local and statewide responses to the prison industrial complex, especially efforts emanating from communities of color. This brief examination of the prison industrial complex offers a framework for interrogating the interplay between race, class, gender and capitalist accumulation in Oregon.

THE PRISON INDUSTRIAL COMPLEX

In the 1970s, Angela Davis formulated the idea of the prison industrial complex (PIC) to describe the growth of the prison industry. She describes the prison industrial complex (PIC) as "a complicated system situated at the intersection of governmental and private interests that uses prisons as a solution to social, political, and economic problems . . . It includes human rights violations, the death penalty, industry and labor issues, policing, courts, media, community powerlessness, the imprisonment of political prisoners, and the elimination of dissent."[2] The United States spends roughly forty billion dollars annually on maintaining its prisons, and close to one hundred billion each year to support the entire criminal justice system. Between 1971 and 1992, government spending on prisons increased from 2.3 billion dollars to 31.2 billion. In 1995 alone, money allocated for university construction dropped by $954 million, while expenditures for prison construction jumped by $926 million dollars.[3] In 1996 alone, construction began on twenty-six federal prisons and ninety-six state prisons throughout the U.S.[4]

Within such an environment, where excess money is funneled away from social services to institutions of social control, and where notions of criminality are linked to racial signs, black youth have suffered significantly. The shifting emphasis on building and populating prisons has resulted in a massive increase in prison populations, especially black and Latino males. Between 1970 (prison population, 200,000) and 2000 (2,000,000), America's prison population has increased five hundred percent, as opposed to a forty-five percent increase in its overall population. "There are currently more than 50 million criminal records on file in the U.S., with at least 4 to 5 million 'new' adults acquiring such a record annually. This record sticks with a person, whether or not charges are dropped, or if there is subsequent conviction."[5] As of 2000, the total number of men and women behind bars, on parole, and on probation, had reached 6.3 million, more than three percent of the adult population.

The systematic incarceration of millions of Americans over the last thirty years has not been a universal phenomenon; rather the brunt of the system's force has come down on communities of color. At the brink of the twenty-first century, close to 3,500 black men for every 100,000 were behind bars.[6] In 1990, the Washington D.C.-based Sentencing Project concluded that on a given day in the United States, one out of four black men between the ages of 20 and 29 was either in jail, prison, or on probation/parole.[7] In 1992, the National Center on Institutions and Alternatives released a study on African Americans in Washington D.C. It concluded that on any day in 1991, 42% (4 in 10) of all black males between the ages of 18 and 35 living in the District of Columbia were in jail, in prison, on probation/parole, out on bond or facing an arrest warrant. Similar numbers were found in Baltimore, where 56% of young black men were in prison or otherwise connected to the criminal justice system.[8]

According to the Prison Policy Initiative, the Bureau of Justice, and the Sentencing Project (2004), Latinos, Native Americans and Blacks are all over-represented within Oregon's prison population. For instance, Latinos contribute 8% of Oregon's population, but they amass 11% of its prisoner population; Native Americans face a similar situation, accounting for slightly over 1% of the state's citizenry, yet they represent almost 4% of those locked up within Oregon's prisons. The predicament facing African Americans is even more revealing, as their rates of incarceration exceed national averages (which are already reflective of the Jim Crow conditions in today's prison system). According to one source, "Oregon is one of the lily-whitest states in the nation, and the percentage of its African American population behind bars is even worse than the national average."[9] For example, blacks account for only 1.6% of the state's population, yet they make up 11.1% of the state's prison population. In fact, while 458 of every 100,000 whites are behind bars in Oregon, and 645 of every 100,000 Latino Oregonians are locked up, the number is 2,763 per 100,000 for African Americans. The efforts to criminalize and incarcerate disproportionate numbers of people of color reflect myriad factors that result from inequity within every step of the criminal justice system. National studies, and those specific to Oregon, reveal the impact of racial profiling and target patrols within communities of color as factors that facilitate disproportionate incarceration of individuals from communities of color. Rates of arrest, prosecution, conviction and incarceration, as well as those of probation and parole, further contribute to the existence of Jim Crow conditions in both prisons and the practices beyond prisons that form part of the prison industrial complex. Sewell observes that "The PIC is a part of the colonization process of people of color in the US. . . . The PIC works hand in hand with the processes of gentrification and policing. When wealthier, whiter[10] people and their unaffordable new businesses feel welcome to move in, so do the police to protect them. Gentrification displaces residents by taking their neighborhoods and space and turning it into a white-centric space using the threat of the police and imprisonment against people of color."[11] Whether because of racial profiling induced by gentrification or prosecution resulting from racial stigmas and policy shifts, the last fifteen years has seen the increasing probability that people of color will serve life sentences, facing mass incarceration inside Oregon's most profitable new plantation: the Oregon prison system.

Additionally, over the last decade and a half, Oregon has increasingly spent disproportionate levels of tax dollars on incarceration, leaving the state tills virtually empty. Governor John Kitzhaber, spoke of the shifting priorities within Oregon in 1996: "School districts will cut hundreds of teachers, we will be hiring 1,000 new prison guards. So we won't be teaching your kids, but we'll be guarding them well."[12] The rise of the PIC inside Oregon has also corresponded with increased levels of gentrification, declining school and health care budgets and a shrinking welfare system, all of which impact communities of color inside Oregon in deleterious ways.

OREGON GETS TOUGH ON CRIME

Between 1991 and 1994, coverage of violent crime in the media increased tenfold, with the number of articles in *The New York Times* doubling and network television coverage tripling over this time period. In each medium, the coverage not only amplified a crisis of law and order in America, but also generated fear, by painting the crime problem as one pertaining to people of color. While Oregon did not have a Willie Horton, Nushawn Williams, or Central Park Jogger to generate racialized fear toward the enactment of strict crime and punishment policies, the racialized national discourse that reduced crime to "dangerous thugs of color"—thereby garnering support for more prisons and police—affected the state's support for Measure 11 and a number of other initiatives.

In 1994, almost 70% of voters approved Measure 11, which dramatically changed sentencing guidelines and the overall operation of Oregon's prison system. In an effort to get tough on crime by sending a message to would-be criminals (and enact policy that would reduce crime), Oregon voters were eager to pass a measure that would lead to longer sentences for twenty-one crimes. Specifically, it set minimum sentences for the most serious crimes, including robbery, assault, kidnapping, rape, manslaughter, attempted murder and other "violent crimes." The initial text of the statute read as follows:

> The measure would set mandatory sentences for listed felonies. A court could impose a longer sentence if allowed by law. The measure would bar early release, leave, or a reduced sentence for any reason. It would cover murder and listed forms of manslaughter, assault, kidnapping, rape, sodomy, unlawful sexual penetration, sexual abuse, robbery. All persons 15 and up when charged with these crimes would have to be tried as adults. It would apply to crimes committed on or after April 1, 1995.

Capitalizing on the racialized fear so prevalent in the national political discourse, and the efforts of supporters within Oregon to generate additional fear through statistics, voters were sold on the idea that "1 crime [occurs] against a person every 9.9 minutes," with homicides happening every two days and rapes as often as every 6 hours.[13] More than simply focusing on numbers, proponents played on longstanding representations of crime threatening Oregon's white children, with numerous stories appearing about the murders of young white girls, many of them involving perpetrators of color.[14]

The support for this measure cannot be understood outside the localized and national context in which Willie Horton, and countless unknown men of color, signified a danger warranting tough-on-crime measures. The prominent narrative used to garner support for Measure 11 reflected the centrality of racial appeals to the ongoing support for the policy. Ronita Sutton testified before an Oregon House Subcommittee on Crime and Law during an April 26, 2001 session, at which she expressed opposition to HB 3934, legislation proposed by Governor Kitzhaber, which would have significantly weakened Measure 11. "My son Christopher Sutton was murdered in '98. Excuse me, this can be a little difficult sometimes. He had just graduated from high school. But three weeks before leaving for college, a gang member mistakenly identified a car he thought belonged to a rival gang member and started shooting into it and shot and killed my son."[15] References to gang members and inner city community represented an implicit racial appeal, as did the ubiquitous commentaries about the relationship between poverty, parenting and crime, all of which played on the longstanding rhetoric regarding crime being a derivative of a culture of poverty. "While these criminals and their enablers are crying for a 'second chance,' they've already had multiple chances. Good citizens don't get themselves into the situation of being convicted of crimes, and good parents don't let their kids fall into that lifestyle."[16] In the end, voters overwhelming bought into the idea of reducing crime through increased incarceration, facilitating the growth of Oregon's prison system. They bought into the idea that Measure 11 would result in safer streets and that it would "bring back the idea that the criminal justice system means justice for all—not just the criminal, but the victim and society."[17]

THE NEW SLAVERY

As early as the 1970s, Supreme Court Justice Warren Berger called upon the state to turn prisons into "factories with fences."[18] In recent years, Senator Phil Gram announced that he wants "to turn every federal prison into a mini industrial park."[19] While prison labor is nothing new, dating back to the days of indentured servants, slavery and chain gangs, the advance of the prison industrial complex has ushered in an era of greater reliance on and profitability in the exploitation of prison labor. Companies using prison labor or reaping prison profits include: Boeing, IBM, American Express, Compaq, Honeywell, Motorola, WSU, Revlon, Pierre Cardin, G.E., NIKE and TWA. Extrark offers a sizable cheap labor source, providing prisoners to Microsoft, Starbucks, JanSport, and US West for packaging and "literature assembly." Eddie Bauer and Victoria's Secret, who pay prisoners 23 cents an hour, utilize prisoner labor for packaging and manufacturing purposes. "Given all this hard work going on in the big house it would appear that America's 1.8 million prisoners are becoming a Third World within, a cheap and bountiful labor reservoir already being tapped by big business and Uncle Sam alike."[20]

The rise of the prison industrial complex is not purely a result of corporate greed and its effort to secure cheap labor and profit from others' misery, but a manifestation of the 1970s economic downturn. Beginning in the 1970s and continuing through the 1990s, America's multinational corporations moved manufacturing plants overseas and into less populated suburbs. The movement of jobs from already depressed black communities left many black families in dire straights. A 1982 report, authored by the California legislature, concluded that South Central Los Angeles neighborhoods experienced a fifty percent rise in unemployment, and a significant drop in purchasing power in the wake of deindustrialization.[21] In a mere three years, the median income for black families had dropped by $2,500 to about $5,900 dollars yearly.[22] In 1985, Midwestern cities experienced unemployment rates of fifty to seventy percent for black teenagers.[23] The increased profits, the ease of relocation, and the examples set by other U.S. companies left inner city blacks, especially youth, without many options.

By the mid 1980s, U.S. companies extensively relied on offshore production, primarily exploiting women of color to produce their goods abroad at minimal cost.[24] An amazing eighty percent of U.S. companies' revenues resulted from production outside of the United States.[25] Technological changes, in terms of improvements in satellites, communication (fax, e-mail) and transportation, facilitated companies' abilities to produce goods overseas without moving offices from the U.S.[26] Additionally, the United States government enabled this process, enticing U.S. corporations with trade agreements (NAFTA) and tax-breaks. This overseas move is to the advantage of the corporations and the U.S., and to the disadvantage of working-class communities in the United States and those nations who were subjected to these neo-colonial practices.

In the wake of the systematic exportation of jobs overseas, and the continued gutting of social services, those from urban communities of color increasingly represented a surplus population within capitalist America. A series of structural adjustment programs (free trade; SAPS, free enterprise sounds; shrinking funding of social programs and education), which sought to stave off the economic downturns of the late 1960s and 1970s, left huge segments of America's population without an economic future. Such structural changes not only resulted in plant closures, a gutting of social programs, an increased number of part-time jobs and horrible working conditions, but also facilitated a heightened level of state violence and control. Beginning in the 1970s up to the present, there has been a dramatic increase in both state support of the criminal justice system and the number of black youth spending part or all of their life in jail.

FINALLY, A SLAVE STATE: OREGON AND PRISON LABOR

In 1997, Oregon voters passed Measure 49. The passage of this measure put an end to a yearlong dispute over the differences in federal and state minimum wage laws concerning prison labor. Measure 49 mandated that the Oregon Department of Corrections put to work all physically and psychologically eligible inmates. Measure 49 built on precedent set by Measure 17, which was passed in 1994. Measure 17 mandated that "all prisoners must work 40 hours per week, and requires the state to pro-actively market prison labor to private employers."[27] Not only did Measures 17 and 49 require eligible inmates to work, they required the Oregon Department of Corrections to do so "in a business-like manner and enable the development of partnerships with the private sector."[28] As a result, the Array Corporation "entered a joint venture with the Oregon Department of Corrections to market and operate Prison Blues."[29]

Prison Blues was not new to Oregon inmates when Measures 17 and 49 were passed. This operation was originally established by Inside Oregon Enterprises, a division of the Oregon Department of Corrections. It manufactures jeans, coats and shirts that are worn both inside and outside the prison walls. Prison Blues has become popular both in the states and internationally, resulting in "more work opportunities for more inmates to work in the factory making our authentic, prison-made blue jean brand."[30]

Prison Blues' motto is "made on the inside, to be worn on the outside." The company's catchphrase is more than simply that: it is indicative of the relationship between prison labor and the private corporate sector of the U.S. and is one of the greatest social injustices taking place within our borders—the colonization of a socioeconomically marginalized population for the purpose of profits for those "on the outside." Despite promising economic, ethical and social benefits to inmates participating in the prison labor industry, in actuality, Prison Blues serves as a model for how corporate America has invaded America's criminal (in)justice system

The Prison Blues factory is housed "on the inside" of the Eastern Oregon Correctional Institution in Pendleton, Oregon, a medium security prison, housing about 1,500 inmates.[31] The factory is staffed primarily by private sector employees in cooperation with state correctional officers who oversee about 50 factory employees. The Prison Blues informational material, available on its website, proclaims that while taking tighter security issues into consideration, the factory mirrors the industry standards practiced "on the outside." Despite the violent and oppressive realities evident within a medium security institution, Prison Blues' management maintains that it provides an environment that is "bright and energetic, designed to maximize productivity, and most of the workers appreciate the time they can spend at work."[32] Requests for first-hand observation of the "bright and energetic" factory were denied due to security concerns, but one must wonder how many workers truly "appreciate the time they can spend at work." If employment is mandated by state law for every eligible inmate, it begs the question: what has prison, punishment and rehabilitation come to mean in the state of Oregon?

Prison labor in the U.S. serves multiple purposes, not just simply offering inmates who may otherwise be bored or suffering from cabin fever, something to do for eight hours per day. In Oregon, prison labor is not even an option for inmates: Measures 17 and 49, in reality, took away the choice to work or not away from inmates, turning Oregon prisons into a modern-day "Prison Slaveocracy."[33] Eligible-to-work inmates in Eastern Oregon Correctional Institution work because of the voter-imposed laws of the 1990s.[34] The private sector utilizes prison labor because it is a surplus population "ripe for the picking;" a community marginalized by capitalism "on the outside" is now forced to serve those very same interests "on the inside."

Proponents of the prison industrial complex argue that inmate labor is meant for the benefit of the inmates if, or when, they are released back into society. "Inmates who stay in the program throughout their incarceration will reenter the outside world with new found job skills and a work ethic."[35] There are two problematic issues evident within statements such as these. First, inmates, through their experiences working in the Prison Blues factory, may learn skills that they did not have previous to their incarceration. That is a reasonable claim. However, in an economy that is vastly and inexorably globalizing in many spheres, there is little demand for skilled garment workers in the U.S. in the 21st century. According to Gordon Lafer, "[P]risoners who do pick up skills often are being trained in jobs that do not exist, or do not pay living wages, in the free economy." He continues, "[S]ince the garment industry has moved almost all production out of the country in favor of lower-wage workers in the developing world, Oregonians leaving prison cannot expect to find family-wage jobs sewing blue jeans."[36] Second, proponents of the Prison Blues factory who claim that prisoners lack a "work ethic," as does the author of the Prison Blues website, make the assumption that all people in prison are lazy. The economy plays an integral part in the prison industrial complex. A rapidly globalizing economy has meant the loss of many American jobs to overseas companies and contractors who can find surplus populations that will work for cheap. It isn't necessarily about poor work ethic or laziness, but the absence of high-wage earning jobs, to which the P.I.C has contributed over the last thirty years. The loss of stateside jobs, then, directly perpetuates both the cycle of poverty and the prison industrial complex.

When the economy goes into recession, the supply of decently paid jobs will shrink; more and more working class people will fall into poverty, and some number of these will engage in nonviolent crime (shoplifting, writing bad checks, drug possession) as a way of getting through. Those arrested will be incarcerated for long sentences and put to work for private companies, where their labor will serve to eliminate many more decently paying jobs on the outside, thus reproducing the cycle.[37]

While Prison Blues employees are not necessarily taking decently paid jobs away from those in the free world, they are still very much a part of the system of reproducing poverty and inequality.

It is questionable that what Prison Blues employees "gain" in the factory can in actuality be considered to their personal benefit. The years in between the passage of Measure 17 and 49 were characterized by a work stoppage in Oregon prison factories. Once Measure 17 established that it was required that all eligible inmates work a full-time job on the inside to "work at least as hard as the taxpayers who provide for their care,"[38] governmental officials, along with their corporate partners, had to decide what to pay prison laborers. Measure 49 ended a year-long debate over conflicting state and federal wage laws, resulting in the establishment of the "prevailing industry wages" of $6.68 to "well over $8.00 per hour."[39] While the Prison Blues website touts the existence of the "prevailing industry wages," presumably a major benefit of prison labor systems, further exploration on this particular site reveals the reality of inmate wages: "Inmates pay their own way with their earnings. Eighty percent is withheld from their earnings by the state of Oregon to pay for their incarceration costs, victim restitution, family support, and state and federal wage taxes."[40] The author continues, "The 20% left can be used for voluntary family support, to pay for continued education, buy items at the prison canteen or deposit in a savings account."[41] Working out the math of an inmate's "take home" pay, 20% of the base pay of $6.68 an hour is $1.34 an hour. For an eight-hour day, the pay is $10.69. A forty-hour week brings in $53.44. This is not much if an inmate wishes to fulfill the desires of family support and continued education—such a pay check would not come close to supplementing an income available on the outside (minimum wage), let alone the luxury of furthering one's education. Not only is the monetary compensation for hard, forced labor minimal for inmates, the benefits are non-existent. Prison employers:

> pay no health insurance, no unemployment insurance, no payroll or social security taxes, and no workers' compensation; they pay no vacation time, sick leave, or overtime. Prison workers can be "hired," fired, or reassigned at will. Not only do they have no right to organize or strike; they also have no means of filing a grievance or indeed of voicing any kind of complaint whatsoever: for example, they have no right to circulate an employee petition or newsletter, no right to call a meeting, and no access to the press.[42]

If the goal is to have inmates work as hard as tax-paying citizens once re-leased on "the outside," to support the cost of their incarceration, should they not also be honestly paid the wages of hard-working free[43] citizens? And if prison inmates are expected to work just as those who work in factories, mills and in malls towards the same goals (family support, higher education, accu-mulation of capital, etc.), should they not also reap the benefits of that labor, having access to health care and unemployment benefits? And if they are working "at least as hard as the taxpayers who provide for their care" (addi-tionally, consider the fact that 80% of each inmate's wages is withheld for in-carceration costs), should they not also have access to their First Amendment rights to assembly, press and free speech? If the inmate employees at Prison Blues are expected to "walk the walk" of unincarcerated citizens, then it should follow that the state of Oregon do more than "talk the talk."

CONCLUSION

The following editorial captures the recent history of the prison industrial complex in Oregon, with its increased reliance on punishment over rehabili-tation, on using prisons as a source of profit through growing industry and its utilization of cheap prison labor.

> Kevin Mannix's vision for using the setting of new prisons to develop new pop-ulation centers sounds like a model for a police state where our economic well-being would depend on prisons and prisoners. Businesses would spring up to provide services to prisoners, and colleges would develop to educate prison guards, police and probation officers. Prison labor would be used to build and maintain the communities so that all could be constructed at lower cost.
>
> Can this sick and twisted view of the world really be Oregon's future? Why do we need prisons to locate decent schools, transportation and medical facili-ties in Oregon communities? Why do we need prisons to practice good land-use planning? And why not offer community development jobs at living wages to people living in the community?
>
> True, with the passage of Measure 11 and Measure 17 (both sponsored by Mannix in 1994) we have at our disposal an unending supply of inmates who will serve long sentences without possibility of parole (Measure 11) and who must work while in prison (Measure 17). Never mind that they are paid wages well below the minimum and they have no work-safety regulations, sick time or any other benefits . . .
>
> I believe that our prisons should be located in plain sight in the communities near where prisoners (used to) live. Prisoners need the support of family and friends if they are to successfully reintegrate themselves back into society.
>
> Lorraine Heller, Southwest Portland

What is missing from this editorial's analysis is how the history of the prison industrial complex intersects with the persistence of white supremacist discourses and practices inside and outside of Oregon. The effort to mobilize support for "tough-on-crime" movements, resulting in longer sentences, more prisons, and mandates on prisoners working, benefited from implicit, and sometimes explicit, racial appeals. The resulting system impacts communities of color in particularly destructive ways. To begin with, it reduces support for state institutions, such as education, welfare, health care, and housing. And it moves people of color into Oregon's newest industrial plantations. In facilitating the on-going destruction of communities of color, and creating a perpetually incarcerated slave-like labor class of disproportionate numbers of people of color, Oregon's prison system is not "sick and twisted." It is rather a capitalistic endeavor guided by and reflective of white supremacist state violence.

NOTES

1. <http://www.mapinc.org/newscecj/v03/n090/a01.htm>
2. http://www.criticalresistance.org/index.php?name=materials#whatcr>
3. Angela Davis, "Masked Racism: Reflections on the Prison Industrial Complex," *Colorlines* (Fall 1998).
4. Christian Parenti, *Lockdown America: Police and Prisons in an Era of Crisis* (New York: Verso Publishers, 2000), 213.
5. Jerome G. Miller, *Search and Destroy: African American Males in the Criminal Justice System* (New York: Cambridge University Press, 1996), 7.
6. Allen Beck and Page Harrison, United States Department of Justice, Bureau of Justice Statistics, Prisoners in 2000, 11, table 15.
7. Miller, *Search and Destroy*, 7.
8. Miller, *Search and Destroy*, 7–8.
9. Abby Sewell, "Books Behind Bars," *Clamor Magazine* 30, (Jan./Feb. 2005), retrieved 10 July 2004. <http://www.clamormagazine.org/issues/30/media.shtml>.
10. The author seems to use the term whiter to describe white people and people of color with connections and money.
11. Sewell, "Books Behind Bars."
12. Oregon Mandatory Minimum Sentencing Law: Measure 11, retrieved 1-July 2004, <http://www.angelfire.com/ms/oregonmeasure11>.
13. Measure 11 Arguments, retrieved 10 July 2004, <http://www.crimevictimsunited .oreg/measure11/measure11arguments.htm>.
14. Sewell, "Books Behind Bars"; a search of articles and editorials surrounding Measure 11 further illustrates this point.
15. Ronita Sutton, "Testimony before Oregon House Subcommittee on Crime and Law." 26 April 2001. Retrieved 10 July 2004, <http://crimevictimsunited.org/ measure11/lettersstatements.htm#sutton1>,

16. This letter from Robert Blacksmith appeared in *The Oregonian*, 10 Feb. 2000.

17. Measure 11 Arguments, <http://www.crimevictimsunited.org/measure11/measure 11arguments.htm>.

18. Parenti, *Lockdown America*, 230.

19. Parenti, *Lockdown America*, 230.

20. Parenti, *Lockdown America*, 231.

21. Robin Kelley, "Kickin' Reality, Kickin' Ballistics," in *Race Rebels: Culture, Politics and the Black Working Class* (New York: The Free Press, 1994), 192.

22. Kelley, "Kickin' Reality, Kickin' Ballistics," 192.

23. Robin Kelley, "Playing for Keeps: Pleasure and Profit on the Postindustrial Playground," in *The House that Race Built*, ed. Waheema Lubiana (New York: Vintage Books, 1998), 198.

24. Walter Lafeber, *Michael Jordan and the New Global Capitalism* (New York: W.W. Norton & Company, 1999), 55.

25. Lafeber, *Michael Jordan and the New Global Capitalism*, 55.

26. Home of Nike.

27. Gordon Lafer, "The Politics of Prison Labor: A Union Perspective." In *Prison Nation: Class, Courts and Convicts*, ed. Tara Herivel and Paul Wright, (New York: Routledge, 2002), 120.

28. Prison Blues website. Retrieved 10 July 2004, <http://www.prisonblues.com/ qa.php

29. Prison Blues website. Retrieved 10 July 2004

30. Prison Blues website. Retrieved 10 July 2004

31. Prison Blues website. Retrieved 10 July 2004

32. Prison Blues website. Retrieved 10 July 2004

33. Dan Pens, "Oregon's Prison Slaveocracy," Corp Watch, May 1, 1998, retrieved 10 July 2004. <http://www.corpwatch.org/article.php?id=857>.

34. Only a small segment of Oregon's prison population, because of the nature of their crime or short length of sentence, is exempt from working.

35. Prison Blues website. Retrieved 10 July 2004

36. Lafer, "The Politics of Prison Labor," 125.

37. Prison Blues website. Retrieved 10 July 2004

38. Prison Blues website. Retrieved 10 July 2004

39. Prison Blues website. Retrieved 10 July 2004

40. Prison Blues website. Retrieved 10 July 2004

411. Prison Blues website Retrieved 10 July 2004

42. Lafer, "The Politics of Prison Labor," 122.

43. Throughout the paper, we use the term of "free" as a way to distinguish between those incarcerated and those living outside the Oregon prison walls.

Appendix A

Ethnic Minorities in Oregon: an Annotated Bibliography

Richenda Wilkinson

There is a significant disparity in the representation of Oregon's various ethnic groups in the published literature. For example, the histories of Oregon's Native Americans and Japanese Americans are much better documented than those of any other groups. For the sake of brevity, it was necessary to be more selective when recommending resources pertaining to these two ethnic groups. On the other hand, this bibliography's section on Oregon's Hispanic Americans is much more inclusive due to the striking lack of publications on the subject.

This bibliography focuses on works that will provide the reader with supplemental resources on the history of ethnic minorities in Oregon. An effort has been made to highlight materials that are particularly appropriate for use in teaching students of various ages. The featured resources address all historical time periods, but books based primarily upon archaeological research have not been included. In addition, works that provide a broader historical overview of the experience of ethnic minorities in Oregon were preferred to those sources that focused more narrowly upon the story of an individual or a particular event.

The works included in this bibliography were selected for their accessibility to the general reader. For this reason, dissertations and other unpublished works were not included, even when they offered the best or only coverage of a specific subject. However, information on relevant digital collections and primary source repositories has been provided to encourage readers to explore the vital, but often underutilized, resources to which they provide access.

I would like to thank my colleagues at the OSU Libraries for their help with this bibliography. I would also like to thank Patricia A. Gwartney for her suggestions. You may contact Dr. Gwartney at the University of Oregon for a list of videos related to the social demography of race and ethnicity in Oregon.

AFRICAN AMERICANS

Books and Articles

Little, William A., et al. *Blacks in Oregon : A Statistical and Historical Report.* Portland: Black Studies Center and Center for Population Research and Census, Portland State University, 1978. Includes history from 1788–1950 and demographic information from 1890–1970, as well as somewhat outdated information on the education of African Americans in Oregon.

McClintock, Thomas C. "James Saules, Peter Burnett, and the Oregon Black Exclusion Law of June 1844." *Pacific Northwest Quarterly* 86.3 (1995): 121–30. Examines the events leading up to the passage of the law excluding blacks from settling in Oregon Territory, attempting to provide possible reasons for the law's passage.

McElderry, Stuart. "Building a West Coast Ghetto: African-American Housing in Portland, 1910–1960." *Pacific Northwest Quarterly* 92.3 (2001): 137–48. Describes the housing situation for African Americans, especially in the fifties when discrimination and housing policies proved insurmountable for civil rights activists attempting to improve the situation.

McLagan, Elizabeth, and Oregon Black History Project. *A Peculiar Paradise: A History of Blacks in Oregon, 1788–1940.* 1st ed. Portland, Or: Georgian Press, 1980. The only comprehensive publication on the history of African Americans in the state of Oregon. Based, in part, upon oral history interviews conducted by the author.

Pearson, Rudy. "A Menace to the Neighborhood": Housing and African Americans in Portland, 1941–1945." *Oregon Historical Quarterly* 102.2 (2001): 158–79. Details housing discrimination against African Americans who migrated to Portland during World War II, focusing on the actions of the Housing Authority of Portland.

Portland (Or.), and Bureau of Planning. *History of Portland's African American Community (1805–to the Present).* Portland, Oreg: Portland Bureau of Planning, 1993. Includes historical information on political and social activities, employment, neighborhoods, and discrimination.

Richard, K. Keith. "Unwelcome Settlers: Black and Mulatto Oregon Pioneers, Part I." *Oregon Historical Quarterly* 84.1 (1983): 29–55.

———. "Unwelcome Settlers: Black and Mulatto Oregon Pioneers, Part II." *Oregon Historical Quarterly* 84.2 (1983): 172–205. Along with the previous article, discusses the political, social and economic climate for Oregon's African Americans, especially during the 1800s. Focuses on the Portland area, where most African Americans lived. Includes charts with demographic information.

Smith, Alonzo, and Quintard Taylor. "Racial Discrimination in the Workplace: A Study of Two West Coast Cities during the 1940s." *Journal of Ethnic Studies* 8.1 (1980): 35–54. Examines the efforts of African American shipyard workers in Portland and Los Angeles in their struggle to combat the discriminatory practices of the segregated union that they were forced to join.

Stroud, Ellen. "Troubled Waters in Ecotopia: Environmental Racism in Portland, Oregon." *Radical History Review* 74 (1999): 65–95. Traces the history of toxic pollution in the Columbia River Slough, which environmentalists and city planners sacrificed as a "natural industrial site" despite the health risks to the large African American and immigrant population living along its banks.

Taylor, Quintard. "The Great Migration: The Afro-American Communities of Seattle and Portland during the 1940s." *Arizona and the West* 23.2 (1981): 109–26. Discusses the large increase in the African American population in these cities and the resulting social changes, including racial tensions and housing problems, as well as increased civil rights activism and anti-discrimination laws.

——. "Slaves and Free Men: Blacks in the Oregon Country, 1840–1860." *Oregon Historical Quarterly* 83.2 (1982): 153–70. Documents the conditions that African Americans experienced in Oregon Territory's early days, detailing the existence of slaves in Oregon despite early laws banning slavery and the settlement of free blacks.

Toll, William. "Black Families and Migration to a Multiracial Society: Portland, Oregon, 1900–1924." *Journal of American Ethnic History* 17.3 (1998): 38–70. Examines the formation of a family-based African American community in Portland in the early twentieth century. Argues that the migration of African Americans in this period led to relatively less racial strife than in other cities.

Videos

Local Color. Dir. Tuttle, Jon, Oregon Public Broadcasting, and Oregon Historical Society. One videocassette (58 min.). Oregon Public Broadcasting, 1990. Portrays the racism and discrimination experienced by Portland's African American community before the 1940s.

ASIAN AMERICANS AND PACIFIC ISLANDERS

Books and Articles

Allerfeldt, Kristofer. "Race and Restriction: Anti-Asian Immigration Pressures in the Pacific North-West of America during the Progressive Era, 1885–1924." *History [Great Britain]* 88.1 (2003): 53–73. Explores the role that Oregon and Washington played in the anti-Chinese and anti-Japanese movements of the period, including the agitation by the Knights of Labor in those states.

Azuma, Eiichiro. "A History of Oregon's Issei, 1880–1952." *Oregon Historical Quarterly 1993* 94.4 (1994): 315–67. An overview of the experience of first-generation Japanese immigrants. Includes many photographs. Part of a special OHQ issue on *The Japanese in Oregon*.

Chiu, Herman B. "Power of the Press: How Newspapers in Four Communities Erased Thousands of Chinese from Oregon History." *American Journalism* 16.1 (1999): 59–77. Documents the almost total lack of newspaper coverage of Chinese residents, even in cities with almost fifty percent Chinese population. When the newspapers did mention the Chinese, they did not publish names but instead referred to them with racist insults.

Corbett, P. Scott, and Nancy Parker Corbett. "The Chinese in Oregon, C. 1870–1880." *Oregon Historical Quarterly* 78.1 (1977): 73–85. A demographic analysis of Oregon's early Chinese community.

Duncan, Janice K. "Kanaka World Travelers and Fur Company Employees, 1785–1860." *Hawaiian Journal of History* 7 (1973): 93–111. Tells of Hawaiian Islanders in the early history of Oregon country, especially their employment with the Hudson Bay Company headquartered in Astoria.

Eisenberg, Ellen. "As Truly American as Your Son": Voicing Opposition to Internment in Three West Coast Cities." *Oregon Historical Quarterly* 104.4 (2003): 542–65. Compares opposition to Japanese internment in Portland, Seattle and Los Angeles. Examines the reasons behind a lack of opposition in Portland relative to the much more vocal opposition in the other two cities.

Ho, Nelson Chia-chi. *Portland's Chinatown: The History of an Urban Ethnic District*. Portland, Oreg.: Bureau of Planning, City of Portland, 1978. A brief history of the Chinese community and its organizations, including many historical photographs and a section on the Japanese in Portland.

Inada, Lawson Fusao, et al. *In this Great Land of Freedom: The Japanese Pioneers of Oregon*. 1st ed. Los Angeles: Japanese American National Museum, 1993. A short overview of the Japanese experience in Oregon with many historical photographs.

Johnson, Daniel P. "Anti-Japanese Legislation in Oregon, 1917–1923." *Oregon Historical Quarterly* 97.2 (1996): 176–210. Discusses bigotry against Japanese immigrants, especially during the 1920s when the Ku Klux Klan became a political power in Oregon. Traces the events leading up to the passage of the 1923 Oregon Alien Land Law and the effects of the law on the Japanese, particularly in the Hood River Valley.

Kessler, Lauren. *Stubborn Twig: Three Generations in the Life of a Japanese American Family*. 1st ed. New York: Random House, 1993. A detailed chronicle of the lives of three generations of the Yasui family of Hood River, Oregon, from the turn of the century until the 1980s.

Katagiri, George. *Nihonmachi: Portland's Japantown Remembered*. Portland, Oreg.: Oregon Nikkei Legacy Center, 2002. A photographic essay based on an exhibit at the center in 2000. Includes very concise information on the historic, economic and social life of Portland's Japanese community up until World War II. Suitable for young adults.

Olmstead, Timothy. "Nikkei Internment: The Perspective of Two Oregon Weekly Newspapers." *Oregon Historical Quarterly* 85.1 (1984): 5–32. Compares coverage of the Japanese internment in two newspapers, the *Hillsboro Argus* and the *Hood River News*, finding that the Hood River paper was much more sympathetic to the plight of the internees due to the editor's familiarity with the Japanese community.

Powell, Linda E., et al. *Asian Americans in Oregon: A Portrait of Diversity and Challenge*. Corvallis, Salem: Oregon State University Extension Service and Oregon Agricultural Experiment Station; Oregon Dept. of Education, 1990. Primarily historical essays on Chinese, Japanese, Korean, and Southeast Asian Oregonians.

Stratton, David H. "The Snake River Massacre of Chinese Miners, 1887." *Chinese on the American Frontier*. Ed. Arif Dirlik and Malcolm Yeung. Lanham, Md: Rowman & Littlefield, 2001. 215–230. The story of the bloody, two-day massacre of thirty-one Chinese miners in Eastern Oregon, for which no persons were ever convicted. Provides some background on the anti-Chinese sentiments of the time and the government's ineffective response to the atrocity.

Tamura, Linda. *The Hood River Issei: An Oral History of Japanese Settlers in Oregon's Hood River Valley*. Urbana: University of Illinois Press, 1993. Relates the story of the first-generation Japanese who immigrated to the Hood River Valley in the late 1800s to 1920s. Details their lives in Japan, the early years in the U.S., relocation to internment camps and their situation after World War II.

Videos

A Family Gathering. Dir. Yasui, Lise, Ann Tegnell, and PBS Video. One videocassette (VHS) (58 min.). PBS Video, 1989. The story of the Yasui family of the Hood River Valley, focusing on their experiences during and after the internment.

Moving Mountains: the Story of the Yiu Mien. Dir. Valazquez, Elaine. One videocassette (58 min.). Filmakers Library, 1989. Describes the experiences of Yiu Mien refugees from Laos, describing their traditional lifestyle in their homeland and their struggle to adjust to a new way of life in Portland.

Turbans. Dir. Andersen, Erika, Carol Ruiz, and Kavi Raz, et al. 1 videocassette (30 min.). Distributed by NAATA, 1999. Explores the struggles of a Sikh immigrant family in 1918 Astoria.

Digital Collections and Primary Source Repositories

Oregon Nikkei Legacy Center: 121 NW 2d Ave., Portland, Oreg., 97209. (503) 224–1458. <http://www.oregonnikkei.org/>. The collections at the Japanese American history museum include photographs and videotapes of oral histories.

LATINOS

Books and Articles

Buan, Carolyn, ed. "The Hispanic Presence in Oregon." Spec. issue of *Oregon Humanities* Summer (1992): 1–40. Very brief articles on the history, origins, arts and culture of Oregon's Hispanic population. Has some overlap in content with the book by the same editor listed below (*Nosotros*). Suitable for young adults.

Dash, Robert C. "Mexican Labor and Oregon Agriculture: The Changing Terrain of Conflict." *Agriculture and Human Values* 13.1 (1996): 10–20. Discusses union efforts to organize migrant farm workers in the Willamette Valley, focusing on the

1995 campaign to organize strawberry harvesters. Also traces the history, politics, and labor structure of Oregon agriculture.

Dash, Robert C., and Robert E. Hawkinson. "Mexicans and 'Business as Usual': Small Town Politics in Oregon." *Aztlán* 26.2 (2001): 87–123. Examines political mobilization in Woodburn, especially in attempts to influence housing and education policy. The author concludes that local, decentralized democracy is not always more inclusive of all community members.

Gamboa, Erasmo, Carolyn M. Buan, and Oregon Council for the Humanities. *Nosotros: The Hispanic People of Oregon: Essays and Recollections.* Portland, Oreg.: Oregon Council for the Humanities, 1995. The only book devoted to the subject. Concise articles and ample illustrations make this book appropriate for children and young adults.

Gamboa, Erasmo. *Mexican Labor & World War II: Braceros in the Pacific Northwest, 1942–1947.* Seattle: University of Washington Press, 2000. The most comprehensive of Gamboa's several works on the experiences of Mexican workers in the Bracero program in Oregon, Washington and Idaho.

———. "Mexican Mule Packers and Oregon's Second Regiment Mounted Volunteers, 1855–1856." *Oregon Historical Quarterly* 92.1 (1991): 41–59. Relates the vital role of skilled Mexican mule packers in supporting the efforts of the volunteer militia, especially during the Rogue River war.

Maldonado, Carlos S., and Gilberto García. *The Chicano Experience in the Northwest.* 2nd ed. Dubuque, Iowa: Kendall/Hunt Pub. Co, 2001. A well-organized overview covering demographics, political activity, labor, education, history and culture. The data for Oregon is presented alongside Washington's and Idaho's.

Slatta, Richard W. "Chicanos in the Pacific Northwest: An Historical Overview of Oregon's Chicanos." *Aztlán* 6.3 (1975): 327–40. Although much of the data cited dates from the 1970s, this remains one of the only articles to discuss the social, political and economic condition of Chicanos in Oregon.

Valle, Isabel. *Fields of Toil: A Migrant Family's Journey.* Pullman: Washington State University Press, 1994. Chronicles the daily lives of a migrant family for one year and through three states, including Oregon. Touches upon such issues as immigration, housing, health, labor laws, and education.

Videos

Aumento Ya! A Raise Now!: The Story of PCUN's Tenth Anniversary Organizing Campaign. Dir. Chamberlin, Tom, Martha Gies, and PCUN, et al. One videocassette (50 min.). Pineros y Campesinos Unidos del Noroeste, 1996. Portrays the strike of Latino migrant strawberry pickers in the Willamette Valley in 1995.

Nuestra Visión, Nuestro Futuro: Our Vision, Our Future: The Oregon Latino Youth Video Project. Dir. Oregon Latino Youth Video Project, Northwest Film Center (Portland, Oreg.), and Oregon Council for Hispanic Advancement. Two videocassettes (60 min.). Northwest Film Center, 2003. Short films created by 49 teens from Bend, Ontario, Gresham and Portland, documenting what it is like to be Latino in Oregon.

The Oregon Story: Agricultural Workers. Dir. Oregon Public Broadcasting, United States, and Dept. of Agriculture, et al. One videocassette (57 min.). Oregon Public Broadcasting, 2001. A history of agricultural work in Oregon, focusing especially on the contributions of Hispanic workers.

NATIVE AMERICANS

Books and Articles

Beckham, Stephen Dow, and Christina Romano. *The Indians of Western Oregon: This Land was Theirs*. Coos Bay, Oreg.: Arago Books, 1977. Drawing upon archaeological and documentary sources, discusses the history and culture of the Indians of Western Oregon in a way that is accessible to young people. Includes many photographs and illustrations.

Buan, Carolyn M., Richard Lewis, and Oregon Council for the Humanities. *The First Oregonians: An Illustrated Collection of Essays on Traditional Lifeways, Federal-Indian Relations, and the State's Native People Today*. Portland, Oreg.: Oregon Council for the Humanities, 1991. Includes sections on traditional lifeways, contact with Europeans and essays on the tribes' heritage-recovery projects. Brief articles and ample illustrations make this book appropriate for children and young adults.

Collins, Cary C. "The Broken Crucible of Assimilation: Forest Grove Indian School and the Origins of Off-Reservation Boarding-School Education in the West." *Oregon Historical Quarterly* 101.4 (2000): 466–507. Provides a history of the early years of the school, focusing on its founding director Melville C. Wilkinson and the hardships that students endured under his care. Includes the text of Wilkinson's correspondence about the school.

Douthit, Nathan. *Uncertain Encounters: Indians and Whites at Peace and War in Southern Oregon, 1820s-1860s*. Corvallis: Oregon State University Press, 2002. Details Indian-white relations in Southern Oregon, from the activities of the Hudson Bay Company to the Rogue River War and subsequent Indian removal to reservations. Also focuses on personal relationships, particularly between white men and Indian women, by drawing on oral narratives.

Fisher, Andrew H. "Tangled Nets: Treaty Rights and Tribal Identities at Celilo Falls." *Oregon Historical Quarterly* 105.2 (2004): 178–211. Portrays the struggle between the federal government, the Columbia River Indians, and the reservation Indians to regulate tribal fishing rights and to negotiate compensation for the destruction of traditional fishing sites with the construction of the Dalles Dam.

Haynal, Patrick. "Termination and Tribal Survival: The Klamath Tribes of Oregon." *Oregon Historical Quarterly* 101.3 (2000): 270–301. One of many articles that discusses how the Klamath tribes came to be terminated, the restoration of tribal status and the lasting effects that termination had upon the tribes.

Rosenthal, Nicolas G. "Repositioning Indianness: Native American Organizations in Portland, Oregon, 1959–1975." *Pacific Historical Review* 71.3 (2002): 415–38.

Details how Indians who migrated to the city formed social and political groups to maintain Indian identity, and how the next generation of urban Indians created their own organizations that reflected their own understanding of urban Indian identity.

Schwartz, E. A. "Sick Hearts: Indian Removal on the Oregon Coast, 1875–1881." *Oregon Historical Quarterly* 92.3 (1991): 228–64. The story of the deception that allowed the termination of the Alsea reservation and the removal of its inhabitants in order to allow settlers to exploit the abundant timber stands on the land.

Spores, Ronald. "Too Small a Place: The Removal of the Willamette Valley Indians, 1850–1856." *American Indian Quarterly* 17.2 (1993): 171–91. Focuses on the various treaty negotiations and the ultimately successful efforts to remove the Valley's tribes from their ancestral lands and congregate them onto the newly formed Grand Ronde reservation.

Stern, Theodore. *The Klamath Tribe: A People and Their Reservation*. Seattle: University of Washington Press, 1965. A very detailed history and ethnology of the Klamath tribes, especially since the formation of the reservation.

Stowell, Cynthia D. *Faces of a Reservation: A Portrait of the Warm Springs Indian Reservation: Text and Photographs*. Portland, Oreg.: Oregon Historical Society Press, 1987. An extended photographic essay on a variety of individuals from the reservation. Includes a history of the reservation and its people.

Sturtevant, William C. *Handbook of North American Indians*. Washington: Smithsonian Institution. For sale by the Supt. of Docs., U.S. G.P.O, 1978–. See Vol. 7: Northwest Coast, Vol. 11: Great Basin, and Vol. 12: Plateau. Each chapter includes a bibliography and the prehistory, history, language, and culture of a particular tribe.

Ulrich, Roberta. *Empty Nets: Indians, Dams, and the Columbia River*. Corvallis, Oreg.: Oregon State University Press, 1999. Portrays the relations between the federal government and the Columbia River Indians since the construction of the Bonneville Dam, specifically relating to the government's failure to fulfill its treaty obligations, and the effect that government policies have had on the tribes.

Zucker, Jeff, et al. *Oregon Indians: Culture, History & Current Affairs, an Atlas & Introduction*. Portland, Oreg.: Western Imprints, the Press of the Oregon Historical Society, 1983. The most thorough overall resource on the native peoples of Oregon. Contains many useful maps, charts and illustrations.

Videos

The First Oregonians. Dir. Johnson, Larry, and Oregon Council for the Humanities. One videocassette (10 min.). Oregon Council for the Humanities, 1991. A companion to the book detailed above.

Horses of their Own Making. Dir. Newman, Jim, and Oregon Public Broadcasting. One videocassette (58 min., 30 sec.). Oregon Public Broadcasting, 1993. Details how the early settlers and the federal government systematically deprived Oregon's native people of their land, livelihood and traditions.

Digital Collections and Primary Source Repositories

American Indians in the Pacific Northwest Collection, University of Washington Libraries: <http://content.lib.washington.edu/aipnw/index.html>. "Provides an extensive digital collection of original photographs and documents about the Northwest Coast and Plateau Indian cultures, complemented by essays written by anthropologists, historians and teachers about both particular tribes and cross-cultural topics."

Tamastslikt Cultural Institute: 72789 Highway 331, Pendleton, Oreg. 97801. (541) 966–9784. <http://www.tamastslikt.com/>. Houses photos, documents, reports and other archival material related to the history of the Cayuse, Umatilla and Walla Walla Tribes.

First Nations Tribal Collection, Southern Oregon Digital Archives: <http://soda.sou .edu/tribal.html>. A digital collection of documents, books and articles relating to the indigenous peoples of southwestern Oregon and northern California.

MULTICULTURAL MATERIALS

Online Collections and Primary Source Repositories

Columbia River Basin Ethnic History Archive: <http://www.vancouver.wsu.edu/ crbeha/> A database of digital collections containing documents, images, articles and oral history interviews about the region's ethnic groups, selected from the collections at five repositories in Oregon, Idaho and Washington. Focuses on people identified as having African, Asian, European or Latin American heritage. Includes tutorials and lesson plans for interpreting and teaching about the resources.

Helvoigt, T., et al. *American Indians, Blacks & Asians in Oregon's Work Force*. Salem: Oregon Employment Dept, 2000. <http://olmis.emp.state.or.us/olmisj/ SiteIndex>. Contains data from the 1990s, including charts that compare the three ethnic groups' general demographic, business ownership and labor data.

The Northwest Digital Archives: <http://nwda-db.wsulibs.wsu.edu/search/index .asp>. A database that provides access to over 2000 archival and manuscript collections in Oregon, Washington, Idaho and Montana. Includes about 250 collections pertaining to ethnic minorities and civil rights in the Northwest.

Oregon Historical Society: 1200 SW Park Ave., Portland, Oreg. 97205. (503) 222–1741. <http://www.ohs.org/>. Extensive collections of manuscripts, photographs, maps, audio/visual recordings and published material related to the history, culture and activities of ethnic groups in Oregon. Oral history collections of Japanese Americans in Oregon, Albina Ministerial Alliance and Hispanic Americans of Oregon.

Oregon State University Archives: <http://osulibrary.oregonstate.edu/archives/>. 121 The Valley Library, Corvallis, OR 97331. (541) 737–2165. Houses a variety of collections related to ethnic groups in Oregon, including the Native American Language Collection, and the Braceros in Oregon Photograph Collection. In addition, the OSU Libraries have launched a new initiative, the Oregon Multicultural Archives, which will comprehensively acquire, preserve and make available collections documenting cultural and ethnic groups in Oregon.

University of Oregon Libraries, Special Collections and University Archives: Knight Library, 15th and Kincaid St., Eugene, Oreg., 97403. (541) 364–1907. <http://libweb.uoregon.edu/speccoll/>. Particularly strong in their materials relating to Oregon's Native Americans, with over fifty collections, including the Southwest Oregon Research Project (SWORP) and the papers of Alvin M. Josephy, Jr. and Joel Palmer. Also houses collections relating to the Japanese internment, the Oregon NAACP and the Ku Klux Klan.

Index

Mexican migrants, 4; application of Jim Crow laws, 95; oral interviews with, 94–96; poverty programs and community empowerment among Oregon's, 93–108; sentiment against, 210. *See also* Latinos
Meza, Lorenzo Alvarez, 140
Micnhimer, Carolyn, 2–4
Microsoft, use of prison labor, 230
Middle Eastern heritage, 187
migrant children, special school opportunities to, 98
Migrant Health Act (1963), 100
Migrant Ministry, mission of, 99
Migrant Ministry Council, 99
migrants: agribusiness industry's dependence on, 93; assistance programs for, 97–100; health reforms for, 99–100
Million Dollar Club Restaurant, 81–82
mining: Chinese work in, 118; Japanese work in, 118; in John Day, 66–67
minorities: denial of right to testify in court, 28; denial of voting rights, 28
miscegenation law, vi, 6, 8, 27–37; California Supreme Court ruling as unconstitutional, 35; debates over passage, 31; as discrimination against Indians, 34; durability of, 30; efforts to repeal, 30; enforcement of, 31; history of, 27–37; provisions of, 31; racial categories of, 34–35; repeal of, 35–36; shaping of regulation of marriage, 30
Mixtec farmworkers, vi, 136–47; in Comité Pro Obras de San Agustín Atenango (Public Works Committee of San Agustín Atenango), 137; improving conditions for, 139–41; language of, 136; in Organización de Comunidades Indígenas Migrantes Oaxaqueños (OCIMO), 137–38; in Organization of Indigenous Oaxacan

Migrants, 137–38; in Pineros y Campesinos Unidos (PCUN), 136–37, 138, 139–41; staying connected and, 141–45
model minority stereotype, 10
Modoc Point, 165
Modoc wars, 154
Montana, exploration of, 17
Montejano, David, 95
Montes, Sonny, 105
Monument, Chinese in, 66
Morales, José, 104
moralistic culture, 201
Morgan, Sam, 32
Motorola, use of prison labor by, 230
Mount Angel College, 105
Mount Angel Seminary, 99
Mount Tabor, 70
Mubarak, Hosni, 189
Mujeres Luchadoras Progresistas (Women Fighting for Progress), 146
multicultural materials, annotated bibliography on, 247–48
multiracial children, 5
Multnomah County: Arabs in, 23; Latinos in, 22; Native Americans in, 19
Museum of Warm Springs, 4

Nader, Ralph, 187
Natatorium, 177–79
National Association for the Advancement of Colored People (NAACP), 86, 87–88, 97; discrimination against African Americans and, 80–81, 82; fight against segregated housing, 83; Portland branch of, 206–7; repeal of miscegenation law and, 36–37
National Board of Censorship, 87
National Center on Institutions and Alternatives, 227
National Register of Historic Places, 1
Native American Leadership Institute, 206

pattern of, 35; transmission of
property and, 33
white timber operators, Chinese in,
66–67
Wilcox, Marie, 36
Willamette University Sociology
Department, 99
Willamette Valley, v
Willamette Valley Immigration Project
(WVIP), 138
women: Arab, 185. *See also* Chinese
women; Japanese women
Woodburn: Mexican origin population
in, 93; opportunity center in, 101;
tejano settlers in, 107
Woods, George, 30
workforce stereotype, shift in dominant,
117

work furlough program, 54
World War II (1939-1945), 124, 203,
207–8, 211; conditions for Black
Oregonians, 90; labor shortage
during, 93
WSU, use of prison labor, 230
Wu, David, 215
Wyden, Ron, 54
Wyoming: exploration of, 17;
miscegenation legislation in, 28

Xing, Jun, 1, 118

Yahooskin band of Paiutes, 154

Zamora, Felix, 120
Zapotec migrants, 140
Zappa, Frank, 187

Contributors

Kera Abraham is a reporter with Eugene Weekly, an alternative newspaper in Eugene, Oregon. Originally from Pittsburgh, Pennsylvania, she earned a master's degree in journalism from the University of Oregon and a B.A. in environmental science from the University of California, Berkeley. Her master's project examined the changing identity of Arab Americans post-9/11, and she has published hundreds of articles on various environmental, social, and political issues in Oregon.

Robert C. Dash is Professor of Politics at Willamette University. He received his Ph.D. in Political Science from the University of California, Riverside. Dr. Dash has published many articles on Latinos in Oregon, which include "Latinos, Political Change, and Electoral Mobilization in Oregon," *Latino(a) Research Review* 5:2–3 (Fall/Winter 2003); "Mexicans and 'Business as Usual': Small Town Politics in Oregon" (with Robert Hawkinson), *Aztlán: A Journal of Chicano Studies* 26:2 (Fall 2001); "Globalization: For Whom and for What?," *Latin American Perspectives* 25:6 (Nov. 1998); "Mexican Labor and Oregon Agriculture: The Changing Terrain of Conflict," *Agriculture and Human Values* 13:4 (Fall 1996); and "Mexican Dreams, American Reality: One Family's Journey," *Diálogo* 1:1 (Spring 1996). Currently he is working on a research project on politics and literature in Latin America.

Ed Edmo (Shoshone-Bannock) is an internationally acclaimed poet, playwright, performer, traditional storyteller, and lecturer on Northwest tribal culture. He was raised at Celilo Falls, Oregon.

Erlinda Gonzales-Berry is Professor of Chicano/a and Latino/a Studies and Chair of the Ethnic Studies Department at Oregon State University.

Gonzales-Berry has published extensively on Chicano culture and literature. She received her Ph.D. from the University of New Mexico. She is co-editor of the following books: *Herencia: An Anthology of Hispanic Literature of the United States; The Contested Homeland: A Chicano History of New Mexico; En otra voz: Antología de la literatura Hispana de los Estados Unidos; Las mujeres hablan: An Anthology of Nuevomexicana Writers; Recovering the U.S. Hispanic Literary Heritage, Vol. II.; Pasó por aquí: Critical Essays on the New Mexico Literary Tradition 1542–1988.* Gonzales-Berry is currently working on a book on immigration from Mexico to Oregon.

Sarah Griffith is a Ph.D. student in History at the University of California, Santa Barbara. Her previous works include, "Border Crossings: Race, Class, and Smuggling in Pacific Coast Chinese Immigrant Society," *Western Historical Quarterly* 35: 4 (Wiinter, 2004) and "Relocating First-Generation Chinese Immigrants through Primary Documents," *History News* (Spring, 2003).

Jessica Hulst received her B.A. from Washington State University in 2005. She is currently a graduate student in American Studies at New York University.

Linc Kesler is Director of the First Nations Studies Program at the University of British Columbia. He has a Ph.D. in English from the University of Toronto and has also published in early modern studies. Currently, he is working on developing web-based video implementations of projects such as the one described in this volume, and on a major three-year grant project, the Aboriginal History Media Lab, with Canadian Aboriginal filmmaker Loretta Todd.

David J. Leonard is an Assistant Professor in the Department of Comparative Ethnic Studies at Washington State University. He received his Ph.D. from the Univeristy of California, Berkeley in 2002 from the Department of Ethnic Studies. He has written on sports, video games, film, and social movements, appearing in both popular and academic mediums. He has two books, on sports films and African Americans, set to be published in 2006, with another examining race and the NBA scheduled for early 2007. His work has appeared in *Journal of Sport and Social Issues, Cultural Studies: Critical Methodologies, Game and Culture,* as well as several anthologies including *Handbook of Sports and Media* and *Capitalizing on Sport: America, Democracy and Everyday Life.* He is a regular contributor to popmatters.com and *Colorlines* Magazine.

Elizabeth McLagan is Adjunct Professor of Creative Writing and Composition, Portland Community College. She received her MFA in Poetry from

Eastern Washington University. She is the author of *A Peculiar Paradise: A History of Blacks in Oregon* (Georgian Press, 1980).

Janet Nishihara is the Academic and Counseling Coordinator for the Educational Opportunities Program at Oregon State University, where she has worked since 1983. She has a Ph.D. in Educational Leadership from the University of Oregon and a master's degree in College Student Services Administration from Oregon State University. A sansei (third-generation Japanese American), she was born and raised in Eastern Oregon. Her current research interests include Asian American history, identity development among college students of color, and multicultural competence in professional preparation programs for student affairs professionals.

Peggy Pascoe is Associate Professor and Beekman Chair of Northwest and Pacific History at the University of Oregon. Her previous publications include *Relations of Rescue: The Search for Female Moral Authority in the American West, 1874–1939* and "Democracy, Citizenship, and Race: The West in the Twentieth Century," in *Perspectives on Modern America: Making Sense of the Twentieth Century,* ed. Harvard Sitkoff. She is currently completing a book on miscegenation law in U.S. history.

Dwaine Plaza is an Associate Professor at Oregon State University in the Sociology Department. He completed a doctorate at York University in Canada in 1996. He has written extensively on the topic of Caribbean migration within the international diaspora. His most recent publications include: (2004) "Disaggregating the Indo and African-Caribbean Migration and Settlement Experience in Canada;" (2004) "Caribbean Migration to Canada: Mobility and Opportunity 1900–2001;" (2002) "In Pursuit of the Mobility Dream: Second Generation British/Caribbeans Returning to Jamaica and Barbados;" (2001) "A Socio-Historic Examination of Caribbean Migration to Canada: Moving to the Beat of Changes in Immigration Policy;" and (2000) "Transnational Grannies: The Changing Family Responsibility of Elderly African Caribbean-born Women Resident in Britain." He is the co-editor of a book entitled *Returning to the Source: The Final Stage of the Caribbean Migration Circuit* (2006) published by the University of the West Indies Press.

Lani Roberts, Ph.D. is Assistant Professor of Philosophy at Oregon State University; she has published "One or Many," and "Barriers to Actualizing Compassion," both in *Philosophy in the Contemporary World*. She is currently finishing an article on a feminist critique of moral relativism. Her main research interest is the structure of oppression.

Patti Sakurai is an Assistant Professor in the Ethnic Studies Department at Oregon State University. She holds a doctorate in English from the State University at Stony Brook and has written on Asian American literature of the 1960s and '70s, pedagogical issues in Ethnic Studies, and the Japanese American internment camps. She is currently focusing on film work and recently completed a short film on anti-Asian racism in corporate media and the significance of alternative community radio.

Lynn Stephen is Distinguished Professor of Anthropology at the University of Oregon, whose work has centered on the intersection of culture and politics. Her Ph.D. in Cultural Anthropology is from Brandeis University (1987). She is currently completing a forthcoming book titled *Transborder Lives: Indigenous Oaxacans in Mexico and the U.S.* Her three most recent books are *Zapotec Women: Gender, Class, and Ethnicity in Globalized Oaxaca* (2005), *Zapata Lives!: Histories and Cultural Politics in Southern Mexico* (2002) and *Perspectives on Las Américas: A Reader in Culture, History, and Representation* (2003), co-edited with Matt Gutmann, Felix Matos Rodríguez, and Pat Zavella.

Robert D. Thompson, Jr., a graduate of University of California, Santa Cruz, Sociology, is Assistant Professor in African American and Comparative Ethnic Studies at Oregon State University. He is currently working on a book about the life of *Shirley Graham-Du Bois: A Life In The Struggle.*

Richenda Wilkinson is a Social Sciences and Humanities Librarian at the Oregon State University Libraries, where she specializes in Anthropology, Ethnic Studies, and Foreign Languages. She is working on several projects related to library services for diverse populations, including a survey of tribal college library services. Wilkinson received her Master of Library and Information Science at San José State University.

Jun Xing is Professor of Ethnic Studies and Director of the Difference, Power and Discrimination Program at Oregon State University. Dr. Xing received his Ph.D. in American studies from the University of Minnesota, Twin Cities. He taught at Carleton College, Emory University, and Colorado State University before assuming his present position. He is the author of *Baptized in the fire of Revolution: the American Social Gospel and the YMCA in China, 1919–1937* (1996); *Asian America through the Lens: History, Representations and Identity* (1998), and co-editor with Lane Hirabayashi *Reversing the Lens: Race, Ethnicity, Gender and Sexuality through Film* (2003).